ARGENTINA:
A Nation At The Crossroads
Of Myth And Reality

ARGENTINA:
A Nation at the Crossroads
Of Myth and Reality

by Ricardo Zinn

Robert Speller & Sons, Publishers, Inc.
New York, New York 10010

The author wishes to thank:

Alicia Zavalia Brandt, Marcelo Raul Marillan and Carlos Perez Rovira for their valuable assistance in research and selection of data and also because, despite the fact that they do not share many of the interpretations and proposals included in this book, they carefully analyzed the first draft and suggested intelligent modifications.

Thanks also to Lidia Matta de Roca for her solid collaboration in essential support work.

My special thanks go to Dan Newland, translator of the text of my work.

Thanks also go to Laurence W. Levine, Esq. and Jon P. Speller for their assistance in preparing the U.S. edition of this work.

Preface

During my 35 years of involvement in the private and public
sector, much of which has been spent in the South American
continent, I have had the privilege and usually the great pleasure of
meeting many distinguished people in all areas of life. I have also
been a close observer of the political and economic scene both in my
own country and in the countries where I had been fortunate enough
to serve my nation as Ambassador — Costa Rica, El Salvador,
Mexico, Spain and Argentina.

This interest in people and events and the chance to live and work
in these areas for a long period of time as an Ambassador required me
to do a great deal of reading which I enjoy very much.

Sometime last year I had the opportunity to read the English
translation of Dr. Ricardo Zinn's book *Argentina... A Nation at the
Crossroads of Myth and Reality*, which was published in Argentina
in 1977 and when asked to write a few words as the introduction to
the American edition I was delighted to do so.

Dr. Zinn is one of the many people I have met during my tenure as
Ambassador to Argentina and I found him well versed on the
Argentine scene and also on the world scene. We have had several
interesting talks and I valued his thoughts.

I have always had a long standing interest in Argentina predating
my designation as Ambassador in 1972. The years my family spent

in Argentina as Ambassador were some of the happiest of my life — although some of the most difficult and challenging.

As I said at the Argentine Chamber of Commerce luncheon, June 28, 1977 in a speech published in the July issue of Vital Speeches:

> For more than forty-five years, one of Argentina's distinguished features has been the discrepancy between potential and reality, a discrepancy that has mystified foreigners and frustrated Argentines. Seemingly poised on the threshhold of social and economic modernization, in the 1930s the country was graced with human and natural resources that led most observers to group Argentina with Canada and Australia and others slated for developed status: Argentina has instead become a synonym for political instability and economic mismanagement. The nearly twenty presidents since 1930, only two of whom completed constitutionally elected terms: the cyclical boombust economic pattern: the intense social and political factionalism, and, most recently, the massive explosion of political violence and hatred have all left deep scars. Understandably, domestic and foreign observers alike continue to wonder whether the country's potential is to remain indefinitely unrealized. I believe the time has come for this realization."

Dr. Zinn's book will go a long way in presenting the Argentine problem to the world and for that reason alone it is a necessary and serious work.

Dr. Zinn's book is the first in my memory that tries to explain Argentina's history with no attempt to color it one way or another. It is frank, truthful and very much to the point. It is very much needed and it is a valuable contribution to the present day history of Argentina.

In an era when there is so much lack of information on the political and economic history of Argentina it is refreshing to see not only the first book of its kind published in English but one of the best. It is only with the frank and open exchange of ideas and knowledge, so that the American and Argentine people get to know each other well, will we develop the kind of good relations we both want.

This book should be an added contribution to that flow of ideas and knowledge.

Robert C. Hill

June 22, 1978

PROLOGUE

My father, who was a German theologian, and who believed in a rigorous life of religious self-denial, never was able to understand that the majority of Argentine citizens look upon high level public service as an honor or a sacrifice. Instead, he taught me that it was merely a calling, a duty which could only be evaded if a person was sure that he could not be of use to the community.

This way of thinking, which places the country above the changeable political positions of each government, includes taking the hard decision of serving, even under the worst government, it you are convinced that you can contribute, if nothing else, at least to lessening somewhat the damage done to the Nation.

Believing firmly in this premise of *"ad maiora mala vitanda,"* I have cooperated each time my services have been required: In 1961, in 1968, in 1970 and in 1975. This, by no means, implies that I have no political stance (this book demonstrates clearly that I do have), but it does suggest that serving my country in whatever way I am capable of doing has priority over my political beliefs or personal convenience.

This is why, though never having been a Peronist, I accepted the post of Secretary of State for Economic Programming and Coordination in May of 1975. I cannot hide the fact that the decision was not an easy one. I could see that the country was being pushed toward political suicide, through uncontrolled and misrepresented populism, in which the ruling party and the main opposition group coincided, and only after a long interview with the future Economy Minister and some deep soul-searching did I conclude that there was a possibility — even if a slight one — of introducing a certain amount of socio-economic realism, which could break somewhat the almost inevitable fall. But when a non-demagogic economic scheme was first applied populist forces of all persuasions began doing their best to hamper it, and the effort failed. Those 48 days that I served in the government, however, were a rich experience, which permitted me to see, from the inside, the workings of those who, either intentionally or unintentionally hinder the growth and maturity of the Republic.

RICARDO ZINN
January, 1979

Table of Contents

PART SIX: PROSPECTS FOR THE EIGHTIES

APPENDICES

Introduction

When approached with the idea of the publication of this English edition, the author hesitated for a long time because he wasn't convinced that the book in English could serve a useful purpose.

Nevertheless, as of November, 1976, a number of events in the West began giving credence to the central themes of the book and made the author realize that it was worthwhile for the book to be available outside the restrictive limits of its Argentine readership.

A true test case, which can be useful for all Western nations which follow the difficult path to liberty and justice, can be found in the process of destruction brought on by populism in the economy and institutions of the Argentine Republic — a process which was accompanied in its last stages by demagogy and guerrilla warfare and which ended with a military takeover on March 24, 1976. The author is aware of certain members of the United States State Department's newly formed "Human Rights Office"* who do not believe that Argentina is an important nation and therefore condemn her for alleged human rights violations, while excusing Russia and China. The author does not believe that this is a sound policy toward the Argentine nation, as it is a double standard in any case and reflects a total lack of reality or understanding of the holocaust Argentina has undergone in recent years.

* This office was created in 1977 by the U.S. Congress.

Guerrilla warfare and terrorism are world phenomena, forming a part of the Marxist aggression launched against the free world, centered on those countries which have pseudo-democratic populist regimes and where the social organization is based on the remnants of colonialism.

Marxism itself is nothing more than the ideological tool of an imperialist world power whose internal problems oblige it to continuously expand its frontiers and areas of influence by subversion and aggression.

On March 24, 1976, Argentina ended a prolonged period of misgovernment marked by various populist regimes, and it began an era of reconstruction on which the Republic should be refounded.

The process has been hindered by internal and external difficulties of all types, including the following:

1. The initial existence of a fighting capability among guerrilla forces which permits them to continue a dirty war, which has cost the Argentine government and people human lives, material resources and concerted efforts in all areas other than the task at hand — to rebuild Argentina.

2. A chaotic situation within the economy characterized by an inability to pay off foreign debts in 1976, the fracturing of the country's socio-productive mechanism, and an inflation rate of more than 30 per cent a month. Though the problem of balance of foreign payments was carried out swiftly and efficiently, the elimination of inflation has not proven to be such an easy matter.

3. A world campaign organized by European and Argentine leftists which is being fostered in the U.S. to run down the international image of Argentina and which publicly supports self-exiled leaders of Argentine terrorism.

There is an almost complete lack of books in English which explain the recent history of the Argentine Republic and which relates this history from an Argentine point of view.

This book, in its English edition, is designed to try to at least partially fill in this gap. It is also designed to show that the illness which Argentina has recently suffered through, and which was finally overcome with the March 1976 coup, is a generalized epidemic which is attacking a number of countries around the world today.

Perhaps the publication of this book in English will be a step in the educational process which must take place between the Argentine people and the United States people — after nearly a generation in which this exchange has been lacking. The process must start, and hopefully this book will give it impetus.

Violence in Europe and growing Soviet domination in Asia and Africa, carried out through bloody coups in some cases (Ethiopia, Afghanistan, South Yemen) and through war moves using Cuban troops together with Russian materials in others (Angola, Ogaden, Zaire, etc.) confirms the thesis that the vain attempt to set up a subversive bridge across the Southern Cone of the Americas drew its inspiration from the same source. The attempt failed because of three main factors:

1. The incapacity of populist-Marxists to infiltrate military ranks in Argentina, Chile and Uruguay.

2. The failure of guerrillas in Argentina to occupy an effective area in the province of Tucuman which was to serve as a base of operations for Cuban troops (1973-1975).

3. The overthrow, backed by the U.S. government, of the Salvador Allende regime in Chile. This was America's last coherent act until the present time in its foreign policy as regards Latin America. Perhaps one day the people who today defend the Allende regime, and condemn the American and world effort to stop it, will have enough experience to realize what it would have meant if Allende had succeeded. I suggest that those who attack what nations did in Chile read about what is now happening in Cambodia, Vietnam and Ethiopia.

In 1976/77 Argentina overcame Marxist guerrilla aggression and freed itself of the populist government which was terrorism's accomplice, without foreign help and in a demonstration of its own moral reserves and profound Western and Christian convictions.

And thus began the construction of a free society within a republican, representative and federal framework made to fit local and geopolitical circumstances through which the country will be passing in the last quarter of the 20th century.

Argentina has passed through a painful process in which its republican institutions, which were in full force in 1920, deteriorated and were nearly destroyed when the red flag was flown even in the country's universities and ministries. The country has also shown that it could later make an heroic recovery. It is because of this that Argentina is capable of serving as a paradigm for the West, although we have a long way to go to re-establish our nation and people to the place we once had.

That painful process is an example of the dangers a society lets itself in for when political liberty is confused with demagogic freewheeling.

That painful process is an example of how progressive statism leads to the building of a totalitarian machine which makes a democratic society become something unrealistically utopian.

That painful process is an example of how populist governments tolerate or even make pacts with extremists due to their poor interpretation of what the "will of the people" means.

That painful process is an example of how Marxist populist power in its last stages bends the will of society through fear and terror (seen today in the actions of Italy's Red Brigades).

That painful process is an example of how Cuba and Moscow train guerrillas and give them logistical support and how a western country can lend itself to being a sanctuary in which those guerrillas are sheltered between one attack and the other, with the only condition being that they respect that country. The future accumulation of killers in a single place causes that country to face the consequences of its fallacy.

That painful process is an example of how, in the last stages of armed aggression, it is absolutely necessary for the nation's security organs, represented by the armed forces, to remain intact, since they are the final custodians of the Republic. It is essential that the unity which they showed to the Argentine people and to the world remain intact.

In Argentina, neither internal nor external aggressors were able to suffocate the patriotism and unity of the armed forces which took over in the most critical moment and saved the nation from destruction. And while it is fashionable in some quarters to look down upon the military, it would be well to remember that military men are citizens in uniform and that all nations call on them.

The United States has many examples of this in peace and in war. Fortunately for the United States, you have not ever experienced an armed civil war of the sort we have had and I wonder what the reaction would be if many of your leaders and officials had to live with armed guards and daily attacks on their lives. During the 1860s your soldiers were called on to defend the nation internally.

Nevertheless, relations between the two countries have never been optimum. Misunderstandings and rebuffs have marked the way through the 178 years of history the two countries have shared. For many decades Argentine schools taught the Monroe Doctrine (1823) as being one of the positive factors of the 19th century which has prevented new European moves to recolonize lost American territories.

Later the Roosevelt Corollary (1904) and the intervention of the U.S. in the Caribbean put a new slant on the application of the Monroe Doctrine. In recent times, without resorting to the Monroe Doctrine, the U.S. has unilaterally exercised sovereign rights which affected other countries in the area during the Cuban missile crisis (1962) and when its interposition prevented a communist takeover in Santo Domingo (1965).

Nevertheless the U.S. fell down in its decision not to impede the installation of a Soviet satellite regime in Cuba.

The overthrow of the Salvador Allende government in Chile can be counted as part of a period in which the U.S. exercises its power to defend areas which directly influence its security and keeps them from falling into the hands of world powers which it opposes geopolitically and which could use these zones as bases for the installation of armaments which would put the U.S. in imminent danger.

Argentine-U.S. relations can be broken up into different periods according to the various stages of America's imperialistic battle for world hegemony.

Until World War I the U.S. was a world power in embryo, and its principal strength was economic, as it had only demonstrated its fighting capability in limited conflicts like those of the Philippines and the Caribbean.   The process of territorial annexation had practically ended, a process which typified the American epic of the 19th century.

There was probably no other power which grew territorially in such a spectacular way as did the U.S. in the 19th century through war, negotiations, and purchases.

Until well into the second half of the last century Argentina, which had achieved national independence in the second decade of the century, was unable to organize its institutions and present a judicially organized national framework.

During that period differences between Argentina and the U.S. were tremendous.   The U.S. had begun its triumphant expansion and, except for the Civil War era, presented no doubts as to its national coherence.   It is because of this that the philosopher of Argentine organization, Juan Bautista Alberdi, and the mentor of national construction, Domingo Faustino Sarmiento, constantly resorted to the example of the U.S. when proposing models of constitutional and judicial organization, and of economic and educational organization for the country.

Once national organization had been achieved, based on the Constitution of 1853, in the latter years of the 19th century, Argentina arose as the undisputed first-place power in Latin America and a policy of reciprocal jealousy and forebodings of future confrontations developed between the two countries.

In the First World War the U.S. took up its role as a top world power even though it was still balanced and somewhat contained by the still existing British Empire and other colonial powers.

At the same time as the U.S. was affirming its world presence Argentina was entering a period of populism and chauvinistic nationalism which not only killed its chances of becoming a world power, but also kept its leaders from recognizing factors which were to affect the whole world. Argentina continued to believe that the world leader was Great Britain and that that leadership would come under fire by Central European powers in the inevitable brother-against-brother war, which was to be a consequence of the diabolical Versailles pact.

The Second World War marked the beginning of the period of *"Pax Americana"* and within the first decade after the conflict the U.S. position was unquestionable.

Nevertheless, the consequences of half the world's being handed over to Marxism at Yalta began to be progressively obvious. Argentine leaders, led this time by Peron, were once again mistaken in their geopolitical position when they foresaw a conflict between Russia and the U.S. within the near future.

It was because of this that Argentina took up its non-aligned and Third World position even before the birth of the Third World.

In 1955, with the overthrow of Peron, Argentina assumed a more realistic policy regarding the U.S. Slowly but surely Argentina developed the consensus that the U.S. was, and would remain, the leader of the West and the mentor of *"Pax Americana."*

As this feeling deepened in Argentina the U.S. began to lose its vocation for leadership.

First with Vietnam and then with Watergate the U.S. appeared to assume the role of the number one world leader by virtue of circumstances and not by vocation.

This history shows that until Argentina was nationally organized, reciprocal criteria of the two countries never coincided. Argentina today recognizes America's position of leadership and finds it desirable. It also seeks and needs coherent American geopolitics. American leaders, on the other hand, seem to be embarrassed in their role as geopolitical heroes and try to find ways to philosophically justify an unclear position, which is even considered by the American public itself to be, at best, confusing.

Latin Americans realize that the U.S. plays a leading role in the fight to keep the banner of liberty and western culture flying high. What is not understood is why the government of Mr. Carter and the U.S. Congress (1978) wishes to oblige Latin American countries to end their resistance to armed Marxist aggression, to reduce their defences and give a new opportunity to their enemies. We Argentines believe that this new contradiction corresponds to a dark period in American life which began with the "strategic surrender" recognized in Paris (1973) by Dr. Henry Kissinger with the Communist leaders of North Vietnam and the Vietcong.

The lack of conviction of the U.S. to triumph over the Soviet Union in the war in Indochina meant that millions of South East Asians would have to live in sub-human conditions under the Communist regimes of Vietnam, Cambodia and Laos. This first defeat in the history of the United States also put an end to the "*Pax Americana*" and marked the beginning of a new period of Soviet territorial expansion: Vietnam, Angola, Ethiopia, Afghanistan and South Yemen mark the road to triumph the Soviets are following to reach their goal of dominating the regions which surrounded Europe and the U.S. and of cutting off communications with the rest of the world without having to enter into a direct conflict with the U.S.

Then, after Vietnam, came the Communist coup d'etat in Portugal, which, although it was overcome, left the country in a state of economic ruin and political chaos; the rise to power (partial for the moment) of the Communists in Italy; and the increasing strength of the leftists in France.

The only area in which there has been a decrease of Marxist power has been in the Southern Cone of the Americas.

It would seem that the Administration in Washington is ashamed of the fact that the enemy has not triumphed in Chile, Argentina and Uruguay and is even prepared to defend the enemy under the banner of Zaire, Angola, Ethiopia, etc., to name only the newest Marxist zones.

The Watergate affair — the causes and effects of which only the American people can judge — has caused a lessening of the power of the executive branch in Washington. It has also brought about the dismantling of part of the CIA (Central Intelligence Agency) operations network and the beginning of an era of demagogic politics in which, in the absence of real leaders, politicians who try to win the people's support through populist practices have appeared.

Also, after Paris (1973), the U.S. was to recognize the Russian theory of limited sovereignty which has been applied in Soviet satellites of Eastern Europe for the past 25 years and which is beginning to be expanded to cover the new regions in Africa Cuban soldiers are winning for their Soviet masters. In 1974 and 1975 the theory of negotiable regions — complementary to that of limited sovereignty — was about to be applied in the Argentine Republic; this happened without anyone in the U.S. — not the public, nor the press, nor the Congress, nor the Administration — moving to support this Republic which was living through a holocaust of populism and terror.

Only the silent and measured efforts of the late Ambassador Robert C. Hill signified that Argentina had an ever-present friend. His knowledge of local idiosyncracies and of the national and geopolitical problems of the place to which he had been assigned distinguished him as one of the most capable U.S. diplomats ever assigned to Argentina.

The United States, as a Western power has an ambivalence to borders which complicates its life, makes diplomacy difficult and directly affects Western countries, including Argentina.

The borders which the United States must defend are far from its geographical frontiers, are spherical and take in the entire globe. Over the last 15 years, these frontiers have gotten even farther away.

Meanwhile, the political boundaries of the United States are those which its political maps care to recognize. That is to say, from the standpoint of responsibility, its boundaries are immense and indefinite, while from the standpoint of rights, its boundaries are finite and perfectly known.

The area of influence which runs from its own boundaries to those of the aggressive powers is the area of responsibility of the U.S.: thus its obligations are probably greater than its rights.

Without the enthusiastic conviction of the United States that it should defend the West the latter will disappear in a wave of armed Marxist aggression. The West recognizes the unquestionable U.S. position of leadership and is thus willing to listen to its opinions on western defense. Nevertheless, western nations want to maintain their boundaries and the free will which arises from their complete sovereignty and thus naturally reject any attempt by the U.S. to meddle in their internal affairs. This is especially true when these internal affairs have nothing to do with western defenses, but with how each nation wishes to govern itself.

The average U.S. citizen has little if any information on Argentina. American newspapers bring up Argentina — and other countries which are not world powers — only in order to print sensationalistic news, stories which in some way damage the image of the country.

It is seldom that *The New York Times* or *The Washington Post* publish favorable news about Argentina. This is not to say that they are discriminatory, since journalism the world over tends to give disagreeable news preference over positive news. This trend has been accentuated since the internal convulsions caused by Watergate took place.

On a recent visit to Argentina (about June 25, 1978), Henry Kissinger admitted in a television interview that, despite having been Secretary of State for eight years, his knowledge of Argentina had not been sufficient about what was going on in the country at that time. It should be remembered that it was precisely during this period that Argentina suffered the armed aggression of terrorism and Marxist guerrillas and was forced to defend itself without the help of any friendly power.

English-language books on Argentina are scarce, and except in broad-ranging reference books, encyclopedias as it were, the existence of Argentina is ignored. It should also be realized that action by official groups in Argentina aimed at representing the country has been sparse and inefficient. With only a few recent exceptions, the Argentine embassy in Washington has not bothered to make Argentine reality known to public opinion makers in the great northern power structure. This situation, in which the U.S. public lacks knowledge of what Argentina stands for, also exists in other top-ranking countries in the West.

Nevertheless, for Argentina the case of the U.S. is much more serious due to the unquestionable links between the two countries.

Undoubtedly, Argentines know more about the U.S. than Americans do about Argentina. This is an unquestionable fact, even if it breeds some understandable, but unjustifiable, psychological reactions on Argentina's part.

Argentina's opinion of the U.S. has been placed within the framework of a love-hate relationship described by Carlos Rangel in his book, *"The Latin Americans: Their Love-Hate Relationship with the United States,"* which was recently published in the States.

Argentine citizens have a profound respect for the institutions and political maturity of the U.S. They wish that Argentine institutions would resemble those of the U.S. and that American political stability could be imitated by the Argentine Republic. Argentines also admire U.S. economic power and the country's efficiency, which they consider next to absolute.

On the other hand, Argentina envies the U.S. its material and technological successes, but is willing to accept this technology and share in the results.

Argentina scornfully rejects the diplomatic clumsiness which has characterized American policies in all political theaters since the time of Theodore Roosevelt.

According to Argentine criteria, the U.S. has time and again tried to play a "big-brother" role in Latin America. It has done this without subtlety and without coming up with solid reasons why it should be able to take this part. It generally takes up the role in the name of some ideal which could not, rationally at least, be applied to the situation in which it is used.

Much less prized by Argentines is American cultural materialism and in some ways Argentina agrees with what Solzhenitsyn expressed at Harvard, where he said that the focus of American culture produced a drop in the defense of the country's basic ideals.

All of this translated itself into the deep sadness of the Argentine citizen when the U.S. was defeated in Vietnam.

The Argentine knows about the existence of the United States and needs for it to be powerful, since without the U.S. the West, including Argentina, would disappear.

ARGENTINA:
A Nation at the Crossroads
Of Myth and Reality

Chapter I

Crisis or Decadence?

A Clean Slate

An observer in the next century who wants to typify Argentina through some important characteristic of its people could refer to the Argentines as a people without a memory.

We are instilled, not only in the course of our everyday relationships, but also through the strongest public declarations, with the thought that we should *never look to the past,* so much so, in fact, that the so-called "clean slate" — to which each community official points when he is placed in the position of recommending that we forget something — has become a categorical ethic.

It is strange, but Argentines have overlapped the concept of *memory* with that of *vengeance* and have thus managed to confuse *historical amnesia* with *magnanimity.* Already in Justo José de Urquiza's proclamation to the people of Buenos Aires, the very day after the battle of Caseros, he suggests that they "forgive all the injuries"[1] and boldly affirm that "we are all friends and children of the great Argentine family." Some of these "friends," members of the "great Argentine family," would go on to stab him to death with blind fury in the San Jose Palace on Monday, April 11, 1870. As it happens, forgetfulness, like national goodwill, clashes with justice.

This curious inclination has contributed to the immaturity of Argentina. While adult nations move *consciously* along the pathways blazed by their history (which is processed and converted into experience) we are induced to be born each morning in the arms of a

1. Proclamation of February 4, 1852.

benevolent moral romanticism which keeps us monstrously paralyzed. Argentina, as a country, looks more like an old adolescent
every day.

But certainly this clean-slate attitude is only another bit of fiction
with which we numb ourselves in order to avoid facing reality. In
spite of our nomadic psychology, which leads us to camp glibly
along the broad pathways of emotion, time moves relentlessly
onward, errors accumulate in our history, and to these mistakes are
added the results of a permissive, self-indulgent and self-destructive
attitude. It does no good for us to forget, as long as there exists a
truthful memory which changes our psychological flight into an
unquestionable indication of a *decadence* that is reaching its final
stage.

The word *crisis* has been hovering over our heads, breeding short-
term reasoning and impregnating the emotions of the nation for some
years. There is nothing nicer — despite the drama of it — than being
convinced that the country is in a state of crisis, since a crisis is a
mutation of normal circumstances, which ends in either collapse or
salvation. A crisis is an accident limited in time, a rough but finite
period that has the advantage of being speedy, resolving itself, for
better or for worse, in a relatively brief time span.

How seductive a crisis is to a country which prefers fast results to
good ones! It is for this reason that we have accepted the crisis —
because of this, and also because in accepting a crisis each of us (the
men and women of today as well as the collective ancestors of
today's Argentina) only has to swallow a very limited dose of the
responsibility for it. A crisis is also more readily acceptable, because
it does not necessarily lay all of the blame on the country itself, since
it is always possible that foreign activities had something to do with
its origin.

While it is possible for a crisis to be a storm blown over our
country's history by foreign winds, decadence is a long and personal
illness, which requires a considerable period of development and of
which pertinacious errors — by commission or omission — are
symptomatic. The creators of decadence, the protagonists (as it
were) of decadence, are nearly always internal weak points in the
country's political body, but whose weakness is not always evident.
This makes it difficult to lay the blame.

As painful as it may be for us to admit this, admitting it is
definitely the only way for us to change what continues to be an
implacable reality.

Some political researchers have managed to come up with a

consoling euphemism by diagnosing the country's problem as a *chronic crisis*. This cute intellectual trick setting out to define the situation with a combination of two terms, which, by nature, are contradictory, is not strong enough to cope with the force of the painful evidence that *Argentina is not in a state of crisis. Argentina is living at the bottom end of a period of decadence which has gradually eaten away the vital centers of its structure.*

It is not difficult to see how different a crisis is from decadence when one compares the characteristics of the one state to those of the other.

A crisis is generally an explosion, while decadence is a shrinking process. A crisis erupts and interrupts, while decadence is a prolonged evaporation and corruption of qualities which once existed. A crisis is not necessarily negative. Decadence is. A crisis can take place within a specific area of a nation's structure (we have seen political, economic and energy crises) and although this type of crisis may drag in related areas of interest, it does not necessarily imply a chain reaction throughout all areas. Decadence, on the other hand, implies a general decline of all sectors — though not all areas falter at once or for the same reasons, as decadence is a gradual process which affects different areas at different times in history. Finally, a crisis is always a fiery, intense occurrence, while decadence consists of stages of unevenly accelerated debility.

It is necessary, however, to be aware of an important phenomenon. Decadence usually ends in a crisis, and since the will to live of a people is, in most cases, stronger than its will to die, the crisis at the end of the period of decadence is usually seen as a hope-giving collapse, which allows. not for survival, but for revival.

In the fields of philosophical thought and artistic creation, these characteristics are more clearly noticeable.

When decadence reaches its lowest depths within the cultural area of society, the crisis occurs as an expression of liberty to open new roads.

When much-abused reason begins to wear thin and can no longer answer the substantial riddles presented by man; and philosophy, after having been greatly strained by Kant and Hegel threatens to fall into rhetorical decadence, the deep Marxist crisis rears its head and via the oblique path of a sub-religion infatuated with ideas of redemption promises to resurrect an already worn out line of philosophical thought.

Although Marxism was originated to counter this methodology, by opening the way to the success of applied sciences — sociology and psychology — as a replacement for philosophy, the Marxist crisis is capable of creating a reaction which will awaken philosophy and put it in a position to continue the *search for truth* beyond the half-truths of neurotic activism and those contained in the avalanche of slogans with which the Marxists make thought tractable.

The Radical Presence

AUTHOR'S NOTE: Socialists and anarchists of Marxist origin made their presence known in Argentina at the end of the last century with the influx of immigrants from Europe.

The concepts they brought with them and began to strive to put into practice in Argentina inspired the birth of the Radical Party and other Socialist political groups. Also taking part in, and leading the Radicals in the beginning, were conservative politicians, who, because of the social immobility of the Conservative Party, did not have access to positions of leadership and who found within the Radical folklore the ideology and opposition that would permit them to get into power through a political process. A typical example of this conservative wing of Radicalism was Marcelo T. de Alvear.

Thus, the Radicals have come to constitute a somewhat significant expression of a leftwing political view in Argentina today. This is not only true of the party's statist proposals, but also of its social, judicial and philosophical views, which situate it to the left of some other socialist groups.

★　★　★　★

Cycles are usually long in the world of politics. In the history of Argentina as a nation to date we have only had one big crisis: We have witnessed the Argentina which grew until 1910 and then was paralyzed with the advent of universal suffrage. Then came the decadence which began with President Hipólito Yrigoyen in 1916, resulting in the final crisis the end of which we have not yet seen.

The crisis which came to a head in the second decade of this century was partial, like all crises, and it was rather simple in terms of cause and effect. We are dealing here with a reserved and somewhat unmanageable country, a country born with a tremendous sense of privacy, a luxury which it is permitted by virtue of the fact that its small population is out of proportion to its vast land area. Suddenly this country found itself absorbing a flood of restless immigrants of varied origin and Argentines had to *move over to make room for them* in every field, including politics. The fabulous power of a mobilized society was thus set in motion. It was a force which could have been used to drive the country forward to greatness, but it was misused instead as a springboard for the banal conquests of political bosses.

The founders of the country abdicated and retreated, instead of mixing with the newcomers and absorbing their strength and using it as a source of power for attaining national objectives. This made way for the creation of an "Argentina gringa" (foreign Argentina).

The cost of modernizing our democracy was high: The country fell into inexpert hands and its growth began to deteriorate. With the rise of Hipólito Yrigoyen (head of the Radical Party) to the presidency, an emotional political style was enthroned in which reason was cast to the wind, being replaced by lenient, disorderly standards which weakened the country's creative capabilities.

From that time until the present day (1976), the Radicals have constituted a constant and decisive political presence: Radicals have taken part in every government — with the exception of that of José Uriburu and that of Agustin Justo — since Yrigoyen's day. (They have been called Orthodox Radicals or Renegade Radicals, but they were all "sons" of Yrigoyen just the same). They were, of course, seen in the government of Marcelo T. de Alvear; they appeared in the Roberto Ortiz agreement; they were in the revolutionary government of 1943; they helped Juan D. Perón found his first political party and later showed up in his government; they held the Interior Ministry during the government of Pedro C. Aramburu; they held top posts in the government of Arturo Frondizi; they acted as substitute officials for provisional President José Maria Guido; they returned officially to power under Arturo Illia, only to retreat in the first stages of the Argentine Revolution and later turn up in the Interior Ministry under Alejandro Lanusse, during whose term in power the return of Peron was planned; under Perón the Radicals served as opposition party legislators while trying to please the Peronist government.

It cannot be denied that they have been actively present in the major portion of the country's political life for the past 60 years and that they have been busy nurturing, backing or inducting a populist Utopia for all of that time. Many of these "sons" of Yrigoyen were capable, extremely honest men who were gifted politicians.

Imagine what they would have been able to accomplish if, on top of their invaluable love for freedom and their substantial respect for civil rights, they would also have possessed a sense of greatness!

Argentina at the Turn of the Century

In the early years of the 20th century, **Argentina** had one of the most solidly based and prosperous economies in the world. Its strength lay in its land, its resources, its climatic conditions and its geographical location. Its prosperity lay in the men of that time, forward looking politicians who had intelligent plans and the capability to execute those plans.

But all of the action was at the beginning.

In his *Industries and Wealth of Nations* (London, 1896), Michael Mulhall states that in 1885 Argentina had a gross internal per capita income similar to that of Germany, Holland and Belgium. Per capita income figures for Argentina were higher at the time than those for Spain, Austria, Switzerland, Italy, Sweden and Norway and inferior only to those of Canada, the United States and Australia.

In 1910, Argentina's economic picture was that of a country which was moving along roads of which it was sure, headed toward firm goals. Argentina was taking confident strides on the land it was cultivating. While Argentines awaited the harvest, they founded rich and powerful cities. The figures that marked the country's progress made predictions of accelerated growth in the future an obvious conclusion. The future, undoubtedly, promised unprecedented prosperity.

There was an awareness of the advantages the country possessed which developed through the sacrifice that came with the nation's battle for independence from a foreign power and for its civil rights. Argentines knew that they lived on a broad, fertile and varied land that was blessed with a mild climate. And there was something more: Beneath the visible topsoil, there lay a mysterious and unexplored subsoil that was loaded with possibilities. Of this, an Irishman visiting Argentina in 1905 said: "In the heart of Argentina's ground, someday they are going to find more working wealth than all the merry gold the conquistadors dreamed of."

It was not all that foolish to suppose that the pace which had been maintained until that time would lead the country to a brilliant destiny. Or at least that was what all of the excited people who attended the 1910 centennial celebration in Argentina believed. This memorable celebration made international news. The fact that festivities were attended by princesses, presidents, great thinkers and 50 ambassadors was proof of how far Argentina's international reputation had reached, even before the civilized communities of the world's large countries began to anxiously keep themselves up-to-date through modern electronic means.

There was nothing to make anyone think that something would happen within a few short years that would change the course of the nation. What came between us and our desire for greatness? What unpredictable downfall undermined our strength? What action or mistaken idea, which upset the national will, or at least the will of those in decisive positions, had the malignancy to tie our hands when we had the future at our fingertips?

It happened at about the middle of the second decade of the century. Was it the worst of times? Was it the best of times? Did someone foresee what would happen? Was it the result of a sole, dark and deliberate act? Or was it the result of multiple weaknesses?

The historical researcher, of course, does not have a complete catalogue listing the parts of each important movement beneath the nation's surface. Will we someday be able to diagnose the exact cause of our nation's infirmities?

I believe that every Argentine should research the problem as thoroughly as he is able, employing all the patriotic rigor he can muster, even though this may not totally answer the riddle. That is one of the purposes — and not the least important — of this book.

One thing is painfully sure. In the same year that Europe descended into the fires of historical uncertainty, Argentina's tendencies toward growth and prosperity slipped out of balance and the country began to slide with a vengeance down the international ladder. From 1916 on, the national pulse was altered, carrying the country into a period of dangerous decline.

No nation lives isolated from the rest of the world. Argentina, in the midst of World War I, was not isolated. But at the same time, nothing pulled Argentina toward the cauldron of fire and steel in which civilization was boiling. No catastrophe had knocked us out of balance; no epidemic had whittled our population down to a critical minimum.

Nevertheless, during the war years a sinister constellation appeared in the Argentine sky. We had no crisis. It would have been logical for us to have one, since the sparks of crisis cast a livid light on most other nations at that time. What happened to Argentina, however, was not a crisis, but the initial episode of something far more serious: decadence.

In economy, trends are much more important than absolutes. A crisis can damage absolute values. A trend can be made up of a series of crises in which absolute values are successively affected.

Decadence is the unwarranted continuance of a trend. And it is one of the gravest illnesses a State can contract.

A crisis (or recession) in a country of high potential represents a change of trend. This could come, for example, in the form of a change which causes a drop in production. It is a serious problem in terms of its effect on the people, but it does not affect the nation's ranking in the world.

In big countries, like the United States, for example, the moment a crisis or change of trend becomes evident, the full force of the country's administrative machinery is set in motion to take corrective measures and find a solution to the problem. This happens because it is understood that prolonged negative trends affect the absolute position of the country. In the case of Argentina, however, we have heard and read in the dense outpourings of our political leaders since the beginning of the country's decline that foreign enemies are responsible for our frequent crises. These politicians have not managed, or perhaps have deliberately not tried, to see that these critical stages all have the unmistakable characteristics of a prolonged and progressive process of self-destruction.

This fall, for some paradoxical, historical reason, carries the men in government or in influential positions close to the government on its back as directors or pilots of the crash, and it is they who make it unavoidable. They seem to exercise a sort of "anti-power." While the country is being led to ruin, they try to divert the public's attention by laying the blame on foreign enemies whose varied and complex actions are given such names as "international sinarchy" (a sort of external plotting against Argentina), "imperialism" and "multinational conglomerates." One of the symptoms most often indicative of decadence is this laying of blame on external factors. Always accompanying the accusations are populist preaching and demagogic acts.

The true objective of these creators of ruin, who are capable of maintaining a sort of Olympic calm in the midst of the disaster they permit or breed, is certainly a topic for serious, delicate and dangerous research. But let us instead have a look at the proof and the consequences of the public misfortune we are analyzing here.

Economic Electrocardiogram

Statistics are to the economist what the electrocardiogram is to the heart specialist. They both provide a valuable means for checking the efficiency or inefficiency of a system. During positive economic periods series of statistics reflect trends and favorable circumstances that government leaders and legislators can use to the nation's advantage. When these indicators begin to show that a situation is negative, the publication of these negative statistics demonstrates confidence in the maturity of the system and that the right of the community to know what is going on is highly regarded.

What we are trying to do here is compare the evolution of Argentina with that of the rest of the world. The dates given here are limited according to the availability of data. The figures published reflect the points of change in national economic trends. The years in each case are excellent reference points to indicate the political changes that accompanied these economic incidents.

Argentina in Isolation

The development of Argentina's foreign trade as from 1910 is in itself an eloquent source of information as to the policies of the men who ruled the country from 1916 onward. All evaluative, socio-logical and economic studies prove that trade is one of the means by which those countries which do not take in entire continents can increase their wealth, complement their economy and bolster their culture. The smaller and more industrious the population, the higher its level of trade per person.

You will notice in this first set of statistics that Argentina is practically the only country in the world whose per capita trade figures have decreased. This could only have taken place through economic shrinkage produced by inefficiency or induced delibera-tely for some other reason.

World Trade Per Capita and Argentina's Ranking

Year	Ranking	Argentina in dollars per inhabitant	In first place	Dollars per inhabitant
1913	8th	209	Belgium	355
1928	10th	274	New Zealand	559
1948	15th	198	New Zealand	542
1964	30th	110	Belgium	1,235
1973	28th	129	Belgium	2,498

Source: Federico Pinedo's "La Argentina: Su posicion y rango en el mundo," and the United Nations Organization's Statistics Annual for 1974.

Appendix I details the development of the 30 countries which participate in the major portion of world trade. In 1913 the Argentine Republic was eighth on the list and its trade level per capita was equal to 59% of the per capita level of first-place Belgium. By the time the Radicals were bumped from power by the Peronist government in 1948, Argentina had already slipped seven places in the rankings and its percentage comparison to top ranked New Zealand was only 37%. With the end of the first Peronist regime and before the beginning of a new Radical government the country had dropped another five rungs on the international ladder and its per capita volume was only 9% of that of the first-ranked nation. By 1973 we were 28th on the world list and our per capita volume had slid to a mere 5% of that of top-rated Belgium. One must make a real effort to believe in the honestly of these figures when one sees how far Argentina has fallen in 60 years of decadence. By the end of '73, even Nicaragua, Jamaica and Malaysia had surpassed us.

Foreign Trade Per Inhabitant
Percentage Difference with Respect to:

Year	1913	1948	1964
1948	—5	—	—
1964	—47	—44	—
1973	—38	—35	+17

Source: Pinedo; U.N.O.

Between 1913 and 1948, the volume of foreign trade per inhabitant declined by 5%. Between 1948 and 1964 trade dropped by 44%, clearly as a result of Peronist policies. Between 1964 and 1973 the volume of foreign trade per capita picked up by 17%.

Out of 24 countries for which statistics are available, *Argentina ranks last in terms of growth of its volume of foreign trade per capita between 1928 and 1973.*

Within this study, two important sub-periods should be pointed out. The first covers the years from 1928 to 1948: During this sub-period, the country was ranked 15th and its growth rate was less than the average rate of those included in the table. This means Argentina had a 5.7% growth rate while the rest of the countries were growing by about 24%.

The second sub-period takes in the years from 1948-1973. Argentina's foreign trade rate decreased by 1.9% while the three countries immediately preceding Argentina on the list increased their foreign trade rate by an average of 99.4%. The three leading countries on the foreign trade ranking list had an average volume growth in 1948 of 256%. If the top-ranked nations and Argentina are excluded from the figures, the average foreign trade growth rate for the period comes to 402%.

Populist practices tend to cloud the collective conscience of a nation's citizens to the point that a numerically significant portion of the population might ask if a reduction in Argentina's trade with the rest of the world is really important. Do these figures really mean anything? Among those who imparted faulty information to the public, Perón stands out with a climactic speech to a massive crowd in Plaza de Mayo in which he questioned the value of the dollar and even cracked jokes about it.[1]

It is through trade with the rest of the world that a nation obtains the technology and goods that it lacks. The incorporation of new goods and technology speeds the growth of the country. This is true even among the most powerful of nations. Even the United States, which is known and criticized for its protectionist policies, has noticeably increased its overall foreign trade. If we compare the US per capita rate of 100 in 1913 with its rate of 1685 in 1973, it has multiplied its per capita trade with the rest of the world by 17 over the past 60 years. Argentina has multiplied its foreign trade during the same period by only 3.65.

A reduction in trade signifies a decrease in communication with the rest of the world. This is a damaging form of isolation, which, above all, robs a people of a sense of culture that foreign objects — the bearers of a real image, of a way of life, of a style — carry with them; these objects are, in a word, loaded with information.

Part Imports Play in the U.S. Gross National Product

Year - 1975	
Percentage of GNP provided by imports	6.47%
Percentage of total GNP provided by imports from industrialized nations	3.51%
Percentage of GNP provided by imports from developing nations	2.62%
Percentage of GNP provided by non-petroleum producing developing nations	1.39%

1 Speech made in Plaza de Mayo on April 15, 1953.

Given its great size and power, the US is not significantly affected, in terms of its standard of living, by the part trade with underdeveloped countries plays in its income. The only case in which the US economy's ability to adapt to a rise in the export prices of developing nations has been tested is that of petroleum — perhaps the most critical element in a modern economy.

The statistics point out Argentina's foreign trade difficulties. The highly developed countries trade more heavily among themselves than with the rest of the countries in the world. Thus, a country like Argentina, with a specialized economy, which renounces participation in world trade, is also giving up a prime factor in its growth. The import substitution policy, which the country has followed for decades, has backfired. Instead of substituting domestic products for imported ones, we have only succeeded in reducing our own exports. Our foreign trade has fallen off, but our dependence on foreign suppliers has not. Before, we imported refrigerators and cars. Now we import indispensable parts for refrigerators and cars. There will always be a need for some indispensable imported item to keep production rolling. It was necessary for the country to make its own cars and refrigerators, but it was very unwise for it to reduce its imports proportionately. The cold, hard figures show that Argentina's reduction in trade makes for a lower availability of goods from specialized countries at wholesale prices and for a reduction in the availability of new technology as well. Thus we have limited trade that would have brought up our technological standards. The country has been paying these typically high prices for decadence over the past 60 years.

Even empires like the Soviet Union have had to renounce these autarchic policies. The Russians have been forced to go abroad to buy agricultural products, even when by virtue of their ecology and the vastness of their lands, they should be self-sufficient. They also need trade in order to incorporate goods and technology they are incapable of introducing into their economy. At first the Soviets resorted to industrial espionage as a way of gaining technology from abroad, but this method proved insufficient to close the gap between them and the West, so they have turned now to multi-million dollar contracts as the means for giving a qualitative shot in the arm to their growth. Clear examples of this are deals the Soviets have made with Fiat of Italy and the manufacturers of Mack trucks in the States, among others. The Russians need these foreigners to give them the boost they cannot give themselves.

The realism of the Soviets has been lacking in Argentine leaders for the past 60 years. Instead of observing the entire economic picture and operating accordingly, our leaders have declared our national patrimony inalienable — a patrimony which includes out-dated technology and a potential wealth which lies dormant and is of no service to the community.

The Gross National Product

It is not strange, then, nor is it out of keeping with this policy of reducing our exchange of goods and culture with the rest of the world, that our GNP and working capital have also suffered losses over the long period we are analyzing here.

Growth of the Gross National Product
Average Yearly Rates

	Argentina	Canada	USA	Brazil
1900-1913	6.43	5.49	3.95	n/a
1913-1938	2.87	1.46	1.98	
1938-1948	3.80	5.71	5.14	
1948-1955	1.41	4.87	4.25	
1955-1960	2.95	2.60	2.24	
1960-1970	4.24	5.60	4.08	7.92
1970-1973	4.95	n/a	n/a	n/a

Sources: CEPAL, "El crecimiento economico de la Argentina," 1956; BCRA, "Producto e ingreso en la Argentina"; U.N.O. Statistical Annual; A. Madison, *"El crecimiento economico del Occidente,"* Mexico, 1966.

After an initial period of dizzying growth brought on, as we shall later see, by intensive capitalization, we find that Argentina fell into a long slow-down period. After the abnormal period of World War II, Argentina slipped into real stagnation. Not until the '60s did the growth rate become more acceptable. A 1970 look at the growth of Argentina's Gross National Product, compared with those of the United States and Canada, gives us the following figures:

**Development of the Gross National Product
As of 1970 with Respect to Key Years**

Index for base year = 100	ˌArgentina	Canada	USA
1913 = 1.00	5.66	6.86	6.03
1948 = 100	1.92	2.73	2.23

Sources: CEPAL; BCRA; A. Madison.

The point is that in 60 years, Argentina multiplied the goods available to its inhabitants by 5.6 times, while Canadians multiplied theirs by 6.9 times and even the United States (a mature economy which had already reached hard-to-exceed limits) increased its GNP by 6.03.

From 1948 onward Argentina did not even manage to double its GNP, while Canada tripled its figure and the US GNP rose by 2.2 times.

These figures show that even mature, developed economies like that of the United States managed to grow faster than that of Argentina during the period under study.

The figures show that between 1913 and 1970, Canada saw a rise in its income which was 21.1% better than corresponding figures for Argentina. Meanwhile, the United States, with a much higher income level, managed a 6% higher growth rate in relative terms. The differences are even more significant if we compare figures for the period between 1948 and 1970.

Canada increased its income by 42.1% with relation to that of Argentina and the United States raised its income by 16.2% in comparison.

This analysis gives way to two observations.

Bearing in mind that between 1900 and 1913 Argentina had a higher rate of income growth than Canada or the United States, by looking again at the table, we infer that as we move further into the 20th century Argentina's growth capability reduced steadily in comparison to that of these two countries. If this alone is not sufficient evidence of a process of decadence, we can add to this the fact that the maturity of the US economy obliges it to a slower rate of growth than that of developing nations.

Half-point differences in the growth rate over a 60-year period are of fundamental importance and signify qualitative changes in the standard of living and the world standing of a nation. A continuous growth rate of 8% over a decade produces phenomenal prosperity and exceptional general development, as has been seen in the case of Brazil.

Of the many methods devised to calculate the development of a nation's economy, *adding the total of goods made available to the community in a certain year and comparing that total to those of preceding years,* is a generally used form which gives a pretty clear picture of the rate of development. Extraordinary growth can be achieved under circumstantially favorable conditions or in situations in which the health and stability of the economy are sacrificed. But a study of five years of GNP readings is the best barometer with which to check the highs and lows of a nation's economy, since it measures the quantity of goods and services offered to a country's people over a given period.

In terms of being an absolute figure, the GNP gives an idea of the economic potential of one nation in comparison to that of others. We are not, however, dealing with absolutes here, but rather with the development of the figures over prolonged periods, since, as we have said before, trends are more important than absolute situations.

When the country's Gross National Product does not grow, a lack of opportunity is created for existing and future generations. In a we world based on communication, travel and transportation, a country which does not grow loses its youth, if not through emigration, then through alienation. Argentina has been suffering this painful process for the past 30 years. Whole generations of skilled workers and university graduates have left the country. Youths of diverse social classes have joined sides up against the country, some of them joining the ranks of subversion. Though we cannot minimize the importance of the role foreign elements have played in the organization and handling of guerrilla warfare in Argentina, we must realize that this country which has not grown has been an exceptional breeding ground for just such subversive forces.

The Destiny of Our Youth

Each year, Argentina adds 170,000 young people to its potential work force. These 170,000 young men and women need to be able to count on additional productive capital that will permit them to learn skills under more modern conditions than their parents knew some 20 to 30 years before.

At one time Argentina offered its children growing opportunities, and even opened its doors to the youth of Europe, who were incorporated into the Argentine work force, in the process. Today the country is no longer in a position even to offer sufficient opportunities to its own youth. And the today we are speaking of was born in the *middle* of the process of decadence. The number of young Argentines who leave the country in search of a better future is proof of this. It is not at all unusual to find them in Caracas, Sao Paulo or New York. The only study available on this shows that between 1950 and 1966, 17,000 skilled Argentine workers and professionals emigrated to the United States. How many more must we have lost in recent years! (See Appendix II).

The following table shows the decline in the Argentine population growth rate, which corresponds, oddly enough, to the decline of the country's production and to the reduction in its trade with the rest of the world.

Argentine Population Growth Per Year

(average per period)

1900-1914	4.20%
1914-1937	2.72%
1937-1946	1.20%
1946-1955	2.21%
1955-1960	2.14%
1960-1970	1.55%

Sources:CEPAL, "El desarrollo economico de la Argentina"; INDEC (National Statistics and Census Institute.

These figures correspond to the attitude among the country's leaders that the human and material country bequeathed to them by their fathers was good enough as it was for themselves and future generations and that all they had to do was assume an isolationist, distributionist attitude and maintain the status quo.

It should have been obvious to them that the less effort we made, the less we would have in the future. It was only natural that our inferiority complex would lead us to resent our international equals.

One could argue that a reduction in population has been general in the West and that as people reach a higher economic and cultural plane the population tends to decrease. But the figures below show that Argentina has suffered an extraordinary drop in its population growth which is far out of line with the fall in the population growth rate of comparable countries even though the others have achieved a higher level of material and cultural maturity.

Average Annual Growth in Argentine Demographics

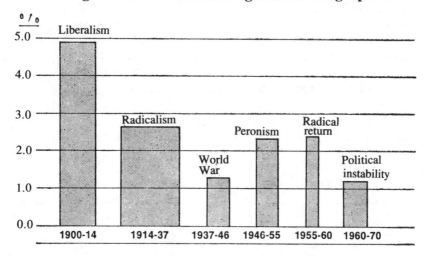

Population Growth Rate in Percentage Per Year

	Argentina	Brazil	Mexico
1900-1937	3.47	2.22	0.87
1946-1970	1.65	2.87	3.24
Difference in rates	-52.00%	+29.00%	+3.72%
	Canada	USA	Australia
1900-1937	2.01	1.43	1.59
1946-1970	2.21	1.53	2.16
Difference in rates	+10.00%	+7.00%	+36.00%

If we establish proportional figures based on figures for the period 1900-1937, we find that Argentina is the only country included in this table which has reduced its population growth rhythm in the post war period.

Countries like the United States grew more in terms of their population after the war than they did during the pre-war base period. Population growth is the result of the effect of the set of policies a country follows. Growth occurs when the country achieves the kind of income level reached in Argentina in 1916. A drop in the population growth rate indicates misgovernment. We should not let ourselves be confused by the situation of countries whose population still lives in a backward state or where the people have suffered centuries of hunger and hardship. In these cases, the growth of a population (which cannot feed, clothe or educate its young) is an entirely different phenomenon. It involves an independent variable which is the cause of its own misfortune.

But if we start with the high income rate in the first decade of the century and add to that the country's vast, unexploited regions, its potential wealth in resources and a land as large as it is untamed, the drop in population growth constitutes an imminent danger of losing our national identity. For here a decline in the birth rate means a decline in hope.

The Nation's Capital

Another chart should be added to those which mark the progress of the GNP, of trade and of population that have so far painted such a dramatic picture of Argentina's decline: that of domestic capital.

By capital we mean all fixed assets —whether they form part of industry or the home — which the population of a country employs to live and work.

As an example of what goes into the forming of the nation's capital we could include: military installations, water works, ports, power installations, public health facilities, aqueducts, factories, research centers, scientific installations, communications equipment, transport facilities, etc.

Stagnation began to take root as of 1914. But the beginning of this process tended to go undetected by the common citizen.

Stagnation became clearly visible in the second decade of the century, when the nation halted its capitalization efforts and entered a period of negligence which was to last until 1955. A new capitalization effort was only seen toward the end of the '60s. During the 1960s the rates became acceptable once again and remained that way until 1973.

The nation's attitude toward capitalization was to seriously hurt its future for a long time to come. The disinterest of those in power from 1916 onward is manifest in their neglecting to create domestic capital.

1973-1976: Decadence Accelerates

National decadence suffered a final acceleration — to the point of virtual collapse — in the three years following the general elections

The following graph shows Argentina's annual development rate per period measured in terms of the country's capital stocks:

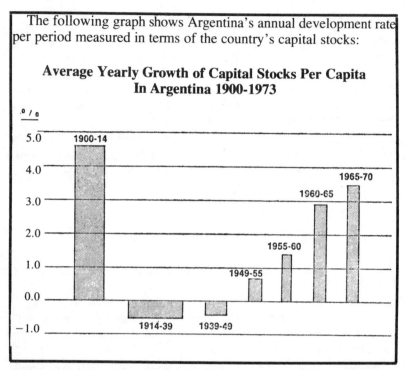

Average Yearly Growth of Capital Stocks Per Capita In Argentina 1900-1973

held on March 11, 1973. The three-year period constitutes a paradigm, a case for study, of the destruction of an economy, and the deterioration of a society and its industry. The figures below reflect the movement of three basic economic indicators during this period.

Year	Growth of GNP	Growth of gross fixed capital investment	Growth of consumption
1973	6.1	0.3	6.9
1974	6.6	5.0	7.2
1975	−1.4	−6.9	3.3

Source: Economy Ministry: "Informes de Coyuntura."

Consumer incentives at the beginning of the period brought an increase in the GNP. New government housing plans also boosted the gross fixed capital investment figure in 1974. But a drop in productivity caused by demagogic national laws and a lack of government authority coupled with a total lack of net reproductive investments were reflected in 1975 — the moment of truth. In spite of the decline of the GNP, the *big spender* philosophy was reflected in the increase in the consumption rate. *The government encouraged the people to devour the nation.*

This consumer onslaught provoked the strangulation of the balance of payments, because it meant that more was consumed than was produced. This, in turn, brought an increase in imports and a decrease in exports. The collapse of the foreign trade sector is a classic symptom of the "consumption without effort" philosophy. The growth rate of our foreign trade for this period supports this:

Year	Export growth	Import growth	Variation in reserves (in US$ millions)
1973	6.0%	−1.8%	731.2
1974	2.6%	20.4%	94.7
1975	−20.4%	−6.3%	−1,094.5

Source: Economy Ministry; BCRA "Annual Report."

Here is another picture of reality:

	Wholesale price level index (Rate of increase/year)
1973	31
1974	37
1975	348
1976 (1st quarter annual rate)	3,090.5

Source: INDEC "Nivel de precios mayoristas" and author's research.

The starting rhythm of 1976 promised a year of hyperinflation and yet, as of March 23, neither the ruling Peronists nor their parilamentary opposition had the slightest idea of how to stop the plunge of the Argentine peso.

1976 Period of Inertia

We witnessed the replacement of the national government on March 24, 1976. A government made up of the Armed Forces took over office from the irresponsible and demagogic civilian government.

History requires that this new government try to reverse Argentina's long decline. If this government realizes that what it is living through is not a crisis, but decadence, it will have a better chance of succeeding. Here we will stick to Argentina's immediate economic future.

The accelerated destructive process the country has been going through cannot be dealt with from one day to the next. The condition of our economic indicators must get worse before it gets better to the point of giving us a solid foundation on which to build self-sustaining growth. So as to avoid having demagogues try to lay the blame for the difficult situation this country is in on Isabel Martinez de Peron's successors, we shall insert here estimates formulated about halfway through 1976 on how principal economic indicators were expected to behave in that and the following year.

We found ourselves in a period of deep recession which had begun in the second half of 1975 and which was caused in general by the governments which ruled Argentina over the 60 years leading up to the 1976 military takeover, and in particular by the governments of Campora, Lastiri, Peron, Luder and again Isabel Peron — that is to say, the Presidents who crucified Argentina for the three years of its history from 1973 to 1976.

Estimates obtained during the course of 1976 and 1977 make significant predictions:

Predictions from 1976-1977

	1976	1977
GNP (percentage variation)	−6	+2
Real wages (percentage variation)	−37	+1
Inflation rate (percentage variation)	+326	+60
Investment rate	16	18

Source: Author's estimates

Thanks to 60 years of decadence we are left with a shrinking country. No policy will be capable of quickly reversing the effects of the figures we have seen in the statistical tables and the estimates (based on the policies followed until March 1976) included here. They point to a sad Argentine future caused by the four generations which have sacrificed the country. Perhaps the government which took over in 1976 will be able to lay the groundwork which will make it possible to permanently halt our decadence, promote national growth and establish the country's geopolitical position. For this to happen, however, it is imperative that future generations understand what caused this decadence and who were responsible for it.

But then, isn't it too materialistic to judge the decadence of a people through the declining figures of its operative wealth?

Actually, money is strangely linked to poetry. They have a basic characteristic in common: the metaphor. Poetic metaphors express a reality by creating another more imaginative, less trivial reality. Jorge Luis Borges takes this a step further when he says: "There is nothing less materialistic than money, since any kind of money is a repertory of possible futures. Money is abstract, money is future time."[1]

And since money is the "repertory of possible futures," its decadence means the decadence of hope and of creative impulses with which to build a destiny.

Argentina's economic decadence is the inclined plane down which we have been sliding for the past 60 years toward fewer and fewer possible futures. It does not matter that analyses show that the acceleration in political activity does not keep a steady pace with the decline in the nation's wealth, since political activity tends to be more arrhythmic than economic activity. But what is sure is that money as an expression of wealth, and politics as an expression of the quality of intelligence placed at the service of the future, will someday have to meet on a dangerous corner in history.

In the previous tables, we have seen how the road to riches can become narrow. If we add a global view of the political situation to this, we will notice that the country's muscle-tone weakens, its motivation crumbles and it finally falls into a tangled web.

From the time Yrigoyen assumed office in 1916 until Uriburu, with the help of the army, kicked him out of his second term in office, Argentina suffered the shock of pernicious inaction. Not even the Radicals had a plan for greatness. Not even Yrigoyen or Alvear were anything more than slow, quiet spectator-presidents, in no way go-getters. Guided by these men, with its muscles still warm from meeting the demands of the creative generation of the 80s, the country left the playing field and took a place on the grandstand where it could passively watch the course of world history go by.

The period from 1930 to 1943 was one of short-term incipiently statist thinking — a period in which the Grain, Meat, Yerba Mate and Cotton Boards, as well as other so-called *regulatory* (a safely

---

[1] Cited by Dr. Rafael Olarra Gimenez in the preface to his book, *El dinero y las estructuras monetarias,* Aguilar 1965.

ambiguous adjective) offices were created. The period was typified by a commodity-based policy, which, by virtue of not being part of a program for the future, ended up taking the drive out of organized creativity and began to break down irreplaceable stimuli for the recuperation of creative action.

At the same time, the people who lived through the constructive last years of the 19th century had begun to die off, and the memoryless new generation was willing to accept policies which offered meager alternatives — a set of non-philosophical policies. The existence of a few men like Savio or Mosconi or of projects like the founding of the Argentine merchant fleet were isolated eruptions which were not strong enough to shake the country out of its slumber.

From 1943 to 1946 we saw the *beginning of the demagogic era* to which populism would later be added. Out of this murky union of populism and demagogy, the crippled Argentina we have inherited was to be born. The eternal, permissive holiday that the Peronist governments comprised, in which the administration declined its duty to lead and elevate the country and instead under the guise of "national conquest," submitted responsibility for the country's political power to puerile populist whims, held a hidden trap. When the Peronists declared that they would do "only what the people wanted" they knew that they had already found the way to make the people want exactly what the government wanted. They were to intoxicate the people with demagogy so that little by little the population would be bogged down in superficial emotions.

Thus, in the final stages of decadence, these demagogy-drugged people were turned into an abject mass. Now it is up to the March 1976 government to move the country into a state of crisis, a natal crisis out of which the country can be reborn.

Chapter II

The Populist Utopia

Quantitative Factor

That amusing line of Sancho Panza's — "Along came the
Saracens and pounded us with sticks: God helps the bad people when
they outnumber the good ones..." — is an excellent way to sum up a
period of political transformation that took place under dangerously
tense conditions. It is worth pointing out that even God is inclined to
consider the *quantitative factor* when he has nothing else to go on in
deciding who is right. The *majority* appear to be right because they
are the *majority;* and if they are not right, it doesn't matter, because
Man has learned that quantity is, in itself, right.

Deformations — in politics — look very much like the original
item, and what is more, they sometimes imitate the original so
closely that they completely confuse those involved as well as
observers of the situation. Populism, for instance, has managed to
do an excellent imitation of democracy.

One of the purposes — among others — of democracy is to let the
country be run in accordance with the judgement of the largest
number of people possible. Because of this, the act of electing —
which should not be confused with mere voting — was a sacred
ceremony in Argentina in which conformity and dissent were
vented.

The populist deformation of democracy works by blotting out
reason, thus inducing unanimous approval. It devalues elections and
transforms them into a bureaucratic corroboration of what *the people*
have already approved of in previous forced *adhesion.*

Conventional cheating methods, such as buying votes or stuffing the ballot box are left behind. Populism brings another kind of fraud, a deeper and more effective technique which comes across as *unquestionable wisdom* and is contained in the dangerous and aggressive slogans which are scrawled on walls and published in the local press. "The people are always right," is one of them. For this sort of movement to operate, it must possess the power of public persuasion — obvious as it was in the case of Peron, or quiet and magical as in the case of Yrigoyen — which works on the masses to inhibit conduct and exalt comportment, or in other words, to hinder the people's reasoning mechanism and excite their primary emotional reflexes.

According to Henry Pratt Fairchild's *Dictionary of Sociology* the difference between comportment and conduct is that comportment refers to a blind and fatalistic way of acting, while conduct implies election, the weighing of bad against good within a system of values or social code of morals. Comportment, then, is composed of natural, purely animal actions, while conduct is made up of actions determined by the will, intelligence and ethical motivation of man alone.

The object in a democracy is to foment meditated, personal decisions; populism seeks an anticipated consensus for every type of test. Despite all this, it is not uncommon for some governments, and also a good portion of the international press, to mistake the pathological (populism) for the sane (democracy).

The dividing line between the two runs right through the delicate area of political propaganda and the path it takes to winning a consensus at the polls passes through an area infected by psychological action and by the clever captivation of the people's affection.

The pathology of democracy is populism, which is capable of turning the concept of the majority into the proliferation of disorderly assent. If a democracy is a government of the people, populism is the abuse by the people, and this invariably generates tyranny.

The Importance of the Minimum Number

Though we Argentines are told over and over not to look back, we should ask ourselves how important the question of number is.

After all, it would appear that quantity is neither a moral nor an intellectual category; thus taking the opinion of the *majority* as a criterion on which to base truth is an attitude akin to *racism*. If racism seeks the handing over of power to people of the same genetic origin, the concept of the majority, as an absolute value, is very similar, with the basic difference that race is a *permanent* condition while adhesion to a particular system is *variable*.

But if we carry this thought through, we find that the impossibility of majority will is not much different than racial aberration. It means that this person or that is good and is right because he *belongs to the group* which thinks the same as he does. The establishment of a group is usually, in itself, enough to generate racism, no matter how large or small the group may be. Thus, the concept of majority is objectionable for the same reasons racism is, except for one fundamental difference: be one white, black, Jew or Gentile, the individual has no choice in what his race will be, while backing one system or another (a decision which places one in the majority or the minority) is presumably a free choice.

What person, who belongs to the majority, is going to sympathize with someone who decided to be part of the minority? Didn't he decide on this of his own free will? Isn't he in a position to change his mind and join the ranks of the winning group if he wants to?

Thus, the essential difference between belonging to a race and belonging to a majority is nothing less than the possibility of *freedom*.

Number, which at first sight seems superficial, acquires the distinctive value of free choice within the framework of democracy. Democracy is based on qualification before quantification, with *minimum number* being as important as *maximum number* to the point that a democracy can be defined as the majority exercising all its power to insure respect for the minority.

But while democracy gives equal importance to the majority and the minority, populism pursues, terrorizes and destroys the minority in order to foment the stupefying uniformity that tames the emotions of the masses. In each populist movement there is a manipulator who profits from the taming of the public. Nazism and Stalinism were two major populist experiences, both of which operated exclusively with the majority, for the physical or ideological elimination of terrified dissidents. It is surprising that after having had these two grave experiences within the same century, agitators and activists are still milking results from this same old formula: *If "all" the people want this, he who does not want it is against the people and is, therefore, guilty of high treason against the people.* And based on this fallacy, rampant violence is permitted. If there is a maximum and unquestionable example of this among modern states, it is under the Marxist system in which the fatherland, in the name of which diverse breaches of justice and human dignity are committed, is replaced by the *people*. Though the rites are different, Marxism is founded on the same idolatry and irrationality as the other systems mentioned.   For Hitler, God was the German people; for the Marxists, God is all the people. The only difference between the two theories is mere geographical volume.

Under Hitler, the Germans were supposed to practice self-glorification, submitting themselves to the idea of conquering other peoples. The Marxist people are taught to be worthy of self-praise by first conquering themselves and then conquering other peoples. This is a practical and opportunistic version of the Marxist theory of class struggle, which replaces vertical (upward) struggle with a horizontal struggle and conquest. These are strange deities who play both God and the lamb sacrificed to calm that god's fury.

But then, who are the people, after all?

The concept of the people is elusive in character. Its semantic trajectory is full of twists and its ubiquitous connotation is not — even by the most subtle linguistic, logical and metaphysical means — easy to define. If we stop to realize that a definition is not enough, that intellectual boundaries must stand the test of empiric reality and that because of this, sociological guidelines may also be useful, things grow even more difficult. For some, the concept of the people signifies a social compound which is the product of associative processes which are integrated on a cultural and superficial level, thus making the people the heart of society. The people are also a universal social constant in a world of historical variables. According to some authors, the people form the cornerstone of culture. According to others, the people are the product and the process of associative personal interaction of individuals and the interaction between their environment and their cultural development.

Populism has resolved this problem by merely replacing linguistic, logical, metaphysical and sociological analysis with simple arithmetic. The people equal all those who belong to a movement. The rest are merely waste matter. They make up the antipeople.

"First the sentence and then the evidence," Alice in Wonderland declares. Find it now and search for it later, populism implies.

The term defined, the concept of the people is raised to the level of an absolute, a prime reality whose demands are manifested in diverse utopias.

These utopias, which are ambiguous by definition, are held in as high an esteem as the words of an oracle, because they emanate from a People, whose voice is that of the magical leader or of the Party. And this voice can thus pontificate on social reality, on science, on economy, on politics, on justice, on education, on culture... well, on practically everything.   If this institution called the People is absolute, then so is any judgement it passes.   And since it is only a short step from being absolute to being omniscient, the People never make a mistake. From this fallacious point of view, everything seems oddly justified.

The passing of industry from its artisanry stage to the mechanized age has been called the Industrial Revolution. The term *revolution* is a good one, since the gradual abandoning of hand craftsmanship and the latter's replacement by industrial machinery, produced a broad qualitative and quantitative mutation, not only in economics, but also in the sociopolitical field.

The machine catapulted the ever-changing face of the entity known as the people to the forefront of the historical stage.

The arrival on the scene of this novel character made possible a coordination of forces, different from the one instituted by the French Revolution in 1789. The rebellion against the feudal system was a bourgeois revolution. The third estate, a highly privileged orphan, was made up of the French bourgeoisie, which numbered about 250,000. The artisans and guild craftsmen formed the proletariat. On the eve of the Revolution, these workers numbered 600,000, but in contrast to the bourgeoisie — which was a relatively organized group — the working class comprised a weak, disorganized mass. The masses did not even have any real political clout under Jacobinic rule.

The Industrial Revolution, once it established its presence among the industrial working class, became the catalyst for the organization of a labor front. From that time on the working class recognized its numerical strength and used it in the struggle for political power. Marx would, some years later, eloquently sum up this metamorphosis by saying that the working class "stops being a class in itself in order to become a class for itself." What do you suppose the inhabitants of socialistic countries think when they see that members of the high bureaucracy can do their shopping in special shops that they themselves are not permitted to enter?

Demagogy: Breeder of Idle Delirium

The demagogy which, for years, has taken the place of democracy in Argentina appears to have a life of its own. Its prolonged control of the management of public administration has left a state of deterioration behind, which will be difficult to erase. Included among demagogy's vital signs in Argentina is the embryo of irrationality which has been planted in the minds of the people. This irrationality has been nurtured by demagogy and has grown to the point that it will be very hard to overcome. Irrationality, contempt for analysis and self-righteous indignation are all weapons in the arsenal with which demagogy wins uncontested victories in questions put before the masses. To analyze is to think, and thought, since it is capable of presenting possibilities beyond those offered by the demagog's programs, is more dangerous than high explosives. Rigorous rationality cannot be permitted by demagogic rulers, because it constitutes the strongest weapon with which to oppose fallacy and demagogy's coat of mail is made of fallacy interwoven with truth.

To what extent has free thought been limited in Argentina? Is it a means for transmitting the indignation that fills us? Wasn't the error obvious of those who suggested that Peronism would destroy itself if it were merely permitted to continue in office? Couldn't they see that in their own downfall the demagogs would drag Argentina's highly prized national spirit into oblivion with them? Wht becomes of a demagog faced with a debate between himself and a group of clear-thinking citizens?

One of the remedies prescribed by the demagog is that of filling the present with current notions or goods of an absolutely immediate nature. This was not invented by Argentina, nor do Argentine demagogs have exclusive rights on it. It is part of an Occidental illness. Oswald Spengler makes this clear in the first few lines of his book on Western decadence. Decadence is an important question that Westerners have not yet studied: It is a question of life and death.

But no one — man or country — can justify his own shortcomings by pointing to those of others. There are very strong reasons why we should not take comfort in others' weaknesses as an excuse for our own. Nor should we justify our fear of asking questions by pointing to the fear of those who should be giving us some serious answers.

The demagogs know all too well how to suspend thought and judgement on the future and how to keep it chained to the short-term and irresponsible present.

It seems absurd in an age when science and technology have reached the summit of far-reaching, long-term thinking, that a people should accept a political attitude which limits the horizon to the most egotistical present.

There are somewhat theological overtones in all this, in that by moving away from God, who combines future, past and present in His eternal existence, society also strays from the legal framework of the commandments and from the code of ethics which governs the individual's present conduct and that of his descendants in the future, and thus the conduct of society in general.

This compass needle, which should be pointing the way to the future, spins about without direction. When it does this, the lost community begins to go around in the desperate circles of the present guided by the empty values of the past.

There are very subtle relationships among politics, ethics and religion that are valid even for lukewarm believers and non-believers, since they are not founded on faith but on metaphysical evidence. No one can doubt, even if his politics are leftist, that it is impossible to instrument any governmental process, unless those involved abide by their own strict laws which must be respected, must not be questioned and the infraction of which brings, in the most extreme case, the downfall and death of the wrong-doer. In other words, there must be laws which regulate actions which affect the future. This happens in any area where man is obliged to represent truth. Now then, the demagog presents a contrary conviction: Man should deal with his existence in terms of the purest present, a present without a future. But as one cannot with impunity say "without future," the phrase is replaced with campaign gibberish like "Argentine Potential" and other similar verbal formulas.

Demagogic delirium over short-cuts to utopia are based on this futureless attitude, the salient characteristics of which are short-term thinking and irresponsibility. The promise which is impossible to keep is believable if the fruits of that promise are offered immediately. It does not matter if the fallacy of the promise is obvious. The mob clings to this promise and puts responsibility for its future in the hands of a new idol. The demagog's assurance is short-lived, but that doesn't matter either. Tomorrow he will concoct another promise, and in spite of its paradoxical and temporary nature, it will have the same delirious effect on the enthusiastic throngs.

The demagog who said: "I have relieved the German people of the heavy burden of thought; my wish is their command," took charge of Germany's future and led it on a downhill race that would drive it to slaughter and ruin in 1945. The German people, massed together in a web of demagogic delirium and prolific propaganda, transferred their historical responsibility to a madman. The generalized irrationality of the period permitted Russia to establish the Soviet Communist hegemony Hitler professed to combat and avoid. Thus, some historical analysts have attributed the Soviets' World War II triumph more to German errors in strategy and to the Germans' unquestioned and arbitrary leadership than to the ability of Soviet generals.

The demagog needs human resources — men and women who are not worried about their future, or that of the community they are a part of — in order to operate. Thus transformed into an insect-like mass, these people will totally lose their individuality. They will listen to promises of immediate benefits. They will barely respond to questions about their limited egotistical hopes. They will only hear the sound of the fury and frustration that drove them to listen to the demagog in the first place.

There is nothing as adverse to the demagog as the people's exercising their analytical capacity to the point of becoming distinguishable as individual persons. The demagog is aware that from that point onward, man acts in accordance with his rationality which requires him to measure his actions today to make them justifiable with respect to the consequences they will have in the future.

This is valid both on an ethical and political level.

In terms of ethics, an act is only morally justifiable if its consequences raise the moral standards of the community and make way for further growth in society's moral traditions in the future. This means that when a moral act is justified, the community does not lose, by virtue of the act, any of the freedom which permitted the taking of a decision to act in the first place. Accordingly, the act could be suicidal, or at least an extreme sacrifice, for the individual, but it would not drag the fate of the community as a whole along with that of the individual.

Acts are also submitted to the criteria of rationality and future on a political level. The foreseeable effects of a political act should approximate the objectives proclaimed by the politician. If, for example, we wish to raise the real wage level, we cannot introduce legislation which reduces the economy's global productivity.

When analyzing a political act or promise, one must project the consequences into the furthest researchable future before passing final judgement. This final judgement must be based on what effect the act or promise will have on the community once the first waves of reaction roll by. It is absurd, on the other hand, to measure the short-term success or monetary backing a political promise has managed to obtain from a mass-minded public which has obviously renounced any right to question the goodwill of the demagog.

The process of *institutionalization* promoted by the government of General Alejandro Lanusse is a perfect example of a typically demagogic, futureless and irrational political act. His government gave legal status and economic support to a populist hierarchy and instrumented the reincorporation of Peronism into the nation's political field. Peronism, Lanusse's group said, was going to eliminate the ills which have caused the Armed Forces to intervene in the governmental process. The result of this policy would become evident five years later, when the Armed Forces again found themselves obliged to take the reins of a country which had fallen into a state of chaos.

The things that happened from the moment in which irrationality first triumphed until the final fall added up to decay. More than 3,000 people have died in an undeclared and as yet unfinished civil war. Power passed in that short period through the hands of Hector Campora, Raul Lastiri, Juan Peron, Isabel Peron, Italo Luder, Lorenzo Miguel and Jose Lopez Rega. The economic damage is reflected in the charts and tables included in this book. The moral damage continues to shame us on the front pages of periodicals both at home and abroad. The demagogic promise of democracy contained in the term *institutionalization* destroyed the last remnants of democracy, and so concluded the destruction of the republic.

The political populist is always a demagog. This fact is seen in the populist's need to constantly generate new ideological demonstrations which permit him to mask reality and to offer the masses the colors and perfumes of paradise, straight from the leader's hand. These political acts make the candidate's future somewhat conditional since the mortgage on these demagogic properties evidently run out, with the promise either not being kept or being kept but bringing eventual harm to the community. Sometimes the damage done is fatal.

We are experiencing the effect of actions of this sort which were taken in the not-too-distant past. The law governing amnesty for the country's political prisoners set free 5,000 delinquents — many of whom joined terrorist groups or gangs of common criminals — between May and June of 1973. The amnesty promise which was a plank in the platforms of the Peronists, the Radicals and other parties involved in the *Hour of the People* received the yes-vote of practically every member of parliament, even though it was a well-known fact that Argentina was fighting a war against leftwing subversion. The amnesty law was the first legislative act of the *people's government* to which power was handed over.

And this decisive act initiated the irreversible development of a destructive process.

History will judge the men who made the amnesty law possible, those who voted for it and those who signed it into law. The military men and civilians who have been murdered by those freed through the 1973 amnesty, cry out against those who opened the jailhouse doors. Some 3,000 people have died in the wave of violence in Argentina since 1973. How many of them died at the hand of the prisoners the amnesty law freed?

The work contract law passed by the People's Congress is another example of the irrational policies induced by populism. The law which, on the surface, appeared to favor the worker by protecting him against all abuse and by giving him social benefits, which, until then, had never existed, ended up causing a violent drop in real wage levels by setting a process of rampant inflation in motion —inflation whose principal cause was a steady drop in productivity, capital and labor from the day the law was sanctioned onward.

Demagogy seeks to place values on false bases which imitate truth, much in the same way as the Scriptures tell us Satan tried to imitate God. In this way, the demagog induces generally fallacious thinking, administered in easy-to-swallow doses of sugar-coated ideology. This false, simplistic thought-substitute is designed to replace real thought, which, to the demagog, becomes more dangerous as it gets deeper.

The demagog's plan is a clever one: It plays on acute and long-term resentments. According to the simplistic populist line of thought: What is the difference between the rich and the poor? The rich live without working. For the people, the rich man is rich, not because he earns more, but because he doesn't work. In this there is a fanciful image of happiness; happiness is more money and less work. The demagog takes full advantage of this vocation for laziness by artificially jacking up wages. But this causes an inevitable rise in prices and the rise in prices brings a new wage rise and so on goes the absurd race which can only end in catastrophe...

But as long as the demagog remains in office, the fantasy is carefully maintained. This fairytale never, however, outlives the demagog that instruments it. The demagog's dominion over the people is not negotiable; it cannot be transferred to a successor even if he himself names the person who will follow him — be that person his protege, his lieutenant or his wife. Tyrants are seldom succeeded by their children. Their plans begin and end with them. Their historical schemes include no future.

Meanwhile, the human spirit is restless. Thus the demagog must protect the idleness he has created to calm the masses by also creating delirium.

Idle delirium, as we shall call it for the first time, is a very peculiar state in which the slim benefits that comprise unfounded prosperity are mixed with ideological stimuli which are part of a doctrine, capable of producing a state of constant delirium, from which the well-indoctrinated masses cannot escape.

The demagog needs fertile social ground in which to take root and develop. This social ground is made up of men and women in whom an illogical yet practicable political act has mutilated Mans's most brilliant attribute: the gift of reason.

Once a sufficient dose of idle delirium has been introduced into society, the great demagogic swindler will no longer have to fear being ambushed by the people he has defrauded. For the moment — and this moment could last 30 years — there remains open to the demagog in Argentina a boundless impunity under the protection of which he can sack the nation, take over its industries, manipulate its money, and worse, wreck all of its possibilities for the future.

Chapter III

Man Is A Geopolitical Animal

Environment Is Not Omnipotence

There are cumulative causes behind decadence. Sometimes a basic error brings the alienation of the nation — in its real status as a nation — and its loss of identity. Perhaps the greatest mistake of the Argentine Republic and its political leaders has been their erroneous placement of the country on the geopolitical map of the world.

During the Second World War, and especially toward the end of the conflict, Argentina was betting on the Axis to win. Later it bet that there would be a new war, this time between the Communist bloc and the Free World. Such miscalculations caused the powers that were to lead the world to push Argentina aside. Worries of a world war between communists and democrats caused us to piddle away our foreign reserves on items which were absolutely unnecessary in a world living in relative peace. These mistakes were accentuated by our adding ourselves to the ranks of the Third World — a true case of geopolitical, social and cultural delirium.

If a nation is mistaken in its placement with respect to other countries, its domestic development policy will remain conditioned to its initial error. That is why we have tried to cover the unmistakable tracks left in the tricky field of history by the only geopolitical animal ever created.

Animal life imposes inevitable behavior patterns, dictated by a standard code, on the individuals of a species. Man, on the other hand, lives in a wide open world and does not find his environment made to order for him at birth. Man must create his surroundings. While the animal is provided for by nature, man must procure an adequate environment for himself by using the raw materials provided by nature to create items more suited to his needs. These items belong not only to nature but also to a society and to a culture.

When the term *environment* is used in connection with human *environment,* it means more than man's mere surroundings; Man's environment actually consists of a system of dynamic conditions, which stimulate or hinder his individual activities and which influence his victory or defeat. In other words, the nation is our overall environment. At the same time, the nation's environment is the world. Thus, from birth, Man is essentially a geopolitical animal.

Ever since Man first appeared, each individual has had to face the problem of placing himself among his peers. Soon Man found that his personality was his own, that it was not a carbon copy of his neighbors'. Sociocultural environment was to have such strong influence over the man-creature, however, as to regulate everything from his speech patterns to his most subconscious value judgements. Its influence would, at the same time, be so subtle that it would come to affect Man's patterns of perception of reality.

Nevertheless, this environment is not omnipotent. It may influence but it does not determine. *Inclinant sed non obligan. To be another.* This is the basis for the structure of what we know, in the broadest sense of the word, as politics, and it has been developed as a concept ever since one being first entered into a relationship with another. Thus each person born is a new fighter who must be prepared to fight not only for his geographical environment, but also for his no less important political environment. The dialectic over being oneself and being another becomes particularly touchy when applied to the status of whole nations.

One of the greatest differences between primitive and modern Man is that the Man of today operates within the guidelines of a tremendous amount of information which has been gathered for him by successive generations. The store of information is what makes each community *typical* and it all began with such simple things as distinctive ways of hunting, of making arms and of butchering an animal. These primitive techniques were stamped on the memories of a couple, a group, a village and so on, and thus formed a repertory of *national* know-how — even if the nation only consisted of a man and a woman.

As time passed one national origin was linked with others until the modern concept of a nation was formed. Thus, those initial techniques which primitive Man developed in order to adapt to the geographical and political demands of his environment, began to repeat themselves. Although they are now seen on a monstrously broader plane, the *being* and the *other being* showed up repeatedly on the international level on which nations confirm their identity and, every now and then, form relationships with other nations. These relationships are important to the extent that organized communities which, despite having had the opportunity, have not associated with other communities, have left hardly any mark at all on world history, and have been left out of the future.

The National Role Is Always International

Just as subjectivity always exists in relation to objectivity, a national role is always an international role. This need for comparison and that other need to battle with one's geography and develop a political stance makes men — who are essentially geopolitical animals — found their existence on a geopolitical concept, which in turn becomes one of the inescapable components of all future concepts.

Geopolitics are relatively new as a technique, but geopolitics, in terms of being an intellectual exercise, have been a part of history since Man first appeared. We nevertheless tend to be given a concept of geopolitics which is mutilated in at least one of its essential aspects.

Space is the territory and everything it contains; time is history. Territory and history are important to a country's relations and form the road on which a nation travels. But there lies a trap in one of these terms. What is usually meant by the word territory? Territory is nearly always used to mean the surface area of a nation and sometimes includes the country's off-shore limits.

We are currently confronted with cases of horizontal vision in nations. This deprives them of a cross-concept geopolitical stance— that is to say, a concept in which the horizontal territory is intersected by the vertical. Four areas are taken in by this double line of vision: under the horizontal heading fall *solid territory* and *liquid territory* while in vertical geopolitics we find *airspace* and *underground territory*. Linked to all this is the variable but important cultural factor. The consequences of this cultural factor will be the development (or lack of it) of the wealth and power which the natural resources of any given country have to offer — on the land, under the land, in the sea and in the air.

This is the environment of a nation. The interaction of culture and geography will yield variable power and will be the deciding factor in whether the country experiences the violent or peaceful expansion all nations need in order to assure themselves of a place among the other nations of the world.

It is not infrequent that people tie themselves to wearisome speculation as to the defensive value of boundaries around the solid surface of a territory while overlooking the fact that frontiers as the theoretical lines of a national, legal and political universe are out of focus when seen through the dual-vision of the geopolitical cross-concept and completely disappear when the possibility of a supra-national structure is contemplated.

Kelsen, already in his day, said that territory should be visualized as an inverted cone, whose tip was situated at the center of the earth and whose base had no limits. In this last sense, his theory was still a bit precarious.

When Bacon said in the 17th century that he who became master of the sea would be master of the world, he was doing nothing more than repeating what Themistocles had said 20 centuries before, in repeating what Mediterranean seamen had told him. Obviously, subterranean, underwater and airspace exploitation never entered their minds, because their respective cultures had not yet developed the technology to place these areas within their reach.

But nowadays, nothing can justify a nation like Argentina not accepting the reality of geopolitical cross-vision, nor that it should fail to compare the dual-angle picture with that of other nations so as to regulate its internal doings in accordance with that is going on abroad. The internationality of a nation, its capacity to *be* in relation to *other beings* will end up being its most intimate and so called "national" success, and from this point on, the nation can break free of the history of frustration and melancholy which have character-ized Argentina, to move on to a series of life-giving successes.

In order to do this, we must reorganize ourselves on a national level, in the way which appears most feasible in accordance with our true geopolitical cross-view. Before this is possible, we must first destroy the myths and taboos, which have nurtured, adorned and celebrated the Argentines' monotonous, complaining mutterings of practically the entire century.

Killing Time

As we said earlier, we must add the dimension of time to the geo-political cross concept. Among the many confusing aspects of our age, one of the most perturbing to a developed sense of reason is that of killing time. The present, *that hinge on which past and future swing, has been pumped up to look like something of untouchable value.* Adhering to the premise that the man of today must *be constantly up-to-date,* the consumption-oriented society has begun with unaccustomed voracity to consume time. Without time to review the past or await the future, this instant-coffee-drinking, speed-reading civilization has limited its world to everyday happenings. Advertising, the press and the business world submit man to an ever more frantic cultural acceleration. Everything included in what today's magazines refer to as "modern living" looks like a gigantic cyclotron designed to split the individual whose vital and shattered nuclei will emanate energy 24 hours a day, a fabulous energy which canot be channeled in time. This modern man's time knows no future and his present is too narrow to take advantage of his tremendous energy flow.

This idolizing of speed, neurotically manifest in the vehicles in which we travel, in our communications systems, in the appearance of a synthesized society full of synopses, condensed books and shorthand, probably masks and at the same time represents Man's desperate perception of his own mortality. The presence of death in the absence of God — signs of which are constantly before us so that no one can possibly forget it — may be the secret stimulus in this free-wheeling race, this vertigo that keeps us encrusted in the present. We do not live in the past and we do not know if we will live to see the future in a world which has proven itself to be particularly uncertain. It is not enough to be a man of *action.* The most *active* of those who put *action* into the present we now call *activists.* What time could we possibly have for reflection? How completely the calm of civilization has disappeared!

The *memoriless people* we mentioned in Chapter I, and the suicidal clean-slate policy, which recriminates anyone who "wastes" the present evaluating the past, form a part of the *currentist delirium* which is invading us and which, with the help of those who try to feed us the fallacious notion that the future is today, is going to also ruin our possibilities of making stable projections.

There can be no deep and creative national reorganization if we fail to change our concept of time. Only with a critical view of the past and a realistic look into the future can Argentina develop a geopolitical stance. A culture which despises historians, eliminates its prophets and nurtures chroniclers is on its way to nothing more than a succession of short-term, trivial lives.

Geopolitics are the channelling of the natural trends of people grouped in nations. Geopolitics work with two variables: One, the dependent one, being vertical and horizontal space with its four levels: solid territory, liquid territory, airspace and underground territory. The other, the independent variable, is time, which includes past and future history, and which is the motivating factor for producing modifications in space.

"Today is moved by time," Goethe affirmed and we Argentines had better get moving right now in search of the time we have lost.

Nevertheless, although people were won over by the *practicability* of ideology over philosophy — which, given the acceleration of the pace of history, had begun to look like an idle luxury — the shower of controversies which we have seen in the theoretical analysis of ideology have been necessary to make it clear that ideologies are: systems of ideas, subordinated from a geopolitical point of view, which dictate and outline action.

We often hear the word ideology modified by the adjective false, but here we should ask ourselves, false in what respect? Ideologies are not based on the *criterion of truth* but on the *criterion of need*. Ideology may be convenient in the context of a geopolitical concept and only in this way can it be untrue to the natural wishes of a nation to grow and expand. But we must not tolerate ideology's becoming a substitute for philosophy. Philosophy *seeks truth* and its entire strength is employed in this search. Ideology employs *truths which are beyond its reach.*

If philosophy breeds a moral, a moral breeds an ideology. But an ideology can be invented outside moral guidelines and these ideologies which have a toxic effect similar to that created by a false illusion, will make victims of countries which lack geopolitical power. To keep a nation healthy, there is nothing better than to give it an offensive and defensive weapon with which to ward off the assaults of such ideologies. The weapon is called a *national ideal,* the true product of a national philosophy. A strong ideal is airtight against any argument, and with time it develops its own arguments, which shelter it and make its growth easier, because it is as strong and fertile as the moral foundation on which it is built.

We must keep this in mind, because in today's world, ideologies walk among us.

Chapter IV

The West Begins
On Calvary Hill

Efficiency and Scruples

Because it is much more than a geographical site, because it is a mode of life associated with freedom, because it knows the solidarity of getting along with one another and because it has built its code of ethics on respect of life, the West begins on Calvary Hill. To leave this out of the framework of politics means omitting the most binding factor in Western civilization. To leave this factor out of the framework of morality means giving in to the employment of any means as long as they are politically useful. And this last practice, which is hoisted like a flag over the cultures from which God has been left out, would undermine the very foundations of Western identity. Generally speaking, we are not far from accepting indiscriminate means on the condition that their perversity is well-masked and that they deliver the hoped for results.

Many Argentines were shocked, when the Watergate case broke in the US, that the pillars of the nation could be shaken by the seemingly puerile business of violating the privacy of the country's citizens. But Watergate is a Western phenomenon, the sudden appearance of a barrier, a moral limit, the passing of which could cause an entire community to crumble. Argentines have experienced Watergates throughout their entire history. Our judicial history is rich with evidence that morality is the essence of the West, and that it is held in much higher esteem than individuality, freedom of trade or the will of the majority.

How far from the West have the people strayed who, blinded by the apparent success of those who "make it" by casting scruples to the wind, opt for immorality and corrupt the basic principles of the way of life! A nation shaken by the discovery of an immoral act, feels, at the same time, the security of knowing that the community is firmly based on a moral foundation which permitted the discovery of the immoral act in the first place, and this feeling constitutes a way of life that no revolution could possibly have the strength to abolish. The Western way of life begins on Calvary Hill.

The "Robinsonian" Nation

We must remember in all this, however, that the world goes beyond the West. There are currently three great powers each of which has its own line of political thought: Russia, China and the United States. With Europe left out because of its inconsistence in international dealings, only the noisy slum known as the Third World remains. These were Argentina's choices. Logically, since the country was living through the bitterest hours of its existence, Argentina formally joined the Third World in 1964 after boasting that its most influential political leader of all time had been a pioneer leader of the Third Position movement.

In Part One of this book, we analyzed the principal factors in the destruction of the moral and creative will of a broad sector of Argentine society. As a natural result of all this, Argentines were too bruised and battered to stand up, look into the mirror-countries and formulate a geopolitical concept.

Just as far from reality as a hermit who has no harmonic relationship with the rest of the human race and in his sterile mutilated form is unable to develop or transmit humanity, is the unrealistic image of a nation, which, like Robinson Crusoe, seeks a self-sufficient and solitary existence.

The nation is the generator of social, psychological and cultural limits, but, like Man, it is something more. It presents infinite possibilities for relationships with other nations and it is through these relationships that light is cast on our opaque psycho-bio-social reality. The nation will thus have access to a different sphere: the metaphysical sphere where the spirit resides. It is within this sphere that those who make up the nation will have the responsibility of fighting the battle for liberty.

Since the people of isolated nations lose their identity, they tend to try to compensate for this loss by relating to a stupid self-centeredness which is elevated to a virtuous position; and at the same time, these people dress a lack of national solidity in the clothes of sovereignty. With its natural sources either omitted or anesthesized, geopolitics will be a useless exercise for these people, who, having lost their constituent structure, will become nothing less than a ghostly flow of something bordering on agony.

Argentine Fantasies

Just as serious as a nation's loss of identity is its loss of meaning.

"We are a great nation," we Argentines used to say before the wheels of the agroimport machinery started to squeak, and we said it with such haughtiness as to add: "God is a criollo." Something made us feel that no matter what we did, nothing would ever go badly for us. This obstinate belief in the fantasy that we were assured *of good luck,* facilitated our tendency to stagnate. When things did start going badly, we invented another childish fallacy: *Negative happenings were the fault of some foreign entity which was jealous of our Eden: if there was a shade of doubt as to whether blame could be attributed to an alien source, we laid the guilt at Lady Luck's door.* We have become so infatuated with this thought, that we cannot tolerate losing. And so we have whipped up a profoundly ridiculous saying: "The moral triumph is ours." It is a saying as versatile as it is ridiculous and can be applied to sports, the quantity of wheat we produce and the quality of our meat. Office workers, cab drivers, professional people and housewives have developed a cult of egocentricity which leaves no room for discussion. But the fact that this egocentricity is for internal consumption only and that the fabulous values it praises are not recognized abroad should be our cue to ask ourselves when Argentina first lost its sense of national meaning. All we need to do to get the figures pertaining to our objective decline is measure the dimension of our subjective complacence.

Not only is it possible for a nation to lose its identity and still preserve a disproportionate sense of self-importance, but it is also possible for one thing to act as a stimulus on the other. In referring to some of the more capricious and arbitrary facts of Argentine national temperament, Lezama writes in his book called *Balcarce 50*: "Argentina appears to be a nation made up of 25 million persons, each of whom is only a child." As this book is being written (1976), Argentina has just come out of its latest demagogic-populist reign and, with its treasury picked clean, finds itself, for the first time, in a truly grave situation. We are no longer a great nation, and God seems to have renounced his citizenship. "Today we cannot fool ourselves: our liberty is at stake once again."[1]

[1] The words of Monsignor Adolfo Nolasco in a tedeum of July 9, 1976.

Now, we are alone, with the world around us, if not hostile, then at least taking a long look at how serious we are in our reorganization proposals. This is our chance to stop contemplating our own interior, to go out beyond our boundaries and take up our rightful position in the world. The demagogic populists tried to limit us to our own backyard, because demagogy is political narcisism.

Culturally and geographically, Argentina falls within the US sphere of influence. This is a fact, and as such, it is neutral. It is not a moral judgement, nor is it an expression of desire. But it is a fact of such power that upon measuring it and recognizing it, we find it is our only choice if we are to attain accelerated development with greater distribution of capital and technology. Whether or not this means giving up sovereignty and surrendering advantages and prerogatives is a matter on which Argentines, not foreigners, will decide. The only other choices are Russia, Red China or the Third World.

Western countries sometimes accept ideology which alienates them from their own culture. This, after all, is a consequence of their freedom. And socialist countries take advantage of this Western freedom of choice. Who would think of infiltrating Western moral fiber via radio, television and the press as has been done behind the Iron Curtain? And yet the enemy circulates among us. In the first stage he manipulates the resentment which exists in society. In the second, he offers a different world — a Marxist world. The intermediate stage is that of the Third World. It is a sort of limbo in which the country is offered poverty and satisfaction with its own misery. Belonging to the Third World is dropping out; it is feeling alone and empty. It ripens a country, makes it want to belong to a new political group.

Of course, the Third World only makes sense to countries with an average income under 150 dollars a month, and only until they manage to *belong* to one or another of the real worlds. It also makes sense to imperialistic recruiters, sent to capture disciples and sectarians in the Third World: Cuba, North Korea and arms traders.

Experts in the sale of Utopia, trained in Lumumba University and in Havana, tempt us with systems of "total social justice;" Everyone earns the same, are the same, have the same identity under these systems, they tell us. They are systems which possess the social justice of an ant hill. Man, on the other hand, can show that he is not an ant. Nor has he been born already strictly conditioned, nor is a world like Aldous Huxley's *Brave New World* a possibility today. All utopias are proposals made out of frustration and which lead to nihilism. And totalitarianism follows nihilism.

We should think about the significance of Argentina's having been included among the links of the Third World chain. We should think about those responsible for its inclusion and about what penalty they deserve, historically if they are dead, and judicially if they are still alive.

But before it can make the right choice, Argentina must regain its sense of identity and its sense of meaning. Not knowing who we were and being convinced of our insignificance could drive us straight into the Third World's arms. We might, in such a case, even wave the Third World flag and be content to have enrolled in a community specialized in the distribution of misery, anti-culture, irrationality and guerrilla warfare.

No nation can fall into the depths of its own insignificance and still conserve its sense of responsibility. And the fact is, that we must have a sense of responsibility if we are to undertake a geopolitical stance.

Ideology: A Geopolitical Tool

When Condillac used the word *ideology* — cleanly and aseptically — for the first time, he could not have imagined the frightening destiny which awaited the term in the mouths of Marx and his followers.

There is no other semantic concept as explosive, as wild and hard to tame in the appeasing network of univocality as that of *ideology*. Rome was — avant la lettre — the ideological boiling pot of the Old World, but in those days, an expansionist policy consisted of exporting military campaigns together with an imperialist culture. The empire's concept of Law — programmed or spontaneous — traveled aboard the logistical trains the Roman Legions composed and because of this, the concept of Law and War runs throughout Roman history.

Having incorporated and developed numerous theories, the Romans eventually taught their system of Law to the Greeks and added Greek theories to their own; this combined legal system then spread the length and breadth of the Empire, jolted Rome of 200 B.C., was finally passed around the world, and still affects most law books today.

Although encyclopedists had not yet hallowed the word ideology, since this had not yet been invented, Rome exported a culture from which we today would be able to pluck ideological concept. But we should bear in mind, that this ideology would merely be the involuntary result of thinking, a way of life, a way of putting an intellectual exercise into practice. What an odd turn this process had taken over the centuries! Today ideology comes first, the next step being to put this Marxist ideology into operation, and then to generate a culture, a way of thinking, a way of life, a way of putting an intellectual exercise into practice.

This gross overdevelopment of ideology, this mushrooming of a type of thought which is not even the most basic form of philosophy, is hardly a spontaneous result of cultural development; it is, instead, a handbook of guidelines to which a culture is supposed to mold itself and it only shows that through the intellectual and metaphysical poverty of modern man, philosophy has been replaced by ideology.

Though they throw concepts off the balcony only to have them come back in through the window, most ideological theorists insist on describing ideology as a partial presentation of reality which is affected by extratheoretical factors. And since the national role is always international, the partiality of ideology — outlined by ethical, racial, economic and historical factors — will be the complex result of the focal and projected vision of men.

Powerless to change the past and stuck with a precarious present, the ideologists are left with the outside world and the future as a field in which to play their geopolitical game. In ideology, they find a tool, which even if it is not of use in the search for Truth, helps to calm anxiety.

It was not necessary to wait for Napoleon to insult the ideologists to realize that *men sometimes have mad thoughts,* because this had already been demonstrated 200 years earlier by the Baroque philosophers; but it took the coming of Marx, Manheim, Pareto and Durkheim to demonstrate that ideologists are full of fantasies, that their power of persuasion runs deeper than that of the naked truth, and that they can be mystifying, materialistic and alienating, as was shown in Russia where ideology was employed as a camouflaged landing force to lead the way for a geopolitical stance based on imperialistic expansion.

Nevertheless, although people were won over by the *practicability* of ideology over philosophy — which, given the acceleration of the pace of history, had begun to look like an idle luxury — the shower of controversies which we have seen in the theoretical analysis of ideology have been necessary to make it clear that ideologies are: systems of ideas, subordinated from a geopolitical point of view, which dictate and outline action.

We often hear the word ideology modified by the adjective false, but here we should ask ourselves, false in what respect? Ideologies are not based on the *criterion of truth* but on the *criterion of need.*

Ideology may be convenient in the context of a geopolitical concept and only in this way can it be untrue to the natural wishes of a nation to grow and expand. But we must not tolerate ideology's becoming a substitute for philosophy. Philosophy *seeks truth* and its entire strength is employed in this search. Ideology employs *truths which are beyond its reach*.

If philosophy breeds a moral, a moral breeds an ideology. But an ideology can be invented outside moral guidelines and these ideologies which have a toxic effect similar to that created by a false illusion, will make victims of countries which lack geopolitical power. To keep a nation healthy, there is nothing better than to give it an offensive and defensive weapon with which to ward off the assaults of such ideologies. The weapon is called a *national ideal*, the true product of a national philosophy. A strong ideal is airtight against any argument, and with time it develops its own arguments, which shelter it and make its growth easier, because it is as strong and fertile as the moral foundation on which it is built.

We must keep this in mind, because in today's world, ideologies walk among us.

Chapter V

Do-It-Yourself Kit

Winning the Heart of the Continent

While the battle between David and Goliath was being relived in the form of the Russo-Japanese War and as Chile and Bolivia were laying down their arms in South America, a polished and urbane Scot, Sir Halford Mackinder, took an impeccable study to the Royal Geographic Society in 1904 to demonstrate the correlation between a country's geography and its history.

He thus staked a claim in the brand new field of geopolitics, outlined earlier in the ahistorical and thus one-sided theories of Sweden's Kjellan and Germany's Ratzel, and became the direct predecessor of contemporary geopoliticians.

"A victorious Roman general, upon entering a city in the midst of the rapturous splendor of triumph, had a slave with him in his chariot who whispered these words in his ear: Do not forget that you are mortal!" Some winged cherub should whisper to our statesmen during their dealings with the enemy that he who rules eastern Europe has won the heart of the continent. And he who rules the heart of the continent dominates world government and he who rules over world government dominates the world.

The geopolitical strength of land power could not have been more carefully and at the same time coherently expressed.

Mackinder's reasoning was not proven correct until many years after his brilliant presentation before the Royal Geographic Society. After crushing the Russian Czars, the Soviets, having turned into the ideological watershed of the world, conquered the Nazis in one of the bloodiest battles of all time: Stalingrad. It began in 1943.

What a heavy responsibility for Mackinder's whispering cherub! He had to remind France, Great Britain and the United States that if the Russian State beat Germany, it would be the most powerful country on Earth. It was the ultimate in natural fortresses, a territory which fit like a glove against the heart of the continent.

It would have been impossible for Mackinder to have known how complex geopolitics would become with the introduction of new factors and conditions which were to modify the correlation of forces, the new clash of realities which history would bring, but from then on, his warning served as a symbol for the West.

Communist China had not yet stepped into the bright lights of history. Not until six years later, in 1949, would the People's Republic be born and with it a new form of communism, more virulent for Peking's Muscovite brothers than for its enemies overseas.

A starting point for new directions with respect to old geopolitical ideas on the battle between land power and sea, air and later nuclear power, it would break down the offensive efficiency of land and sea powers and would temper the Russian wave of expansion, which would be obliged to sharpen up its ideological methods in order to continue its expansive aggression.

Dialectic Symmetry

"Learn from your enemies." Haushofer suggested to his disciple Ewald Banse at the pompous Institute for Research on Germanism, which was generously supported by Hitler. Learning from the enemy meant discipling Germany so as to be able to reach the government's geopolitical goal. After all, this was Mackinder's formula for winning the heart of the continent. And out of the unfounded idea of the superiority of the German race, the geoideological theory that each geographical zone should be utilized by a race which possessed certain qualities was set down.

By placing what was *going to happen* in current reality *before it happened*, slanting a bit of biology here, a bit of political science and strategy there, the Institute for Research on Germanism managed to rationalize the most immediate objective of Germany's international policy: territorial expansion in the face of the threat of suffocation due to the population explosion.

Until that moment, geopolitics had never gotten beyond the speculative stage; it had not yet overflowed the banks of the university classroom or broken out of the limits of intellectual circles. The theory of a biologically superior race, with all the horrors it bred from this stage onward, brought the subsequent Nazi ideology, the madness of which became evident in its international moves and multiple aggressions perpetrated between 1933 and 1945.

It is a good idea, then, to show why the strategy and tactics of the Soviets do not appear to be very different from those of the disciples of Haushofer and Hitler. If we replace the words *Nazi* and *race* with *Soviet* and *Russian*, the geopolitical scheme of worldwide communism will appear with total clarity.

If the best life is that which is individually or socially worth living, the positive or negative value of a geoideology lies in the cultural norms it seeks to instill, which is to say that geopolitics is a branch of the great moral tree.

And just as all congruent morals are founded on ethics, so too must ideology — a dominant factor in geopolitics — be based on a philosophy.

Man — and especially the Argentine — needs a philosophy in which to anchor his geopolitical stance. He needs a love of knowledge, a vocation for universally valid and dogged respect for unfailing truth. and all of this calls for an extra effort, a stubborn and vigilant vow of poverty as regards compromises of any kind so as to bring the death of ideology and the birth of philosophy.

Dialectic Asymmetry

When the Brazilian IV Army stationed in Minas Geraes marched on Rio one day in 1964 and opened the way for the officers of the Advanced War School to take charge of the country, the foreseeable end of the populist projects of Goulart permitted Brazil to pull out of its political and economic starvation.

Field Marshal Castello Branco gave his backing to the idea that the military government should last ten years without any possibility, even in the distant future, of elections, and General Golberry do Conto e Silva established the bases for a national security policy in his *Geopolitics of Brazil*. These ideas laid the groundwork for a concrete democracy, hic et nunc and assigned Brazil a role as the South Atlantic representative of the West and of the United States. This idea was already being borne in mind when Brazil sent an expeditionary force to Europe to fight in Italy on the side of the Allies.

Headed by the circle of "sobornnards," as the Brazilians call the officers of the Advanced War School, the Brazilian revolutionaries, influenced by Thomas Hobbes via Golberry, and intolerant of the vices of "the system" to the point of dissolving parliament in 1969, reiterated the need for modern economic organization which would be capable of building an economic dam to stem the flow of galloping and endemic inflation. And this was achieved. Although statistics do not give the causes of historical facts and processes, they do show the effect: the effect of a correct geopolitical choice.

As Brazil was taking off in 1964, Argentina was formally joining the ranks of the Third World. The results of this move are clearly in view and it would be superfluous to raise a finger to point out those responsible.

The Reality of the Southern Cone

The Latin American continental union dreamed of by Bolivar survives today in the soft melancholy rhetoric of philanthropic speeches and in the preaching of jurists and diplomats on the integration of nations and of Pan Americanism.

But is Latin America a unit? This unity is, perhaps, more of a part of Bolivar's lost and remote paradise than of geopolitical reality, more of a myth than anything concrete. It is, however, legitimate to consider Latin America as a whole, by virtue of its cultural, historical and linguistic links. It is beneficial to do so, because with the idea of Latin American integration in mind, a frame of reference can be built for correct geopolitical development.

The idea of a Latin American international policy is not a direct objective of Argentina, but a consequence which is as desirable as it is difficult because of the conflicting interests of the big countries, Argentina, Brazil and Mexico.

Before broadening our geopolitical stance to take in the enormous area which begins at the Rio Grande and ends on Cape Horn, Argentina should consider its more immediate responsibilities. We should respond to those countries which make up our geographic habitat — the countries of the Southern Cone.

Because Argentina should have two geopolitical objectives:
1. The assumption of an identity and a meaning as a nation in the complex pattern of international power and in its capacity as a Western nation.
2. The forming of a policy with respect to Uruguay, Chile, Paraguay and Bolivia, countries whose destiny is tied to that of Argentina and whose international positions give them a two-way option: Argentina or Brazil.

Statistically, the Southern Cone looks like this:

Southern Cone: Basic Figures (1973)

	Population	Km^2	GNP in millions of dollars	Popula- tion Growth % (1970/73)	GNP Growth %
Argentina	24,286,000	2,776,889	40,000	1.5	3.7
Uruguay	2,992,000	177,508	2,351	1.2	−1.2
Paraguay	2,674,000	406,752	769	3.9	5.0
Bolivia	5,331,000	1,098,581	1,146	2.6	4.5
Chile	10,229,000	756,945	6,517	1.7	4.5

Source: U.N. American Statistics and own sources.

Argentina is the natural market for the Southern Cone and it is also the natural supplier. Buenos Aires is the Great Metropolis. It may be the capital of Argentina, but it is also the Great Metropolis of the Southern Cone. Traditionally Argentina has been at the service of its neighbors in tims of need, no matter what the politics of the country that was in trouble.

Just by looking at a map of Latin America, one obtains a clear idea of the reality of the concept of the Southern Cone. Nevertheless, it is useful to confirm that commercial relations between the countries which make up the Southern Cone have already demonstrated an elevated level of integration that goes beyond that of any other region in Latin America.

If these figures are compared with the internal trade figures for the Andean Pact, they show, unquestionably, that the Southern Cone is a reality which should be assumed politically, and that the Andean Pact is a political idea which does not respond to geographic and political reality. (See Appendix III).

In order to begin integrating Argentina with its immediate neighbors, the country should effect a program of physical integration, a program of economic balance and integration, one of cultural integration, one of harmonization of internal and external security measures, as well as one to multiply our own markets while giving solid support to our neighbors. To all of these should be added a program to increase the purchase of manufactured goods. Because if integration means yielding, only the strongest can promote an international get-together and inevitably, the stronger the whole, the stronger the strongest.

Reciprocal Trade in the Southern Cone (1974)
(in thousands of U.S. dollars)

	Uruguay	Chile	Paraguay	Bolivia	Total	% of total
Imports from Argentina	79.737	191.283	51.567	69.607	391.64	9.96
Exports to Argentina	14.423	179.351	42.978	46.261	283.013	7.73
Difference	65.314	11.932	8.589	22.806	108.641	
% of total imports	18.3	8.5	26.0	18.4		
% of total exports	3.8	8.8	24.9	16.3		

Source: Various issues of *Financial Statistics;* Indec.

Mutual Realities

Nevertheless, before an adult and forward-looking geopolitical stance can be conceived of, it is necessary for us to ask ourselves if there are any "missing pieces" — those deficiencies which have impeded us and continue to impede us. We must do this in order to fully understand with a sense of greatness, the time-space, territory-history equation, without which no proposal can have any other value than that of idle speculation.

Argentina has only one option: the free world, the West. The United States, which is part of the West, should consider giving unlimited support to Argentina. This does not signify giving up advantages or prerogatives which would diminish Argentina's power of decision. World reality, on the other hand, has taken the place of the "Big Stick" policy. Big powers should adapt to reality, and Argentina forms a part of the US reality today, just as the US is a reality for Argentina. This does not mean that we should ignore fallacies and defects in US foreign policy which have troubled Argentina even in recent times. Rather, it constitutes the recognition of a concrete situation which should serve as a basis for the formation of our geopolitical policy.

A striking example of this is the way in which Washington and New York have offered to help Argentina out of the absurd financial situation into which it had fallen through its own carelessness and through its policy of unjustifiable sovereignty. And this occurred because the United States is the only economically powerful interlocutor with a general sense of reason in the free world.

Europe appears to have renounced its role as hero in the political world and is willing to live in domestic bliss while the US protects it from outside forces. There is no notable exception among European countries in this lack of initiative to solve their own problems. Europe expects the US to accelerate its economic rhythm in order to improve the European economy. Even China is worried about the lack of backbone Europe is displaying in international politics. France's political moves have only achieved one result: the slowing down and blocking of the European political process. Argentina must have optimum trade relations with Europe, but it is difficult to deal with the Europeans politically.

But there are no good guys and bad guys in international politics. There are only established situations, natural states of affairs which come head-on with our objectives, condition them and result in the formation of a policy. In today's world, the only option proposed will permit us to reach our objective of accelerated growth and increased distribution.

Only the West can give us capital, technology and culture for our growth and for distribution among Argentines. The final objective of any national project should be the formation of the Argentine human being and this must be achieved through the interaction of a growing society; it must be achieved by giving priority first to the Western world and then to the rest of the world.

With the West we will have an easy exchange of creations from similar cultures. From the rest of the world, we can expect their lack of confidence in something new and unusual.

Chapter VI

To Ignore a War is to Lose It

"He who wants only to rest dies quickly."

Insensitivity in analyzing public administration is the direct or indirect consequence of the demagogic schemes we spoke of earlier and will return to later, but it must also be considered in the study of a rare collective anesthesia: *voluntary ignorance of the war factor.*

Over the years, educational methods designed to make Argentines believe in certain falsehoods and to respect the supposed fidelity of these falsehoods from the tenderest years of infancy to the cloistral university level, have succeeded in causing Argentine citizens to forget or voluntarily deny the possibility of war. In order for this to happen, a whole circuit in our information bank had to be rerouted so that our knowledge would be detoured around a chain of concrete data that ties other nations to the reality of war and this lack of knowledge is historically and inevitably fatal.

By looking at the overall list of conflicts included in any good world history book, we draw the conclusion that the six millenia of recorded history represent 6,000 years of battle among peoples, nations and cultures. These conflicts have flared up over political supremacy, geographical expansion or over a need for natural resources. The formal or material causes of these wars are as veried as they are continuous. The generalized characteristic is the dialectics; the warriors collide and unite and it is quite reasonable that historians can use this as a working hypothesis from which they can extract a series of valid explanations. Some are surprisingly clear and summarized in von Clauswitz's hypothesis, a commendable effort aimed at working out the war philosophy enigma. As the pages of the history book continue to turn, we are repeatedly faced with two thoughts of surprising force: *Politics are the continuation of war by alternate means;* and *peace is the interval between two wars.* There are several exact and brilliant differences between war and peace, though the two have such a logical ring to them that the dilettante can easily confuse them with a play of words. One of these constructions goes like this: *If politics are the continuation of war by alternate means and peace is the interval between two wars,* it can easily be concluded that *peace is the pursuit of war under distinct conditions.* It can also be inferred that politics and war are two different names for the same thing which is the continuous flow of political biology, always just a step away from the actual power of war, a progressive and constant movement toward a remote final cause.

Something we soon discover as we look into the nature of the complicated phenomenon known generally as war, is that, among other things, it is a manifestation which represents in human relations an organic process present in any natural state. It cannot escape the attention of the person who knows even basic biology that the world exists through constant war and strife, as does life. Everything indicates that "he who wants only to rest dies quickly."[1]

We don't plan to discuss here the obvious difference in values between war and peace, nor shall we discuss the high-level inter-action between these two which turns them into one. What we should do is accept that there is as close and final a link between the two terms, as there is between the two phases of a heartbeat.

Everything appears to signify that war has been and is a constant in the history of Man. Peoples which have ignored the existence or the danger of war have disappeared. This means that indifference toward war amounts to historical suicide. It is suicide in real political practice. It is suicide in the highest of theoretical realms. This is an old and anonymous principle which is loaded with tragic significance, rich in immediate deductions and which corresponds to this rational outline of inevitability. According to this principle, a desire for peace begins with a readiness for war.

Russian expansion

Classic antagonisms — Egyptian-Syrian, Persian-Chaledonian, Greek-Persian — (listed in Appendix IV) are seen throughout the

---

[1] Homer Lea, *The Value of Ignorance*

course of history. These antagonisms have reached modern times and are setting the stage for the greatest conflict ever known. We are contemporaries and a party to this conflict.

The process which is affecting us was begun in the year 1200 in the principality of Moscow. In 1280, this process formed the embryo of the nation which was to set out to achieve, and has done so, the greatest territorial expansion and the greatest political dominion in history. That country is Russia.

The Russians have manifested a morphology of war might which goes beyond being a temporary political policy and has grown to be permanent and incontinent. We are touching upon this as a theme for historical and philosophical analysis, which certainly merits an entire lifetime of meditation by historian and philosopher alike. It consists of the process of expansion and dominion which began in the Principality of Moscow in 1280; was sustained through the warring Czars: Ivan the Great (1462-1505), Ivan the Terrible (1547-1584), Peter the Great (1672-1725); a process which after conquering Siberia, swallowed up Caucasia and Turkestan; and which, undaunted by a change in leadership in the 1917 Revolution, formed the Third International upon the conclusion of World War I. We were to find this same army designing a new map of the world in 1945 when it conquered the Balkan satellites and East European countries and we were even to see its uniforms and its stellar symbol on the Middle American island of Cuba, in Southeast Asian Vietnam and in the Angolan heart of Africa. At one time or another the autocrats' killers take up the project planned by their victims. This is an irrefutable demonstration of the survival and the supremacy of geopolitics over politics within the framework of the Socialist revolution and its imperialistic projections.

The study that ignores this expansive wave in its analysis is fragmentary and mutilated. It is not possible to study the development of any country in the world without taking Russian politics into account. It is not even possible to recall the peregrinations of relatively Socialistic countries without observing how the Russian power machinery has dealt with them. Hungary (1956) and Czechoslovakia (1968) immediately spring to mind, since both countries tried to form Socialist systems independent of Moscow's influence, but without taking the geopolitical objectives of the Soviet Union (which covers a sixth of the earth's surface) into account. A conflict involving Communist countries outside Soviet administration — China, for example — would not only be historical and geopolitical, but also ideological.

Elsewhere in this book, we have attempted to establish the difference between ideology and philosophy. In the ideological confrontation between Russia and China we see that ideologies which proclaim a "truth" that is subordinant to their geopolitical strategies, though apparently united by a common philosophy, clash virulently.

The gigantic Russia's behavior with the Third World countries is always the same — along this road to war and its resulting maximum expansion — because it is not based on a political philosophy but on ideopolitics. This consists of channeling its aggression toward the lines of least resistance so as to bring as little retaliation as possible from the West. The countries the Russians pick off are sitting ducks, sheep without a shepherd, and they can be brought into the Soviet battle for an end in which they themselves will never participate.

The War Over There

In this atmosphere of varied force in which bombings, crime, treaties, deals, business, bankers and spies alternate, the visits of Western Marxist Socialist party leaders to Moscow every year to pick up instructions are easily explained. It is all part of the same incredible plan which governs those who are ordered to steal millions and those who become millionaires.

On the surface, we see isolated incidents, sudden movements, flare-ups, retreats and advances. These are the great and small movements which form a part of the international war for Russian Communism declared by Lenin in 1919 as a means of conquering the world. Those who study the ins and outs of the history of the last two centuries will find surprising similarity of actions in the annals of Communist diplomacy and the archives of the Czarist chancellory. This unity and finality of procedure affects every country and their politics should take this pressure into account. If they do not, they will be dragged into a destiny which they have not imagined or desired.

In Sir Robert Thompson's book *Peace is Not at Hand,* which was published in 1974, the author carefully analyzes what he calls the Third World War, the start of which he places at the end of the 1940s and which he says Russia is winning.

Thompson says that the people of the United States must become conscious of this state of war and must realize that the credibility of the United States as a superpower is at stake.

A number of things have impeded, until now, a new armed *world* conflict. One of the major causes has been the dissuasive power of

the atomic arsenal — and even that of conventional weapons. Nevertheless, the conflict has taken another expressive route, and the
Russian need to expand creates new forms of aggression all the time.
The so-called *cold war,* which formally began in 1947 and which
"ended" with Richard Nixon's visit to Moscow in 1972, demonstrated the variety of means which can be employed in this type of
non-conventional confrontation. Even if the cold war has been
officially abandoned by the United States, Russia has not given it up,
as has clearly been demonstrated in its intervention in Angola and its
creation of virtual arsenals in Libya and Ethiopia.

Also, from a purely Argentine point of view, the government, the
Armed Forces and the people must become conscious of this state of
war and realize that the survival of Argentina is at stake.

Russian leaders realize that their political stability can only be
assured as long as they have a growing nation. This principle is valid
for nearly all nations. But the rigors of history make us understand
that for reasons that are unclear in some cases or because of
deliberate indifference in others, not all countries do their political
planning in accordance with this rule.

In Russia's case growth is indispensable to subsistence. A regime
with this type of leadership cannot live in harmony with other
systems. It will not stand for comparison. *Consequently,* it is
obliged to try to conquer the rest of the world. It must try to impose
its system on the rest of the world in order to keep the system from
changing. The stability of social machinery composed of institutionalized aggression and misery can only be maintained through expansion. World aggression, represented by multifaceted attacks, is,
for the Russian leaders, a necessity. Those who believe in detente
are taking the same position as Chamberlain. That which was dealt
with and pledged in Paris in 1973 and in Helsinki in 1975 is very
similar to that which was lost in Munich in 1938.

Argentina began to be affected by the operative deployment which
characterizes Russia's dominant action during the strange economic
episodes which took place in our country during the last year of
Yrigoyen's government. At this stage of the game (1928-1930)
Russia managed to introduce a trade force organization (IUIAM-
TOR) in Argentina with full approval of the country's authorities.
This group placed essential items — down to electrical light bulbs —
on our market at prices so far below their own that they could only be
considered a dumping level. This move threatened the very foundation of our incipient national industry for quite some time. It is
interesting to remember the moment in which this devastating

surprise attack was made on us by the Russian power machine, and to make ourselves aware of the pleasant conditions under which the enemy was received. This attempt was limited. The opposition with which one sector received it was one of the causes of the 1930 revolution. It was a typical act of industrial war. Over the course of time and of our national development similar examples have cropped up.

The War in Argentina

As the war goes on on many fronts and in its many forms those who force the action to continue, through eloquence and money, raise the flag of peace among us and accompany it with sermons on pacifism. We see this in the conclusion of and the actions derived from the World Congress of Peace in the '50s and '60s.

Charged with these same or similar continuous and diligent tasks, Argentine leftist leaders have gone to Moscow and to satellite capitals behind the Iron Curtain and their resulting actions have been over-publicized by these leaders themselves.

Argentina has been within Russia's reach ever since the Soviets conquered Cuba, put Fidel Castro under orders from Moscow and made that island nation a stepping-stone to the invasion of Latin America. It was only a few years after Castro took power in Cuba that Argentina's guerrilla war began. Though he would later deny and condemn it, it is clear that Peron used the Argentine terrorists while he was living in exile in Spain. Illia, who was president during the growth of subversion, tolerated it. Politicians sometimes showed prudence on subversion, but at other times idolized it. Soon Argentina guerrillas began using Cuba as a training ground and later they would take refuge there. Argentine-born Che Guevara shot to the top of the list of Marxist saints after his *martyrdom*. Manufacturers and shopkeepers — who madly believe it is all right to make and sell anything people will buy — printed up and sold thousands of posters bearing the face of that paladin of subversion, so that they could be stylishly hung on the walls of bourgeois houses. Young people still dress in guerilla uniform style almost without knowing, in most cases, the meaning of the clothing they are wearing. Protest records have become high-consumption articles, their repetitive and hypnotic promotion being carried out by disc-jockeys. Guerrillas move frequently in and out of newspapers, television and radio shows where Socialist dogma is often cleverly linked with folklore. Standing out in the middle of all this are those who theorized, for the benefit of the naive, that putting these symbols, figures, dogma and arguments of the enemy before the public cannot hurt anything and might even help our cause, since their mass production and subsequent proliferation tend to make them lose importance and force.

While this war machine was coming to life, the Gelbard-Castro pact — an exchange route of singular importance — was born. Via this pact, we sent food and vehicles to the frontlines of the Soviet attack force and they, in turn, sent instructors to Argentina to indoctrinate local Castroites. There was no language barrier — Cubans speak good Spanish. They even have an agreeable little accent; they are romantic and they sing pretty songs. If there was even any question about what they were doing in Argentina, it was only necessary to rattle off a bit of a speech in which one member or another of the Peronist government listed the virtues of pulling down ideological barriers. Thus we soon became the meridional capital of the Communist revolutionary movement. Our northern provinces became direct routes for the passage of subversion to other countries. Our cities became centers for the concentration and outgrowth of Marxist doctrine. There came a moment in which nearly any home could be transformed into a barracks for guerrilla fighters. Arsenals were set up in apartments in residential areas, conveniently located near the theater of action. Urban guerrillas go beyond the wildest dreams of the logistics expert: the guerrilla stores his weapons just a few meters away from the site where he will gun his victim down.

If we examine the results of the guerrillas' efforts, we find that they tend to attack the productive sector of the nation; they seek the physical elimination of business executives, the halting of the country's payment of international debts (a decisive stage in the breaking of an economy); and they alienate youths who have been deprived of cultural and employment opportunities. The orthodox rules of war call more for the disarming than for the destruction of the enemy. Reaching these tacit objectives means slowly but surely weakening the opponent, thus paving the way for the final victory.

Through an unpardonable cultural and psychological deficiency, collective ignorance in such important matters as this war has grown. Thus a complete indifference has been achieved through the hard work and backing of the enemy who developed their campaign through ideological infiltration and subversive sabotage, as well as any other means, to dissolve the cohesion of the country. The enemy must break the country's morale, undermine the population's confidence in its institutions, lessen the prestige of these same institutions, overturn current cultural values, and break down the people's interest in finding solutions to problems. In this last case the enemy clouds thought by destroying discussion.

It only takes a brief look to see what is on the moral and mental horizon for an alarming number of young people undermined by these factors which dissuade and discourage them from doing what they must do to reach any useful or beautiful end. A look at this panorama gives us an idea of how mortified the will to create, the will to resist, and the will to conquer, are in Argentina. Although this chapter emphasizes Russian aggression, we must also remember that China is an imperialistic nation which is obliged, because of its demographic problem and its low level of income, to expand.

The same problems which gave birth to a comparison between Russia and the West for the leaders in Moscow, the same need to expand to keep the people from comparing, the same necessary resentment, form a part of Peking's plan. We have placed emphasis on Russia and Moscow, however, because if it is true that Moscow's plans for expansion move toward the West, China's area of expansion also goes toward the West, which is Russia. Geopolitically, Argentina is in Russia's sights, and it is clearly not in those of China, although this does not mean that it is completely absent from Peking's geopolitical map.

Hypnotic ignorance

Culpable ignorance of the war is linked to a fallacy which is analyzed in another part of this book. It is the faulty reasoning which leads some people to believe that "we have gone as far as we need to go. Nothing should be changed unless it is a change to keep things the way they are; One of the things we have been able to achieve is that we are in a position to watch the battles of others without getting involved, and all we want to do is take advantage of that situation. We have no reason to worry about the problem of those who have not reached our preferential position and we should not come down from that position."

Another fallacious concept linked to the people's indifference to the war factor in this world which Russia plans to dominate is: *the incomparable Argentina* concept. "As we are the best in the world, nothing will take us into a war which is a complicated and painful thing, which affects others who are not as capable or as rich as we are. We musn't think about this." These grave errors originate in the lack of memory which demagogy has provoked, conditioned and conserved. We lack both long-term and short-term memory. It is a condition which is closely linked to the lack of depth, ably induced by planned deficiencies in our system of cultural communication but voluntary ignorance of current events is a lack of immediate critical attention which is impossible to pardon. And even as these pages are being written, the number of casualties among civilians and military men and the volume of material destruction brought on by the subversive war could easily be compared to the figures in a classic war. Although perhaps no one has done a comparative study, it would appear that the relationship between this and conventional war would be shocking. There is no truce in this war. There is no pact which can indefinitely halt the pursuit of this conflict. Incompetent politicians have still not understood what weapons are being employed. The frightening truth is that they do not even suspect that these weapons are being used. But these weapons should be pointed out and should be studied deeply. Never in the history of war has there been such a disconcerting arsenal: drugs, gelanite and Vietnamese directional mines all play a part in it. It also includes flame throwers powerful enough to destroy armoured vehicles but used instead in carrying out of summary executions and it also includes money; money obtained through bribery and through treason, and enough money for the terrorists to stay underground for centuries.

Voluntary ignorance as regards war, is another of the weapons used, and it is the most frightening. Ignoring the war is the quickest way to lose it.

Much research and analysis has been done on the different aspects of the problems which exist in the West and among the countries of the West. Much of this research is truly valuable and contributes to the incessant search for truth which characterizes the liberal-capitalist Western regime.

The majority of these studies, however, suffer from a basic illness which, to some extent, invalidates their conclusions; this illness consists of ignorance of the constant interaction between the West and the non-West and above all, between Russia and the West. In any study of sociological, economic and political values in the last quarter of the 20th century the researcher should not stray from reality; the entire world has been subject to a dialectic of confrontation, interaction and battle for geographical space, natural resources and political supremacy.

Still unknown factors, can, perhaps, change the polarity of the conflict. Perhaps these factors can cause the disappearance or the weakening of the power which currently operates the geopolitical switchboard. This vacuum, however, will produce new disturbances and Argentina is bound to be involved.   There is today no utopian world in which our country can be a mere observer of distant conflicts.   Today, as always, our country must be active or it will be a victim.

Chapter VII

Immediatism and Fatalism

Accepting the Short Term

The absence of a sense of future which appears to have poisoned contemporary society, this "immediatism," which seems to fill the nation's present and that of the West, is not entirely brought on by indoctrination through advertising or by our compulsion to mimic.

Just as man is able to conceive of his own perishability through the idea of death, he is also capable of forming a concept of God and God has been his ticket to eternity. But when God, who represented the future and whose commandments and morals were the guidelines for the existence of the individual within society, was left behind, Man began to walk in the concentric circles of the present which were curiously devoid of immutable values.

It seems absurd that in a world in which technological and administrative techniques are aimed at long-term thinking, cultural horizons have been reduced to only the most precarious present. When Man becomes indifferent to the destiny of his soul, he also becomes indifferent to the future of his community. Humanism shuts us in a trap which makes our soul disappear, strips the individual of his concept of the future and replaces it with an intangible present, the social security of which is by no means liberating.

Atheistic Socialist nations are in a better position to deal with this problem, since although they have eliminated God, their projects bring paradise down to earth and at the same time prudently place this paradise at a distant time which current generations will never be able to reach. Thus they give Man a sort of futurized and semiliturgical scheme, which is naturally linked to its redemptorist ideology, creating a plausible illusion of semi-religion.

Meanwhile we Argentines have continued to struggle in the midst of the dizzying present which will be further complicated by the demagogic utopian games which have tainted our actions with the acceptance of the ephemeral as if it were the absolute, thus stripping us of our sense of historical responsibility toward the future. A promise which cannot be kept becomes credible if political leaders can offer some sort of instant results to the people. These tangible results give the masses the confidence they need to transfer responsibility for their future to their new idol.

Promises of instant gain are not enough; they must be backed by a strong emotionology, which permits the resentment which normally resides in the masses to overflow. Because of this, the demagogue must have a common enemy, a sort of anti-hero which will make him a hero and in the hazardous course of the 20th century history, we have seen the demagogue build up an abundant repertoire of universal enemies which range from Jews to multinationals to oligarchy, to Yankee imperialism and to the sinarchy which we mentioned before.

Since rationality requires that our actions of today be justified by their consequences of tomorrow, irrationality is a part of all demagogic manipulation, and we must bear in mind that this manipulation is not always political, but is sometimes cultural, and it uses mass communications media in order to infiltrate the minds of the people in general. The demagogue is, on a lesser scale, the television MC, for whom all the guests on his program are beautiful, intelligent and important and who also flatters *his* public, which, according to him, never makes a mistake. A newspaper is demagogic if it serves crime news done up in the most repulsive and sordid manner to its readers and justifies itself with the idea that: *what the public wants the public gets*. This contempt for truth, this distortion of values, which places financial success above everything else, contributes to preparing the people for a docile and happy acceptance of the demagogic politician who snatches the people out of their status as free individuals who are responsible for the future.

How far away the domestication of the individual submitted to the God-present's treatment is from the ethical level at which the moral justification of an act is plain if its consequences add to the moral growth of the community! Seen in this way, the suicide of a *kamikaze* is a sacrifice, while the death of a movie fan who has committed suicide because Rudolph Valentino is dead is gravely damaging the community. The first example — though difficult to understand — is a reaction whose logic can be found on a spiritual level and because of this it can be seen as an act aimed at saving the community. In the second case, the fan who commits suicide, in a certain sense obliges, with this act, the entire community to commit suicide. The *kamikaze* — which is a violent and spectacular Oriental version of the sacrifice certain mystic Christians made — reinforces the moral fiber of the community because it is aimed at a future which will permit new sacrifices and which will continue in turn to generate a growing moral patrimony. With the suicide of the fan the community loses a certain amount of freedom since the suicide forms part of an alienating and immediatist wound. In other words, one suicide is aimed at permitting an access to the future while the other occurs because there exists no future.

Political Opportunism and Socialistic Fatalism

If we compare the systems in which individual liberty and private enterprise are respected with those in which these characteristics are absent we find that about 700 million people live in places today where liberty and capitalism — which constitute an insoluble unit — are the community's main guideline.

This information shows just how far this way of life has spread and although the 700 million people take in the populations of countries whose ruling political regimes have been elected by various means and countries whose social security systems possess varying degrees of efficiency, all of them have one criterion in common; capitalism and individual liberty exist in all their countries and is demonstrated empirically through private enterprise and freedom to enter and leave the country. Never in the entire history of mankind has such a high proportion of people and countries lived voluntarily in an atmosphere of continued and growing liberty and production as they do today.

Despite this fact, it is common to find Socialists, Radicals or Peronists, who, upon finding a scarcity of rational argument, justify their populist Socialism by resorting to the argument that: the world is moving inexorably toward Socialism and since these prophets possess an attitude which is common among Argentines, that of looking for an easy way out, they extend this conclusion and come up with the following incongruous premise: We cannot oppose Socialist expansion, therefore I am a Socialist.

In this attitude we find a perfect demonstration of political opportunism, and of culpable ignorance of reality, and of a lack of knowledge, understanding and interest in general trends of the history of mankind. And it is this which leads them to simply become members of the team they think will win in the future. The coercive action of this supposed fatalism is effective in a community which is submerged in idolizing the present and which, because of this, is unable to see the future as part of its freedom. The community thus submits docilely to an inevitable future against which it would be impossible to fight.

Even though the historical path to greater individual liberty and productivity was patented with the coming of the Industrial Revolution which began in England, it had its beginnings in even earlier times. "The air in the city makes the men free" (Stadt Luft Mach Frei) says an old German proverb, which adjusts itself nicely to the era in which cities were expanding.

During the Middle Ages, in the 11th century, trade on both the Mediterranean and seaways to the north was greatly expanded and the effects of this expansion were demonstrated in the corresponding growth of cities — as from the next century — the transformation of western Europe which slowly but surely abandoned feudalism with its lack of freedom.

While life in feudal communities, with its stiff regulations imposed by tradition, created an atmosphere of confinement, the climate among the commercial communities in the city was one of liberty. The cities wanted freedom and got what they wanted, this being especially true of the city which in part five of this book, we consider to be the acid test of a sociopolitical system: free movement into and out of the city. Wealth became stagnant during the feudal period because it was all invested in land. But the decline of feudalism during the 11th and 12th centuries gave wealth a new dynamic fluidity and what is more, a new social mobility was born and became more accentuated with the passing of time.

Since that time there has been an uninterrupted process which has led us to a period in which men with initiative and strength, capability and drive, can choose their socioeconomic role in a system of growing social mobility and a system which is free of the chains of servitude.

Let us take the fallacy into which Socialism falls, when it tries to make its imaginary process appear needed, for what it really is: a typical ideological lie. When Marx proposed his class struggle and the abolition of private capital as an absolute historical necessity, he was restricting human liberty. Just as Hitler said that he was assuming the German people's responsibility for thinking, Marx and Lenin were assuming the responsibility of thinking for all the people on earth. There exists no fatal process in the history of humanity, although when analyzed afterwards or superficially, some of these processes can be used by the ideologues, who, interestingly enough, claim that they were of historical necessity.

The human being is intrinsically free. God gave us the ability to choose freely between good and bad. There can be no historical process which is superior to the will of God, nor which assumes the responsibilities which each individual human being has been given. On the contrary, the more fatalistic a process is, the more precarious it becomes. History itself shows us that none of the pseudo-empires for the last thousand years have lasted very long.

From an ethical point of view, to assume that a process whose moral principles and political ends are repulsive is fatal or necessary, constitutes intimate defeat of the human being. It simply can't be that just because Socialist propaganda has infiltrated us with the idea of the fatality of the Socialist-Marxist process, we, as mature Western men, adhere to this process for fear of having to lucidly confront the truth, or for fear of having to exercise the difficult responsibility of being free.

There is a great danger here. The biggest danger is that because of the way in which this propaganda is spread, it will make us lower our defenses, give up our liberty of our own free will, and convert us into Marxist-Socialists. What this would mean, today, in the last quarter of the 20th century, would be that our country would become one of the many satellite countries which belong to Marxist imperialism. We should realize that to a great extent Socialist fatalism is what has caused modern society to think only in the present, only with immediacy.

The succession of Populists and demagogues, offered to us through our national folklore for the last sixty years as an alternative for capitalism or an alternative for Marxism, has only managed to bring us closer to Marxism.

All these substitutes were given total and unconditional backing for their plans, but none of them — not even the Radicals, nor Peronism — augmented the prosperity of the nation, or made the nation grow or set up valid goals for the Argentine nation, and most important of all, *none of these substitutes raise the level of liberty and sovereignty of the nation and its inhabitants*. The books on this process of decadence and crisis which we analyzed in Part I, were balanced on March 24, 1976.

Now it is clear that there are really only two choices: freedom in a Christian, capitalist, Western world, or an atheist Marxist world with the social security of an anthill and dulled by sterile discipline.

If we insist on following the dangerous lines of insidious Socialist propaganda, it is because even our businessmen and executives have come to believe in Socialist fatalism. It means that even businessmen and executives have come to behave politically as what the Communists themselves cynically define as useful idiots.

Chapter VIII

Members of the Nation

Who and Why

We have already seen how Argentina has forgotten its history and could thus *lose the war by ignoring it.* But if blocking the way to the future and sacrificing ourselves to the almighty present can mutilate us as a nation, then Argentina is short of another item in this depressing catalog of "missing pieces."

The item that is missing is much less dramatic than war; it is somewhat less metaphysical than the future, but is something we should definitely keep in mind: We need to know exactly who the nation's friends and enemies are:

It is obvious that any honest individual of goodwill is the nation's friend, no matter how humble his function within society may be, but what we are aiming at here is to clarify the effect an individual's actions can have within a large group of other individuals. In order to carry out this analysis, we will take into account the amount of direct damage different groups may suffer when faced with the alternative of a country in a state of decline and a country in a state of growth.

A country, viewed in a general sense, constitutes a structured society, and not merely a group of individuals; a member of the society knows and accepts the goals and objectives the society plans to reach and wants his society to reach these goals and objectives — which are coherently outlined in a flexible social project — and he also wants to participate, through his work or other activities, in the future the social project offers him and the other members of his society.

There can be no society without there first being individual members. And just as an anthill is not a society, a society is more than a group of anonymous and indifferent individuals who have turned their individual responsibility over to an omnipotent State.

Growth in a society means a greater number of members — members being taken to mean responsible, active individuals who choose their socio-economic roles in society freely. The nature of the different sectors which are associated to form a country is not being discussed here; simply as an acid test, we shall analyze what sector of society will appear if the nation does not grow. Also, though defections in each group do not make changes in its overall character, we still think it necessary to bear these cases in mind as exceptions to the rule.

In an ideal situation, a member of a country is, necessarily, a member of the government and vice versa. By looking at Argentina's history — and this is because our system cannot be described as optimum — we can see the difference between being associated with the government and being associated with the nation. POLITICIANS: These individuals form a small group but one which has a strong influence on national life. As their objective is to conduct the nation's business (through their actions or through their opposition) it would appear logical that they should prefer to lead an important nation, but so far there has not been a politician who has rejected the presidency because he found that the nation was in a state of decadence. On the contrary, this decadence has been a political advantage at times since it has given politicians a chance to present themselves as heroes come to save the nation. In line with the objective of some politicians, then, the decadence or growth of the country is often of a relatively indifferent value. Thus, they have not necessarily been members of the nation.

INTELLECTUALS: These individuals do not, strictly speaking, form a group, since their work is essentially individualistic in character. Since historically no relationship has been established between the decadence or growth of a country and the decadence or splendor of intellectual life, we could probably say that intellectuals do not work against the nation and they thus become passive members of it. Potentially, however, intellectuals are the most important active members of the nation.

WAGE EARNERS: These individuals form, without a doubt, the most numerous and heterogeneous group. If we consider the isolated fact that they are workers, we could lump them into the category of members; but since their most substantial objective is that of *earning a living,* and if we omit the factor of which political system it is more or less difficult to *earn a living in*, the fact is that they work toward their objectives within a liberal system or within a Communist system. It is obvious that a country which is in a state of decline reduces the field of action of this group, but this does not mean that decadence causes its disappearance as a group. The growth of the nation interests the wage earner as long as it means he will be offered greater social mobility. At times, through a lack of communication, wage earners act as passive members of society, while in order to put the nation on the road to growth they must be made to feel like what, in reality, they are: extremely important members of the nation.

ARMED FORCES: The nature of their function shows the members of this group to be members of the nation. Beyond that, the last fifty years of Argentine history have indicated that on top of being members of the nation the Armed Forces have had to act as syndics, even if our judicial statutes' lack of adaptation to reality have made the group's interventions appear institutional ruptures. We will return to this fallacious concept further on in the book.

CHURCH: As an entity, the Church is always a member of the nation but not necessarily a member of the government.

BUSINESSMEN: If we understand by businessmen that we are speaking of a group with a sense of permanence and if we leave aside the speculators who would surely have a lot to gain through crises and decadence, the group's members in general, by virtue of their work and their proposals, are inevitable members of the nation. We are speaking in general terms; the exceptions do not invalidate the general rule.

If the politicians adapt to new demands they can survive in a Communist state. Intellectuals, wage earners and military men can also survive under Communism. The only group which cannot survive by any means under the jurisdiction of a Marxist state is that of the businessmen. In Marxist nations there are politicians, intellectuals, wage earners and military men, but there are not, and there cannot be, businessmen.

On the whole, avoiding decadence and promoting growth is a moral obligation for politicians, intellectuals, wage earners and military men, but for the businessman, since decadence can bring the rise of the Communist state, contributing to the growth of the nation is not only his moral duty, but also a question of life and death. It is no coincidence that subversive propaganda takes businessmen as the perfect target for its aggression. That is why we must quickly analyze this group whose characteristics demonstrate that it is, by necessity, a member of the nation.

The Role of the Producer

Working in the midst of the nation's fundamental shortages, there is a vigorous business community whose interests coincide with those of a modern and growing Argentina.

Any type of producer is a member of the country, since, when the country has a recession, the producer is the one who sufferes substantially from the impact. This is most accentuated among industrial producers. A business community made up of large companies and strong businessmen whose interests can only be served by a growing country is the best ally of both the nation and the government. It is also a powerful ally for political stability. The overlapping of interests of the businessman and a growing country raises the businessman's fixed active investment. Although all businesses are eventually affected by a process of inflation or decline it is nevertheless the large company, industrial, mining, agricultural or a company which provides survices, which, with its large active investment, technology and labor force, suffers most from decadence and crisis in a nation.

The decadent process in Argentina is also demonstrated in the existence of very few Argentine companies of great size.

The Large Company's Role

The large company within a modern economy is creative. It incorporates scientific and administrative techniques, and above all, it is a generator of fixed national capital. As was shown by Galbraith in *The New Industrial State*, 60% of all US capitalization is effected through its companies, and specifically its large companies, via reinvestment of profits. Besides that, a strong company, a healthy company, is a perfect place for individuals, the inhabitants of the nation, to invest their savings and thus obtain profits and capitalization so as to create an awareness of savings and investment.

The large company phenomenon, expecially that of the large industrial company, or that which applies industrial techniques for mining or farming, has not been sufficiently publicized and, like so many other things, has not been understood by the nation as a whole.

Populism has tried to make us believe that the large company is an enemy and that it is the origin of many of our problems. The role of the large company as an exploiter of our natural resources and a generator of wealth in the nation has been hidden from us. The company which has invested huge sums of money in the nation in the form of active physical assets, stock, administrative personnel, skilled labor, and creative technology, is a member of the nation. Its interests coincide, by necessity, with those of the country. The industrial unit in which the production factors have been invested operates by necessity in the country's favor, since its own subsistence as a techno-structure depends on the country's growth and the country's progress. It should be sufficiently clear today that a large company acquires such cultural independence from its owners that the social and economic phenomenon it generates are the very nature of its existence and are free from the capricious will of the owner.

In most cases proprietorship of large companies is divided up among members of the community. Nowadays ownership of Argentina's large companies, Alpargatas and Celulosa, is divided among hundreds of thousands of shareholders, and these are but two examples. In the United States large corporations have placed their stock throughout the entire social spectrum of the country. The wealth of the companies in this way is reflected in the wealth of the people. It is necessary for these companies to be rich and powerful so that the people can also be rich and powerful. Industrial companies which provide products on local markets have a basic interest in maintaining real wage levels and in a high level of income for every sector of the population, since otherwise demand for their product will drop and they will suffer the consequences of recession.

The Techno-structure

The board rooms of large companies are the training grounds for top government leaders of tomorrow. The state officials will also have an opportunity to sit on the boards of directors of large companies. Human interaction between large companies and the government is created. This dialectic, which many times appears to be contradictory, and to present a conflict of interest situation, is fruitful and generates systems of promotion and control which can bring progress to all. Large companies breed an anxiousness to promote new activities in the state for winning new markets, and for protecting the best interests of local markets. The large company executive is a soldier of the nation in a joint position in the fight for economic growth. His responsibility goes beyond the year-end balance sheet. His prime obligation is the growth of the company. An industrial company, defined in the aforementioned terms, which does not grow, does not survive. This is especially true in a country of medium income and a semi-modern productive setup like that of Argentina.

The responsibility of the executive or the board of directors in a company of maintaining the firm's survival and growth, moves along two equally important and decisive roads: the relationship between the company and the community (which includes the relationship between the company and its own personnel) and the company's profits. A company which makes life impossible in its relations with the community and with its own personnel cannot expect to maintain an adequate growth rate even if in spite of these poor relations the company manages to make circumstantially high profits. In modern states the relationship between companies, their own personnel and community occupies a major proportion of top officials' time. We could say that the community, which is everything, is the prime worry of the modern board of directors. This is not particularly worthy of merit, but it is natural if we bear the fundamental objective of the company in mind: to survive and to grow.

The factors which go into making up a company — its directors, its stockholders, its executives, its personnel, its labor, its suppliers and those who carry out services for it — can only have a better future as the company grows. This future will be no better if the company only makes a profit but does not grow. It has been shown statistically that wages in modern companies depend on the company's size and profitability. Once the minimum level of profitability has been reached at which the company can justify its existence from the point of view of its stockholders, the factor which decides what the factory's personnel at all levels will get out of it is the size of the company. This means growth.

Material Success Is Not A Sin

The problem is that none of what has just been expressed can take place in a broken-down, decadent nation. It is because of this that Argentina must count on the business world as one of the prime factors in its recuperation and transformation.

This will take sacrifice on the part of the businessman, but he will certainly have to make this sacrifice because the gravity of the situation requires it of him, because it is his duty to the community, and because his own existence hangs in the balance. Even in the most socialistic free countries, such as Sweden, the large company, far from disappearing, lives on as a private method of production. Other groups within the nation should also review the prejudices against business and businessmen that years and years of demagogic, populist propaganda has generated in them. Argentina should learn once and for all that making money legally is no sin, that modern, creative capitalism is not shameful, no matter what the ways of the adversary's psychological war have tried to lead us to believe. We must learn that a solid, efficient company with the capability of expanding is a motive for community pride, as is the poet, the researcher or the sportsman who is outstanding in his field.

This is a very important *missing piece* in the attitude of the community. We should replace it in order to face the future and we should do it quickly, because those who are working to split our country are not very far behind us and many naive minds have already been captured among politicians, intellectuals, wage earners, military men and even businessmen.

Chapter IX

National Projects

March and Countermarch

Argentina has lived through 166 years of hazardously independent life, a life of permanently threatened liberty, of convulsively retarded growth and of often-times endangered internal cohesion. Anybody who looked at the path of our history through a timeless optical synthesizer would probably agree that it is characterized by a series of marches, countermarches and halts.

If we looked at the country in terms of geometrikinetics, we would come up with unequal figures, which would displace one another at inconstant intervals. Graphic comparisons of the different segments of the nation's history would give us distinct figures for each segment. There are no periods of more than 20 years which are invariable. The direction of the nation, as a political, social, economic and collective entity, has been changed incessantly. In a certain, sad sense, Argentina is, in terms of its destiny, a nomad, condemned to wander for almost two centuries within the borders of its enormous land mass. That which is Argentine, appears to be lost in the desert, a desert so large that at times the waters that irrigate the territory, the valuable harvests, and the nation's mineral wealth are all covered by limitless dunes whipped up by our confusing and interminable internal sand-storm.

The thread with which the nation weaves its portion of history is of varied color. The weave of one section is different from that of another. In just a decade the pattern has been changed so radically that one segment of the overall historical fabric has nothing to do with the other. In some places, it is tough and resilient and could be counted among the most beautiful in the world. In others, the political weave is so weak that the fabric appears in danger of ripping at any moment. Lately, repeated stripes of blood-red have been added to the fabric.

Until now, those who have taken up the difficult task of trying to figure out the causes of the nation's ills have come up with splendid analyses of the facts. They have outlined well-founded historical accusations. Some of them sharply contrast others, but are, at the same time, curiously reasonable. But everything leads us to believe that the misfortune of the nation is not the product of bad or mistaken actions of its men, but of a fundamental flaw, a negative stone in the foundation of our other shortages.

The nation is afflicted with nostalgia for a national project. Because at the time when the country had a project, its fruits were emancipation and national reorganization. The generation of the 80s conceived a project and lived to make it work. It permitted the country to create an infrastructure and begin to progress. After the 80s came the partial projects, the demagogic projects, and the country stood still. Perhaps we must criticize the generation of the 80s for the lack of adaptability of their project, but the undeniable fact is that the project existed and that it has permitted Argentina to project a future — and to carry out its projects.

The current void, this absence, has a history and a philosophy of its own. Perhaps we should understand that a project is not necessarily a plan. It is not a detailed formula or quantified, instrumental goals. It contains great political and geopolitical objectives and morals. It does not depend upon the mere measurable economic heights to which it can creep. On the contrary, one of the distinctive characteristics of a project is that it should be sufficiently general to adapt itself to changing situations, without the community's having to suffer a break in its life style. This is basically what was lacking in the 1880s project. It was a project for an empty country, which quit being useful when the country filled up halfway.

Actually there have been a number of natural projects at different times. They were positive in some aspects and vain in others. None of them contained enough seeds for the future as to be self-sufficient and to make it through a formulation period. All of them were of isolated value. The only thing they had in their favor was that they offered short-term results, or they were inspired by an idea which had enough backbone to make it through one stage of development.

Nevertheless an important national project, a ubiquitous national project, real because it is ideal, ideal because it is real, and stubbornly guided by the consequences it would have in the future was lacking. A project which would compress so much past, so much intelligence and so much experience as to permit posterior expansion and thus with the passing of time spill over and be absorbed by us and descend from us as a dynamic heritage, would be of unending benefit.

National Emancipation

The first national project was, by necessity, *to create the nation*. We had been a colonial appendage. We became what we were through revolution and emancipation. The word liberty in the period from 1810 to 1820 was nurtured in a context of national sovereignty. All this was a project. That a country would grow out of it had not yet been foreseen. But the rough sketches were there. They gave it character. They were indelible. The most important element was a passion for liberty.

But it was easy to see that this wasn't enough, because, among other reasons, a doctrine capable of protecting liberty itself had not had time to gel. Perhaps this was because in order to achieve liberty it is necessary to know what liberty is, and knowing what it is is the pathway to deserving it. But that was a valuable primary national project even if it was obviously fragile and plagued by limitations. It was isolated and unilateral. So much so in fact that a person of that time might have asked the dramatic question: liberty? *What for?*

The fact that some people did ask this question probably accounts for the fact that it wasn't until half a century later (with everything such a long period means in the infancy of a nation), that a second project arrived on the scene: that of National Organization.

During the period from 1820 to 1853 Argentina teetered between fear and despotism, between demagogy and strangulation, between alliance and treason. It was a national battle in the search for an identity.   It was an exhausting internal polemic on the type of organization the country was to adopt. For lack of a project blood was spilled and stained many areas of Argentine development. If the national project of 1810 would have preserved more carefully the best element inside of us all, it is possible that the Republic would have seen fewer battles and would have been the scene of many more collective triumphs. Because in the desolate history of civil strife, pain is always victory's child.

The 1810 revolution was of economic origin and international character. Its origin and consequences had to do with the high seas.

It followed the weakening of Spain. Similar movements developed for the same reason throughout the Americas. As nearly all triumphs depend more on the errors or incapability of one of the sides than on the strength or strategic organization of the other, time is an important factor. Triumph is as fleeting as the factors which make it possible. This revolution was not preceded by a period of fermentation in which national organization could be discussed. It was the consequence of an imbalance between ever-stronger local interests and those of a battered Spain. It was an imitation of other wars for independence throughout the Americas. It was an echo of the American Revolution, among others.

During those years and totally outside the guideline of a national project, which didn't exist, which no one had laid out, a tragic conflict took place. For fifty years charismatic "caudillos" battled with individual liberty in mind. These are two symbols of the nation and of the period. Both sides went too far, overstepped their limits, and eliminated one another. It was a disproportionate and blind battle between a thesis of authoritarian and arbitrary solitude and an antithesis of free and chaotic multitude, in which many had to die before a clear synthesis could be established. This synthesis appears to have been born in the 80s. But just as it triumphed, it failed. There was a sort of nemesis which devoured the generation which reached its goal, waving its project like a sword. The 1880s model did not adapt to a change of circumstances. It did not have the moral tenacity it needed to keep growing. Because of this we could say that in a way the clarifying synthesis as it stood in the conclusive form, has not cast any real light on our present day circumstances. And this is true, despite the fact that so much and such a paradoxically painful time has passed and that both sides have exchanged as many insults as they have eulogies recognizing both the merits and faults exhibited along the way.

Since then the country has seen an internal upheaval which is tragic in that everyone involved is somewhat right. Count Keyserling would have much to say later about how a tragedy is produced when two peoples who are right battle with one another. We Argentines are perhaps a prolonged example of this. It is also an example of the enigma of this nation that some desolate fighter in the civil war could have asked the agonizing question: Independence? What for?

National Organization

When the battles between the charismatic "caudillos" appeared to be winding down, the nation organized itself according to the typical model of the period, with a federal, representative, republican Constitution.

It was logical for this line to be followed, since our forefathers did not have more solid notions about a national project than we do. The very essence of a national project is still difficult to conceive, because it refers to value levels set by many different people, and to achievement through the work of many more; it must deal simultaneously with the immediate present, with a past one which is not equally remembered by those involved, and the future, the concept of which brings fear and intrepidation together and in which valor must overcome all fright, if the project is to be carried out. Perhaps a national project should be an ideal of the future in a community in which the leaders think in terms of greatness, rather than on a scale of partial interests. It is along these lines that we find an intrinsic problem in the national project: It is a promise made by the entire nation and it is only as good as the word of those who make it. A project being the real together with the possible; it moves from the potential to the kinetic, but it does this by putting its maximum strength at stake in something which does not yet exist, something which is still an idea. It is capable of proving that an idea is the strongest force there is for changing a possibility into a reality. A project is the step from not-being to being, and it is the biggest gamble the human being can make: A national project means risking everything in order to win everything.

There are measures of achievement. Not everything in human terms can be fully achieved. Better said: Nearly nothing can be considered total achievement in human terms. Thus a condition of human existence is perhaps man's most precious reward. No other species does things more or less well. Animals and plants carry out their modest little operations with universal precision. Only Man in his tremendous solitude in the universe can be mistaken, is capable of being clumsy and omitting errors of judgement. But Man is also the only magnificent rebel the Creator made with the built-in probability of reaching something better, something difficult, the perfections which had been denied to all that passed before him. There was a need for a superior creature with the capability to project, and projection is a type of promise. That is why Nietzsche said that Man was the only animal capable of making a promise. If one looks inside oneself and realizes how difficult it is to formulate a personal project, we will have no difficulty in recognizing what an arduous task is that of working out the gigantic dimensions of a national project.

The continental project consisted of making American countries free for their even freer citizens, and to construct and defend a place where private initiative and individual responsibility could exist and develop. This is the project which, in modern times, has permitted the unfolding in the United States of the Watergate drama and has allowed the US to overcome its defeat in Vietnam.

Parts of the 1880s project were not reduced to rubble, nor did they become fossilized; these remnants, which still stand in Argentina, are the truthful structures on which the original project was built. So it was that national organization subsisted, despite some men, who, once in power, turned into the worst kind of poison for the nation. Alberdi was the philosopher of national organization. His contemporaries, even when brought face to face with the critics, were "doers." They showed all the problems of the period with themselves as active parties in the proceedings, and they showed too that where there is a philosopher with an idea, there is a possibility of moving the country into a constructive stage in its history.

Alberdi's project was a dynamic one, a project of leadership, a constructive, instructive, pragmatic project which took population growth into account. In referring to projects included in the Constitutions of Latin American countries of that period, the author of *Las Bases* says: "None of the Constitutions in South America merit being taken as examples for imitation... All of them are reminiscences, treason, reform (or) many times textual (copies) of Constitutions out of the past... They have been done looking inward, some to build up power in the name of order, others to weaken it in the interest of liberty; sometimes to centralize their jurisdiction, other times to localize it, but never with the idea of omitting from constitutional law that which, from its very beginning, it has had against the growth and progress of new states nor to give support to means conducive to reaching this great goal of the American Revolution..."

Liberal Project

The generation of the 80s transformed the letter of constitutional policy into that of a growing, dynamic nation. It was the only opportunity in which two national projects — the political and the practical — overlapped one another in time and constituted the two parts of a continuous whole. Out of that national project came a nation with a high level of ever-growing possibilities. It was a project with adequate formal continuity for time and space. It was the same generation, which, together with the next one, faced the questions of national organization and territorial integration; policies for the conquest of the desert, settling and colonization, transport and education. The generation's policies had to do with the making of a nation.

With all the limitations calendar dates imply, we could say that this was all happening during the Liberal period (1880) during the course of which an important and damaging phenomenon was taking place.

It was a period of undeniable progress which was not accompanied by the growth necessary to give it permanence and future. It is true that as from 1880 there was an attempt at introducing education, transportation, settling and colonization. Important goals were reached. But it is also true that through indifference to agroimport plans, the nation lost vital areas of its social body. These mutilated areas would come to have an odd life of their own — thus, a monstrous life. And they were to put pathological pressure on the nation's political soul.

The agroimport scheme was to finish with the last of the virgin lands, which were not worked beyond their natural primary possibilities. Because no system of agricultural technology was followed, the virgin soil ran out much sooner than it should have in reality. When was chemical technology first applied to the enrichment of Argentine soil? What measures were taken by landholders or the government to take advantage of our real land resources and to thus augment production to cover any bad times to come?

The nation's most important men, both government officials and land-owners, thought everything had already been done.   More perfumes than fertilizer formulas were imported from Europe. More jewelry than drill bits arrived in our ports. More ladies' hairdressers than professors of physics came to Argentina to settle. There was very little interest in diversifying the economy.

If an analyst were to ask what kept Argentina from becoming a leader-nation like the United States, we would be hard pressed to give him a single, sufficient answer.

The generation of the 80s founded a nation on liberal principles — principles which upheld the need to achieve social mobility and ample participation in governmental power. These principles were blocked by the leader-class, which was made up of land-holders. Their lands were among the most productive in the world, and without actually trying to, they had assured themselves of a perpetual income. The higher the level of demand for primary products, the greater their income, since increased production which brought a need to cover this greater demand would have to come from marginal lands which were less productive and which, because of the money it would take to whip them into shape, would have raised prices. This increase protected the land income of the landed class.

If for some reason prices went down all the land-holders had to do was decrease their income, which, without a doubt, would still assure them of a sufficient level of income, given the shortage of fertile land at the end of the last century. The possibility of a drop in sectorial prices was unimaginable in the last quarter of the century, particularly with the coming of the first cattle boom. Land-holders felt assured of income for many generations to come. The predominant political group of that time received and acquired the best and most productive land once the Indians had been evicted for good. The new owner-settlers moved into marginal zones, even though their incomes remained linked to the prime zone.

An end to the occupation of the most fertile lands caused a rise in their price, since from the end of the century onward they became more and more scarce. The coming of the railroads put the finishing touches on the land price rise. The railroads reinforced the feeling of security the land-holders had already had. From that time on they would never have to worry about money again.

It seemed all bets were covered: The future looked promising since the relative shortage of land would be greater all the time and its price would keep going up. This class had reached the summit of a social group's aspirations: It had insured the future of its children and their children. And thus there was no real reason for them to use their energy in creation and competition.

Only a prophet would have been able to foresee a crisis like that of the 30s, after the way foreign demand for leather, wool, grain and meat had increased continually. Any thinker of that time would have laughed if he had been told about the problems lack of fertile land was going to cause. He would have said that this shortage would only tend to increase the exchange rate, thus bringing new activities into export trade and new efficient industries would be established in order to make substitutes for imports. This would have a possible effect on land income, since a higher exchange rate tends to favor primary products: All bets were covered.

The tax system was not developed and multiple exchange rates were not used in the world at that time. Thus, no one could have imagined that the economy would be attacked from that angle. Agrarian reform was mostly a topic for discussion among European intellectuals of the period, and could even be considered a danger to the ruling class.

The scheme's flaw resided in having created a country in which income was assured to many generations through land, while immigrants and criollos who did not participate in power had to work within an economic system which was competitive and of limited possibilities. But the rising classes, new ranchers, farmers and the children of immigrants exercised continuous pressure from 1890 onward with the aim of participating in power, taking power or simply toward achieving a better position in society. They thus used the landholding group as a social reference.

The rules of the game in this system demonstrated that through primary, secondary or third-level activities one could become the holder of economic power equal to that of the landholding class. The economic mobility was there; what was lacking was access to political and social power at the top.

When political mobility arrived with the coming of Radicalism, they found that this power was not sufficient either, since the landholding class had its income insured whereas the rest of the population suffered the slings and arrows of economic competition. The mobility was there, but it was accompanied by insecurity, a condition which the ruling class had overcome.

And so the country's progress was cut off and stagnation set in. The less fluid and competitive the market became, the greater the opportunities were to re-create the situation in which the landholders lived. The 1930s produced the long-awaited change, permitting the formation of a protective industrial group, which felt secure and which began to stand on an equal level with the landholders.

New socio-economic groups began to join the legion of those who did not need to better themselves because nobody competed; expansion was the way to win security. Once the right conditions had been achieved to give protection to business and trade, there was no reason to worry about improving or even maintaining the status quo.

This ideology based on comfort through lack of competition was taken to its extremes with the coming of Peronism — a period in which all production was protected and when security was achieved through the growth of firms. Inflation completed this circle of defense by allowing an artificial growth of demand and the subsequent subsidizing of production. Multiple exchange rates and customs tariffs formed the central part of this scheme in which the new bourgeoisie began to have the same privileges as the old landowning class, and this could only take the country a step backwards. Exclusively upward social and economic mobility is a fallacy, because once the upper zone is saturated all mobility is obstructed.

This is shown clearly in the trade union policy imposed during the different Peronist periods: retirement on the best wage of a person's working life; automatic promotion without taking capability into account; employment security; immobility in public office; and these are only a few of the examples taken from the scheme which mimicked the power reached by land-holders in the early years of this century.

This analysis allows for the suggestion of a few of the reasons political demagogues have exploited values which have been a great expense to the population in general. They have always promised their followers conditions similar to those which at one time only belonged to the landed class. The land-holders' way of life has served as a model for the construction of values for the rest of the community and has taken the nation down the road to institutionalized stagnation and free-for-alls. Unity and drive are not recognized as positive guidelines.

Any real possibilities have been milked dry. Leftovers have been thrown out. Milk cost so little for so many years that it wasn't worth the trouble of saving it. Dehydration was not put into practice for many years and the first plant was installed only after great difficulty, and during a time when leftovers were running short. We would have been able to make Argentina a wealthy nation by breaking into new markets and conquering them, if somebody would have planned ahead. But a fatal idea reigned: *Everything has already been done in this country. If any change need be made it should only be made so that nothing changes.*

This national project was full of unpardonable cracks, omissions, and confusion. The country is so large that it is not worth going to the trouble of dedicating oneself wholly to the nation's affairs. It would get done by itself. A deep crack is opening beneath our feet. It is caused by the fact that we have not paid enough attention to the formation of the individual. "To instruct is not to educate." One who indulges in egotistical and self-centered conduct which takes all the wrong roads leaves no path open to others of his same group. It is a suicidal egotism with social consequences. This causes an unhealthy low in social mobility almost to the point of stagnation.

Thus the nation went through a so-called Liberal period based on the exploitation of an agro-imports economy, which was insufficient for the 24 million people who would eventually come to live in this country. It is much more insufficient for the 40 million inhabitants who should be living here by the end of this century. But then, this inept national project for the future could kill the possibility of the population's reaching this point. In other words, bad government today makes for de-population tomorrow.

At that time no one asked himself: Progress? What for?

Mass Access to Power

The same immigration scheme which was part of the project of the 1880s was the catalyst which took us into a second stage which was to be added to the deprivation we have already spoken of: the stalling, the slowing of social mobility which characterizes the Liberal power structure.

The demographic structure of Argentina took shape during this period. Its cultural form became more defined. The Constitution of 1853 was a reflection of most other American Constitutions from the time of the US Revolutionary War onward. Thus, the process of access of the people to power through the universal vote signified an emulation of world trends.

As of 1890 this mechanism — it is nothing more than a voting mechanism, with absolute abstraction of the consequences of the acts of those elected — began to have an objective of its own. Universal suffrage which until then had held a secondary position in bigger and more powerful countries, suddenly held a place of prime importance. Elections were adored simply because they were elections. The act of electing, the mental function which was activated was more important than the thing being voted on.

This new phenomenon brought about a lack of logic of unforeseen proportions. The favorite candidate, within this deformed school of political thought, is he who guarantees and shows that he is convinced that the most important part of governing is the election of the person who governs. These are the thoughts of the electoralist: I am the best candidate for election by the people because I am sure that there is nothing better, in governing, than to be elected by the people.

And to govern is essentially to guarantee that the people elect the best candidate which is to guarantee... and so on ad infinitum. Along these lines of thinking, it does not much matter what the public officials will do. What is important is how these things take him into power.

This fallacy was the main ingredient in a remedy which had just appeared and which promised to cure political ills: It was called Radicalism. In reality more than an ingredient it was an excipient: Its mission was to accompany the prime substance and make it tolerable.

What was the prime substance, the essential component in Radicalism? That is a mystery just as Yrigoyen as a man was a mystery. Manuel Galvez put it this way: "...the shortage of written documents on the physical intimacy of his person, his strange and mysterious silence concerning himself, a shortage of exact data over the years...have converted the life of Hipólito Yrigoyen, from a literary standpoint, into a series of arduous problems."[1]

What Galvez does not say, or even induce one to suspect, is that the word mystery can be just as ambivalent as nearly all the other things we think we know. For one to call oneself a mysterious person, and nothing more than mysterious, could very well be a velvety way of disguising a lack of content. Generally, when content exists, there is no mystery. Or at least it is usually this way on a human level. And even, at times, on a non-human level. This is why at the end of Oscar Wilde's story "The Secret of the Sphinx" the awsome monster revealed his mystery: "The enigma of the sphinx is...that it has no enigma."[2]

The seeds of Radicalism were planted by the people of the period before Radicalism appeared. It did not reach power alone. It came to power when the ruling class, with which it had battled, decided it could not govern without the support of an elected minority. Few could see the substantial effect of this reasoning, since, as we have mentioned before, the ruling class was not worried about maintaining a political stance. When it finally decided to take a stand, it was already too late, and it made a mistake. Because of this, the ruling class permitted itself to be taken from political power. There is also a worst thought at the bottom of all this. The ruling class was turning Radical and the Radicals were trying their best to rise to the position of the landed class in a transfer of symbols which has occurred throughout history and has usually ended up demonstrating the true identities of those involved in the swap.

Within a few years, a voter majority, conditioned by the political machine Yrigoyen had created, gave him an election victory and handed power over to him. At this precise moment, something happened which was very similar to an occurrence of 100 years before. Someone a hundred years before had asked: Independence? *What for?* In 1916 the question at the start of the Radical government's reign was: Government of the people? What for?

A people's government, in terms of independence and national

---

[1] M. Galvez, "Vida de Hipolito Yrigoyen, el hombre del misterio."

[2] Oscar Wilde's "The Nightingale and the Rose and Other Stories."

organization, is a secondary objective. It does not have self-sufficient value. And since it does not seek a program for the nation, it ends up being nobody's government. It is merely an administrator of national affairs, a group of politicians who do not know where they are leading the nation.

It becomes clear in reading the words of Felix Luna on noted Radicals in the introduction to a book called "Que Argentina queremos los Argentinos?" (Page 26) that Radicalism did not know how to propose a national objective to the nation, once it had managed, through universal suffrage, to take power.

These are Luna's words:

"It was at this time, that the country looked perfect (about 1925), it looked finished, and many sectors figured the only things left to do were merely a few minor adjustments. A paradigmatic piece of literature on this is *Introduccion a la historia de la literatura argentina* by Ricardo Rojas, in which he says there is nothing important left to do in the nation; that it is only necessary to tighten the educational springs and improve electoral practices. He said this in 1918 or 1919."

This lack of a national objective continues to characterize Radicalism, which is content to take a merely institutional role in politics and government. In this sense the leaders of the so-called Liberation Revolution, Illia and Lanusse, whose politics were Radical-inspired, ran governments similar to that of Yrigoyen. They guaranteed the free play of institutions, but they proposed nothing for the country. The false idea of a country which had made it, which had achieved everything it needed to achieve and in which the only thing one needed to guarantee was the upholding of the vote, lasted until the 1930s. The Great Depression then demonstrated that Argentina was not prepared to face a world crisis and the nation began to search for a new future.

What happened to Argentina was that imperative geopolitics came to it from abroad and it was not prepared to absorb their meaning, since its culpably frivolous cultural programs contained not even the slightest inkling of geopoltics.

The FORJA Era

Though Yrigoyen's Radical movement claimed to be nationalistic, in fact it continued, except in a few exceptional cases, to carry out the open economic policies which had been a part of the Liberal system that had gone before it. It was only after the depression of the

1930s that many countries began to ask themselves if, perhaps, the days of open world trade were over and if national autarchy was not the only option left. The question arose in Argentina as it had in the aggressively nationalist Central European countries, and out of this, Argentine economic autarchy was born. The best known group behind this movement was the Fuerza de Orientación Radical del Joven Argentino, otherwise known as FORJA, which, in about the middle of 1935, was preparing an ambitious attempt at revitalizing the badly tattered Radical movement and at introducing a nationalist doctrine, a doctrine which, like all nationalism of that period, was emotional and confusing.[1]

FORJA sided, as did much of the Argentine military establishments of the 1943 revolution, with the Axis during the war, and this placed Argentina on the opposite geopolitical side from the country which would be the number one world leader from the end of the war onward. But FORJA was also infiltrated with the Marxist concept of imperialism which gave it a nationalistic rhetorical pomp that would be a part of Argentine politics from that time on. To the "country that's made it" concept was added the concept that "the nation is not to blame since imperialism is to blame for everything."

Born out of the revolution of September 1930, FORJA was a protest movement, and as such, it was based on resentment, which proves to be a hollow basis for any movement. FORJA joined up with Peronism in 1945, breaking up as an individual movement, and passed its anti-agrarian, emotionally nationalistic, autarchic views on to the disastrous Peronist economic policy. Instead of building a nation which was strong on exports and then industrializing critical, basic sectors on the strength of exports, Peronism, inspired by FORJA, wanted to diminish agricultural activity and built up nothing more than industrial manufacturing activities.

The country would be healthier and more highly industrialized today if agricultural incentives had not been restricted as of 1945.[1] It was FORJA's way of thinking that brought about the disorderly nationalization of public service companies, and which has led us to the current calamitous situation in our rail, telephone and electric services. Under the motto of "We are a colonial Argentina; we want to be a free Argentina," a poor, dependent Argentina has been built.

In the moment of final decline of the British Empire, the moment in which it became obvious that the Empire could no longer exist, all the emotion of the era was centered on an attack against Britain,

---

[1] M.A. Scenna's "FORJA."

which appeared to be an echo of Hitler's speeches in the German Reichstag. If all the strong will the British, who did not have a decent card left in their hand, employed to withstand the wrath of war would have gone into the building of an Argentina, this would have been a different nation today.

The idea of economic autarchy, which was proposed at the end of the 1930s, was imposed on Argentina at the end of the 1940s in absolute ignorance of what was going on in the world outside. This idea, which appeared to perhaps have a spark of economic feasibility in the 1930s, was rendered absolutely absurd by the Second World War, a conflict which made it obvious that a world of open trade was far superior to the setting up of autarchic nations.

Hitler took the concept of autarchy to its extreme, by, among other things, trying to conquer the countries which held the natural resources he needed to keep his autarchy alive. He thus showed that autarchy was impossible even for a Central European state. Even after the Bretton Woods Agreements outlined plans for a world of open trade, Argentina, led by Perón and inspired, to some extent, by FORJA, enrolled in the non-existent world of autarchy and disorderly development.

Social Distribution

After the war abroad which had frozen Argentina's possibilities, a new alternative situation presented itself, and, as had happened in 1914, the wrong choice was made, in an Argentina full of possibilities. The rising generation wanted to participate in the construction of an Argentina present and future. But the absence of a national project permitted national unity to break down. The different factions in the nation's political life began to confront one another with all the verbal, and sometimes physical, violence they could muster.

A blindness grew among businessmen, proletariat and government alike and the cracks in the nation's unity grew wider still. By the time World War II had ended, political, cultural, institutional and moral weaknesses had led to an attitude of personal convenience rather than general well-being. The nation was impregnated with a sordid utilitarianism which saw very few exceptions in any sector of society. It was a time of cynical merchants and preachers of history. And beneath all of them were the rich and promising remains of a broken country. It was the perfect setup for a charismatic leader, who took up the reins of deceit, mounted the horse of power and rode through the land distributing pieces of "the best country in the world."

But the charismatic leader was not distributing the fruits of continuous and progressive growth. It was easier for him to distribute the fruits of the past. Actually, he did not distribut them; he burned them in the home-fires of a flattered public. Thus, led along the road to decadence by Peronist demagogy, Argentina was to pick up social distribution and make it a permanent passenger in the form of a national objective. This distribution was badly carried out, in that what was distributed was not work and a future, but hand-outs from the past. False well-being was distributed, and so was political power to people who were not capable of using it for the benefit of the community. What was being distributed, in reality, was fire.

Both the Radical project, the goal of which was the election of public officials by the people and the social distribution project which we owe to the Peronists, are mere by-products of the Liberal progress project of 1880. Both the Radical and the Peronist projects lack the construction and spirt of sacrifice included in an authentic national project and could, in fact, even be considered "anti-projects." They bear a great portion of the blame for the process of decadence in Argentina, which we analyzed in the first part of this book.

Developmentalism

In 1958, national development was presented by Frondizi and Frigerio as a national program. They presented a list of unilateral, technical ideas, which were founded solely on reaching material goals. A thought which deserves our attention is the following: Material development which is not linked to moral values is a project that can be fit into any ideology. It can be applied to slavery or to liberty. Developmentalism had something in common with Yrigoyenist Radicalism: It had the form of something solid, but it was hollow, an empty shell. It was a movement in name only. Its power did not go beyond the magic of the word "development." It did not fit reality. The roots of these two policies were not firmly planted. Why didn't they respond to the basic questions: Development? What for? Why should the country grow, so as to obtain autarchy, and thus cut down on our contact with the outside world? Developmentalism did not propose an overall increase in exports. It did not lead to better ties with other countries. Instead, it proposed that we use international capital to make ourselves more autarchic and more self-sufficient. It was ap lan which tended to bring greater growth and less independence.

The paradox here is that the main line of ideological defense of most Latin American countries is their commercial interdependence on the rest of the Western world. If one of those countries achieves the building of an autarchic nation in the midst of these ties, it can cut its links with the West and could easily embark on a program made, not by our government, but by some other one.

At any rate, the experiments that were set up when these groups were in power proved to be impractical and contrary to doctrinal sense. The statistics which show the living results of this administration are more eloquent than the concepts themselves (see Chapter One). And while government action was unable to come up to the plans outlined, foreign political corpuscles entered the nation's nervous system, corpuscles which sought to link Argentina with countries in other blocs. These bio-organisms united among themselves to form cellular structures. They supported one another and managed to get into key posts. They stuck close to the top post waiting to get into them. They had never been as close to power as they were then. The brevity of the Frondizi government — brought on by political mortgages he found it necessary to take out in order to get into power — keeps us from being able to make a conclusive judgement on whether his program was or was not feasible. Clear political analysis does not permit conjecture over what did happen.

Summary

A summary of the Argentine process of national projects can be seen in the following way:

1 — The country obtained national independence and reached a very important position among other nations. Geopolitical carelessness has lowered the level reached. The prime objective of the nation, sovereignty, is in danger.

2 — The national organization of 1853 was able to make the country grow but was not able to finish creating it. The last fifty years of history have shown that that organization is no longer adequate in the dog-eat-dog world. Modern brainwashing methods damage the operations of republican institutions. Methods used in means of mass communications act to paralyze the active role of liberty and democracy.

3 — The European type plans initiated in 1880 signified an important step for the nation. It was not adequate however, for

modern times.   The type of leaders it created chose suicide over giving an opening to social mobility. The old elite did not know how· to adapt their project to the new elite. The European model was left behind and today there is no valid model to be emulated. Besides that, the European model began to agonize when Comtean positivisim, which was the rage in Europe and Argentina's intellectual circles for a time, passed its zenith.

4 — The access of the people to power, according to the Radical model, showed itself to be insufficient for a growing country. It also ran into difficulties in trying to run public administration, which it took in its clumsy demagogic hands and carried into a futureless inefficiency.

5 — The Peronists' social distribution project whittled away at the country's resources for 10 years in a daily orgy of demagogy. The only thing which can come of a political machine which spends without producing is the highest inflation ever seen, the greatest uncontrolled rebellion, the greatest myth-making and disillusion which Argentina has ever known. Its final phases saw delinquents standing with the country's leaders in a level of corruption unknown before in the annals of Argentine history.

6 — The developmentists' project was never consummated, and was more of a technical value than it was an accepted national plan.

7 — Thus the country faces the generation of 1980 and is still without a national project. The saddest part of this is that this generation must suffer the erosion caused by the inefficiency of its ancestors. Not knowing what to do with a country or for a country would appear to be the trademark of our leaders.

Full Circle

Every time Argentina has a change of government, politics on the highest level come *full circle*. Everything that was done by the government before is declared incorrect and must be modified. This coming full circle is a manifestation of political demagogy in Argentina. The reasoning is simple: If a change of government hadn't been needed there wouldn't have been a change of government and *of course the change was justified*. And with this the image of the former government deteriorates. The new government can construct an image by merely doing the exact opposite of what the first government did. Thus many policies and government instruments have been destroyed; they have begun contradictory processes and they have put the brakes on valuable initiatives in Argentina, because this coming full circle also affects conflicting economic interests.   The opposing side in the moment of change is the strongest.   It tries to achieve a 180-degree transformation which changes its members into the beneficiaries of a new policy which is not necessarily any more correct than the one before it.   The slogans of change or of great change serve to emphasize even more the process of coming full circle, which thus acquires a position of distinction of its own.   All national affairs and economic factors suffer abrupt and deep variations each time the political forces which regulate their movements change.   With each of these 180-degree turns a number of production factors are dismantled and a number of top businessmen and producers are permanently demoralized.

This signifies that changes introduced in government action should be part of a pre-conceived government plan.   This plan should be brought ready-made into office with the person who takes the responsibility of governing.   A simple program of contradiction which has been the rule until now will not work.   This is because not everything a government does can be wrong.   Some courses of action must be correct.   Some will have no effect one way or the other and will be more of a problem to the community to change them than to leave them alone, at least for the time being.   One thing is certain: An unnecessary 180-degree turn is damaging to many, causes disorientation and benefits only a few.   The real nation goes on working even on the same day of the change of government.   It works according to existing rules of the game, the majority of which are absurd and contradictory.   Nevertheless each time we come full circle we find ourselves in still another contradictory situation.

This round trip characteristic, which nurtures completely opposite positions, will be further analyzed later in this same part of the book. We will take a final look at its effects when we refer to a proposal for the 1980s.

Chapter X

Political Party Platforms
Projects for Consumers

Unasked Questions

The analysis of projects which over the course of time managed to get certain backing from the Argentine community raises questions over what aims they proposed to the Argentine people. A review is useful because even if the projects which were to put into practice or which aborted after a short time, have become obsolete or were unilateral, there might have been among them a program which actually constituted a national project.

We should remember that the last national elections were held on March 11, and August 23, 1973. In the first vote the Cámpora-Solano Lima team was elected and in the second, the Juan D. Perón-Maria E.M. de Perón team was elected. All political parties took part in the election without limitation and freely expressing their political platform.

There are very few Argentines who exercise their right to vote in order to choose a government program. Actually, they vote for candidates whose general ideas are known but they tend to be ignorant of the particular instrumentation of these ideas as they apply to the administration of national growth. Political parties have never placed much importance on distributing information explaining such important issues as: *What* we are going to do, *why* we are going to do it, *how* we are going to do it, and *with whom* we are going to do it.

Within this lack of publicity on the projects of each party there are probably a number of factors, among which the proven demagogic electoral efficiency would have to be counted. This efficiency is aimed at keeping the party from assuming concrete commitments where their fulfillment could be demanded or checked on at a later date.

Voters are tremendously indifferent about what government principles they are voting for. In contrast, they are avidly interested in knowing personal details about the candidate. On the other hand, the printing cost of the government program to be mass distributed, seems superfluous to the financial director of a campaign who is more interested in spending party members' scarce funds on catchy jingles. The disheartening evidence is that, in general, political parties lack specific plans for government and they are nearly always content with high-sounding but hollow declarations, which are very useful in raising the enthusiasm of the masses but which are totally lacking in significance.

Concrete information on party platforms is difficult to come by and the following section of this book has been compiled, only after great difficulty, with what incomplete material we were able to gather.

In Appendix V the reader will find a classified summary of the political platforms presented by major parties which took part in the aforementioned election. Important points of the programs of the following parties were studied:

Justicialist Liberation Front (FREJULI)
Integration and Development Movement (MID)
Progressive Democratic Party (PDP)
Federalist Party (PF)
Intransigent Party (PI)
Popular Christian Party (PPC)
Democratic Socialist Party (PSD)
Radical Party (UCR)

1. System of government and major legislation

These political party platforms confirm what was said when we analyzed the Radical project before. The mere functioning of institutions within the current constitutional system is considered enough to generate a better future and economic growth for the nation.

Most of the parties, including the UCR, agreed in March 1973 on the necessity to repeal repressive laws and other special legal machinery put into effect to defend the country against subversion. Ideological infiltration was already on the move at the time and this made way for the sanctioning of the amnesty law.

The FREJULI platform clearly promises an *ample and generous amnesty law*. The consequences of such a law were foreseeable and are being seen today. The PDP emphasizes defense of freedom and insinuates that the system should defend those who do not respect the Constitution, while at the same time stating that democratic rights can be withheld from no one because of their political beliefs. The political naivete of the 19th century appears here in the last part of the 20th. No one recognized in March 1973 that the nation was in the midst of a grave fight for surivival. They were obviously living within the utopian process of institutionalization. FREJULI introduces a "classist"'twist in speaking of a naming and immobility of judges. A judge's values could be adequate or inadequate according to what social group he belongs to. In other words, in order to be a judge, belonging to a certain group is essential.

The PDP also includes an ample chapter dedicated to justice in which it proposed the elimination of the military command's control over military justice.

The PSD makes proposals which have already been turned into realities in Argentina, like the separation of church and state and freedom of religion.

It is important to point out that in 1973 the UCR, in the midst of a guerrilla war, proposed the revision of the obligatory military service system and the PSD proposed the reduction of military service and a decrease in the number of effective armed forces members, the limitation of the military budget to no more than 50% of the education budget, as well as proposing other limits on armaments.

2. Foreign policy

This is probably the saddest chapter in the political platforms, because it shows the same absolute lack of world perspective which has been in evidence in Argentina since Yrigoýen.

The common denominators among all the programs are, among others: relations with Cuba, which in practice would be beneficial to subversive elements which would obtain logistical support, materials and necessary ideology.

The maintaining of an independent policy, which is to say, ignoring the geopolitical interdependence of the West.

Latin American integration against North American imperialism.

Modification or repudiation of pacts with the OAS and the ALALC (LAFTA).

The foreign policy sector of all the platforms is the most declamatory. It shows a lack of seriousness in the Argentine political climate.

It is worth pointing out that the PDP was seeking "popular participation in the Latin American Common Market, through a Latin American parliament." At a moment in which national parliaments throughout Latin America were not functioning, the PDP proposed the organization of a continental parliament.

There are repeated declarations and enunciations of American imperialism and even of Brazilian sub-imperislism; we did not find, on the other hand, a single reference to the possibility of Russian imperialism or Marxist imperialism. Had Marxists infiltrated all these parties or were their leaders ignorant of the existence of Russian imperialism?

3. Culture and education

The best demonstration of the lack of modern ideas and pace-setting power of our political parties can be found in the backing of education law 1.420 and the university reform by the UCR, the PSD and the PDP. Several other parties also sought to have the teachers' statute put back on the books and called for a thaw in provisional benefits for retired teachers despite the fact that it had already been shown that it was not possible to pay the total amount promised within the statute.

There were a few references to what the education program would contain, but many references were made to numerous mechanisms which should be invented, created or reinstated to give the benefits of an education to everyone.

The unlimited income concept was common to many platforms. Various platforms proposed the elimination of state contributions to private schools or state help being limited to totally free schools. There was no proposal for how to replace the education that was to be taken away.

All of the education proposals, when we get right down to it, were merely lists of benefits for the community with no indication of how they would be financed, what philosophical content education would have, and by what human means they planned to implement such ambitious and incoherent programs. It should be pointed out here that the MID suggests: ''restructuring the university system on a basis of teacher aptitude, oriented investigation, satisfaction of national priorities, and the equal placement of professors and students in university life.'' What the MID did not say was how it planned to carry this out, nor by what means, nor did it give information as to what national priorities would be. This, like many other programs, was made for individuals, to fit individual priorities.

4. Economy

The economic platforms of the political parties set out to satisfy everyone's interests. A good example of this was the UCR platform which proposed more state intervention in various activities as well as more extensive state control over foreign trade, of the financial system and of foreign investment, but it did not neglect to say that the party supported private initiative. It is difficult to understand what model the UCR was following in its national platform, because anyone who was worried about anything could find himself specifically satisfied as long as he did not read the paragraphs that contradicted the promise made to him with a promise made to another sector or with greater state intervention in his own sector.

One of the principal worries included in the political platforms of March 1973 was how to control foreign investment. This worry made for the Foreign Investment Law which was approved in 1973 with participation from nearly all of the political parties and after the passing of which not a single foreign investment was made in the country.

The FREJULI proposed the reforming of the socio-economic structure according to popular Christian national doctrine and we leave it to you to decide what this meant. But as the FREJULI was the party which governed us for three years, we can infer that a national popular Christian economic doctrine is what drove the country into a state of chaos and economic ruin.

In 1973 co-op (labor-business) direction of companies was in style and nearly all the platforms talk about it.

Perhaps the most salvagable platform was that of the Federalist Party, which, even if it did not respond to an economic model, was coherent in a number of aspects and did not contain, like many of the others, internal contradictions.

The PDP proposed a number of tax cuts without saying how it was going to finance the state. It also proposed the elimination of secrecy in the filing of sworn statements. It also declared that it was going to level off the expenses and financing resources of the state, without explaining how it planned to do this despite a reduction in taxes, and in the midst of a drastic reduction of public employment and other mechanisms.

The PI proposed, after all these years, the division of lands in Argentina, complete agrarian reform and the state takeover of all public service companies, communications, and transport, including bus lines. The PI platform is probably the most statist of the group.

The system of official control of prices was proposed by the majority of the parties and was coherently applied by the government which assumed power in March 1973.

As far as public works, transport and energy go, there are endless promises about bringing the national infrastructure up to date. In no case, however, was it explained how to finance or whether there were enough resources in the country to meet the needs of such huge projects, including the ambitious housing programs.

The UCR, the FREJULI and the PPC were in agreement as to monopoly control by YPF of oil interests. None of them, however, cared to say how the country would manage to become self-sufficient in oil and not increase its imports as had been happening over the past five years due to the growing YPF monopoly and a lack of means to explore and exploit oil resources.

The UCR, like the PPC and the PDP, proposed no agrarian reform. No one who wishes to know what was really proposed for the economy by traditional and new parties in their programs of government should fail to read the appendix. There is no better demonstration of a lack of a national project than the recapitulation of the high-sounding campaign promises which were issued in place of serious programs with real objectives that the nation could reach.

5. Labor

Within the UCR platform we find special emphasis placed on broader democratization of union life and the elimination of unions from national political life.

In the rest of the electoral platforms there were new promises of a better life for all workers. Since Argentina has already reached a high level of social legislation, these promises would have been difficult to keep.

There was an explicit promise in the FREJULI platform — and in one form or another in all of the rest of the platforms — of a work contract law, which was actually voted into effect in 1974, and paved the way for a universal drop in productivity.

FREJULI also promised — and later kept that promise — to give special union rights to labor leaders. Co-op administration apears in the UCR platform, in that of FREJULI and in other platforms as well. Other parties reaffirmed workers' stability throughout the civil service.

The PDP denied the state the right to supervise union activities and pretended that the workers themselves should be the only judges of the union. The MID also denied this right to the state. In one form or another, a new power was created within the nation. This new addition which already existed in the 1973 political platforms, was to play a big part in the nation's political life from that date and would contribute largely to the destruction of institutions during 1975 and the beginning of 1976.

6. Social welfare and social security

There is no better demonstration of why we have called this

chapter "Project for Consumers" than taking a look at how the political party platforms handle social security and social welfare. It is hard to think of any social benefit, any right, that the state could possibly authorize to any individual, which has not been foreseen in the party platforms of 1973. When we call Argentine politics a demagogic orgy we had this documentary proof of a free-for-all in which political parties promised to hand out what the nation did not have.

For example, in the area of social security we find veritable manuals which covered everybody, every problem and even permitted retirement benefits for those who simply did not want to work. Jobs were guaranteed. Systems in which employers, workers and the state were to participate were to be created, and tangled bureaucracies were to be formed to administer them; minimum benefits were guaranteed; a social benefits bank was to be created; housewives were to receive retirement benefits; all workers were to be guaranteed the possibility of owning a home; a national social security code was promised; unemployment funds were to be established. No one mentioned the imbalance between the cost of social security and the economy's capability of paying it. During the hour of promise nobody was worried about that. There was also no proposal of a system in which the individual would be responsible for paying into his social security fund.

Public health programs aimed high, especially the UCR program which proposed a complete system of health care equivalent to the best in the world. The UCR platform did not say where it was going to get the funds for this system or how long it was going to take to establish such a perfect system in Argentina. It was a typical utopian plan which promised immediate happiness and which would cost nothing.

None of the platforms emphasized the responsibility of the individual to protect his own health through caring for his ecology and living a healthy life.

Reading through these platforms leaves an unreal utopian taste in one's mouth. Everything that could be promised was promised. There was no prior diagnosis of the possibilities or priorities of the country. What was important was the consumer, who represented the majority, and who believed he could consume more and more all the time. Once the vote was over, diversional substitutes would take the place of campaign promises.

What happened in 1963 (Illia) was a case of unfulfilled demagogy. What happened in 1973 (Cámpora-Perón), on the other hand, was a case in which the country's rulers kept the prime promises of their

political platform, and did so with the support of the opposition:
   Amnesty (law No. 20.508)
   Elimination of repressive legislation (law No. 20.509)
   Foreign investment (laws Nos. 20.537 and 20.575)
   Work contract (law No. 20.744)
   Wage board conventions (application of law No. 14250)
   Urban rents (law No. 20. 519 and others)
   Nationalization of deposits (law No. 20.520)
   Renationalization of banks (law No. 20.522)
   Ministerial organization (law No. 20.524)
   Central Bank Organic Charter (law No. 20.539)
   YPF monopoly control of oil (nationalization of service stations,
                     Economy Ministry resolution 320/74)
   National Grain Board organization (law No. 20.535)
   Professional associations (law No. 20.615)
   Provisional and price control
   Monopolization of traditional exports (law No. 20.573)
   Tax reform (laws Nos. 20.626/27/28/29/30/31/32/43)
   Broadening of retirement benefits (law No. 21.118)
   Mining promotion (law No. 20.551)
   Industrial promotion (law No. 20.560)
   University organization (law No. 20.654)
There have been few times in Argentine history that a government
has had such backing for its program. The nation suffered a full dose
of populist triumph and the carrying out of all its promises. The
officials in this demagogy were mere messengers who acted as
necessary vehicles for the philosophy. The measures they took and
the result of those measures corresponded to an irrational lack of
coherence between apparent ends (growth-independence) and the
concrete means which are characterized by populism. Thus, any
official who tried to introduce a bit of rationality was eliminated in
short order.

Populist Masterpiece: The Hour of the People

   Although it does not constitute a party platform, we should stress
the importance of the alliance — fundamentally Radical and Peronist
— known as the Hour of the People, and which was the cause of
grave incidents in Argentine history during the period from 1973
until 1976.
   The first document of the Hour of the People was put out on
November 12, 1970 and constituted a prelude to the process of

institutionalization which was to be imposed by General Lanusse beginning in March 1971. On July 20, 1972 a document was released to the press in the home of Mr. Rawson Paz and it was entitled Agreement on Guarantees for the Hour of the People. (*La Nacion*, Buenos Aires, July 21, 1972, page 12).

This Agreement on Guarantees was read to journalists in the presence of Mr. Ricardo Balbín, Mr. Luis Leon, Mr. Enrique Vanoli, for the UCR; Messrs. Héctor Cámpora and Alejandro Diaz Bialet for Justicialism; Messrs. Horacio Thedy, Camilo Muniagurria and Leon Platis for the Progressive Democrats; and Vincent Solano Lima and Alberto Fonrouge for Popular Conservatism.

This document and others put out by the Hour of the People demonstrated the ties of all parties which would later follow the policies of FREJULI.

Besides habitual declarations of respect for rights and guarantees accorded by the national Constitution, other concepts which would later turn up between 1973 and 1976 are noteworthy.

"The right to resist oppression is recognized as a non-negotiable faculty of the people to refuse to consent to any form of tyranny."

"No political or economic doctrine, no class, race, religion or faction nor any power factor can pretend to represent liberty by denying it to other groups or other beliefs in the name of a final goal, no matter what it is."

"The death penalty should be suspended."

"The opinion of the citizens is manifested, in a democracy, through political parties. These (parties) should be recognized by the national constitution as a basic guarantee of democracy."

"Penal laws destined to combat crime and punish delinquents should only be dictated by the people through their representatives in the national congress. No penal law should be dictated to repress a profession or adhesion or any type of ideology or religion. Violence as a means of action shall be unacceptable within the Argentine democratic system; its causes will be suppressed in order to prevent it. The only way to guarantee peace is to apply and respect the law."

There is also a long point 14, which speaks out against "the factors of power, pressure groups, monopolies, multi-national corporations, extra-national colonialsitic organizations."

It also proposes "to reserve for our country the dominion over and exploitation of all sources of energy."

The document ends: "We thus describe the Argentina we pledge to bring about in the future. This constitutes a formal and solemn obligation of all undersigned political parties, to the Argentine people, with its sole purpose being to serve the high ideals of transformation in peace, liberty and social justice..."

Rereading the Hour of the People document we see that the dominant trend was already that of disarming the nation in the face of subversive aggression.

Apart from declarations already contained in our Constitution and which no one questioned, ideological liberty was declared beneficial even for those whose aim it was to infiltrate the nation with destructive ideologies, mixing it with freedom of religion which was already an Argentine right which had been exercised for a hundred years.

The basis for the future foreign investment law shows up in the contents of all political platforms of those who believed they could capitalize politically on the foreign investor.

The concept of *dependency* which was the mark of the first part of the government begun on May 25, 1973 is a common denominator in the Hour of the People documents. The basis for the amnesty law and the repealing of legislation which protected the country from subversion showed up in these documents and was to be almost unanimously approved by parliament in June, 1973.

When the period from 1971 to 1976, which represents a continuous period of institutionalization and populism, is judged, the central ideas generated by the Hour of the People should be also judged. The spirit, according to Hegel, is a dynamic force, but in this case the spirit of the Hour of the People was a destructive force. In March 1976 the results of this long period of destruction, the beginning of which was marked by the Hour of the People, were harvested.

For anyone who is thinking of reconstructing a Radical-Peronist alliance with other power factors, this document and its consequences are required study material.

The CGT Economic Plan of 1975

In August of 1975, when the process of political and economic deterioration which would hit its lowest level in 1976 had already made its presence known, the General Confederation of Labor (CGT), a group which linked many of the nation's top trade unions, put out a statement in which it expressed its doctrinal stance on how the government should be run.

This document should be on the desk of every person who is, in some way, involved with the nation's future. It was written by committees which included CGT auditors and the representatives of the country's most influential unions.

It proposed the following things:

"The structuring of an organized community, with the participation of all representative sectors on a strategic, tactical, decision-making level." That is to say, cooperatve administration, self-administration, not only on a business, but also on a national level. Argentina — Chapter 10 — galley 8

"Insure a more just distribution of wealth, which, in its first stages, would mean the increasing by 50% of the wage-earners' income." The highest wage rise figure in Argentine history had not exceeded 42 or 43% and that had been in times of better income distribution. In August of 1975, when the country was in the middle of a deep social and economic crisis, the idea of putting wages up by 50% was one of the causes of a steady upswing in the inflation rate that would be in effect from that time on.

"Modify consumer guidelines imposed by dependence." Was this a Maoist type of mass consumption proposal?

"Move, within Third Position guidelines, toward the integration of Latin America into the Third World as a step toward universalism." What universalism is this talking about? The universalism of the dictatorship of the proletariat, perhaps?

"The state should assume a strategic and predominant role, carrying out a guiding, precursory, business function, acting as promoter and administrator of collective interests." The well-known statist position of Argentine labor was clearly reflected in the text of the CGT document.

"The workers, spinal column of the process, are organizing themselves so that their participation goes far beyond the discussion of salaries and work conditions. The country needs for the workers to define themselves as a social group which is the society to which we aspire..." This proposal, together with that of creating a Naional Project Council with corporate representation and the National Planning and Administration Control Institute, were finishing touches to closing the circle around state and nation which the CGT proposed in August 1975.

"Participation policies should be backed as a form of business administration. The action of the workers in participative business administration should be complemented by representatives of the same level of the industrial and economic branch together." This came at a time when representatives of the Light and Power union managed SEGBA and the Water and Energy company. A railway union representative was running the rail system.

As far as concrete economic measures go, the CGT document was a resume of the Populist document already outlined. Despite this we have seen fit to transcribe some of its proposals so as to avoid pernicious historical amnesia.

At the beginning of this chapter we said that this historical experience had been disheartening, and we really believe that. The poverty of ideas or the total absence of the major parties in the discussion of really important topics in the workings of the nation points up the lack of political substance, the improvisation and superficiality with which those national parties carried out their duties. Demagogic character is the one common factor in all the proposals, as well as a lack of coherence and a complacent attitude with the "clientele."

This means that all these principles constitute the basis for a national project for consumers, not for doers. The distributive trend, without a structure that encourages production is one of the prime political ills in Argentina and which we have pointed out throughout this book. All of this friendly posing, we could almost say, buddy-buddy relationship with the voters and all the talks about their relationship to the greatness of the country, is the best proof we have of how fragile our political structures are.

Chapter XI

Liberty as an Ideal

Basis for the Second Founding of the Republic

In any process aimed at carrying out a proposed goal within a certain society there is an initial moment in which the author of the process asks himself what ideal he is proposing for society. The question is recurrent. It appears time and time again during the analysis, taking diverse forms. How can that ideal to be reached be defined? What should society achieve? What is the most perfect asset to which a society can aspire?

Time and time again the answer is the same: Liberty. Because all other assets, when we analyze them, add up to this ideal of liberty — be they equality, fraternity, welfare or prosperity. The others are all only measures of roads toward liberty. Isn't fraternity an attitude which comes of man's free will and which cannot be reached by anyone but free men? Isn't prosperity or welfare without liberty just plain exploitation? And what, but slavery, is equality without liberty?

The greatest asset a human being has is liberty, which is the synthesis of all the other assets he can wish for and is the result of all the virtues he can possess. It has been repeatedly pointed out that the history of Man, is, in essence, the history of Man's battle in his development toward liberty.

Whenever human thought has gone beyond the mediocrity of its time it has been in the search for a shortcut to liberty. There have been those who proposed utopias and who wanted to see gods instead of men, and faced with the possible death of God, there was even someone who proposed the appearance of a superman. When Man moves away from God the needle of his compass which points to liberty goes haywire, and he confuses liberty with wealth, with security, and with gratification. He identifies pleasure with liberty, short-term present with liberty and, above all, necessity with liberty. Man forgets that the only need which will take him toward liberty is the need for God.

Mankind is an imperfect group composed of imperfect individuals, which it is possible to perfect, but which can never reach perfection. Only a perfect being with infinite power has complete independence. Perfection is a shield against the slavery of passion and His omnipotence keeps Him from being submitted to the will of others.

Within these limitations which the universally hoped for liberty has for Man, we should return to the ideal proposed by our forefathers for the Argentine nation and for all Argentines: *Liberty*. All human dignity is taken in by this word.

Because liberty of the citizens of a nation is the worst enemy of messiah-like caudillos; over the last thirty years there were attempts to replace our illustrious national anthem, a true song to liberty, with the march of a charismatic caudillo's party. Even if proving it is not always instantaneous and easy, there exists a close relationship between philosophical problems and those which Man is confronted with in his political and social life. In other words, a necessary link exists between the theory of liberty which we sustain and the socio-political reality to be achieved through it. Perhaps the cornerstone of the *new republic* which we propose should be a careful re-definition of liberty.

God and Liberty

We know that God is free because He wanted angles to be equal from the center to the circumference and He wanted the inside angles of a triangle to equal two right angles; because He wished for these and other truths to be eternal, and constructed a world of essences; because, although there is no alternative to truth, it was born naturally; because of these things we know that God is free.

Descartes' argument is still good today. It is not necessarily that God wanted such things, but that there are necessary truths, because God wanted it to be that way and just as freely as He created eternal essence, God also created this world of private existence, of action and passion, of contingency and finality.

Since Man can only want what his intelligence points to as being possible; Man can only create on the basis of what has been created before, never from scratch; in God there is no before and after, because He has also created what we call nothing. He understands, loves and creates absolute liberty in a single indefinite perfect act. That is liberty.

Man is tied up in a thousand knots because God wishes it — although He could also not wish it. Man is imprisoned in his body, in his limited intelligence, his often failing will and his lack of direction. But Man is free.

A particle of divine liberty is encrusted in his heart like a diamond, and he uses the word "liberty" at various times and under various conditions with meanings which may appear to be mistaken, but which a deeper look reveals are tied together by an internal dialectic which protects his intrinsic coherence and at the same time is the mark of his unique origin.

Man's conscience before, during and after any voluntary act is witness to his freedom, and affirms without a doubt that the act is his and only his. "Listen to yourself and consult yourself and you will feel what freedom is as you will feel what rationality is," says Bossuet. Moral life is testimony to Man's freedom. Without free will there would be no sense in talking about obligations, duties or responsibilities. And neither laws nor contracts nor advice nor promises would be anything more than hollow sounds if liberty were a myth and Man had everything already decided for him.

Man and Liberty

Man is free because he participates, although imperfectly, in the absolute absence of necessity which is God. And besides having an ideal goal ever present and never reached, Man tends toward liberty. A fortunate hunter of freedoms, Man can never capture full liberty.

Because of this, liberty is not an end, something which can be reached and possessed, but an ideal which is always just beyond our reach but nevertheless real or desirable because of this.

Objectives, goals and ideals ride on the back of a continuum which goes from the concrete to the abstract, form the near to the remote. But there is something which elevates the ideal to the position above goals and objectives: while they are static, the ideal is a dynamic reality.

The only way to define an activity is by looking at the object at which it is aimed, like a target in target practice, but we should not forget that the object is nothing more than a signal which specifies the activity we wish to carry out. Strictly speaking, it is not the target, but hitting the target, which is the goal of our activity, and if we achieve this end by means of the target it is not less certain that we also achieve it through our weapon's sights and through the finger which pulls the trigger.

The specific object is simple, a guidepost in a process of continuing our activity. To achieve freedom is to reach goals or objectives, in that liberating activity from the heart of Man which is aimed at the eternal target of liberty — a target which can never be used up.

A common idea throughout the ages has been that a man of knowledge is a free man. Even if Man was nothing more than a particle of Nature, an element in the cosmos, his consciousness of universal determination alone would be enough for him to feel free. For the Dark Ages liberty was knowledge. And that knowledge could not be reached in a distracting outside world but through folding oneself up into the mysticism of one's own conscience. Both the schools of Plato and Socrates and the stoics of later years reiterated the advantages of casting off passion and material necessities in order to arrive at the much-sought after goal of liberty through purification.

Man, in order to sin, must have liberty, even if only in the big decisions he must make with relation to God. He can serve God freely, as distinct from glorifying Him *necessarily,* by virtue of established order. Because God needs creatures whose unhindered existence makes their love and service profound and agreeable and it is because of this that Man is free.

At the end of the Middle Ages scholars would be torn between two schools of thought: that of Saint Thomas which said that intelligence was the *cause* of the free act, and that of Duns Escoto who said that intelligence was only a condition of a free act. No matter which of these thoughts we subscribe to, our modern western concept of liberty originated with Christian thought.

The Modern Ages inherited this conflict, which already introduced in the Middle Ages, between will and intelligence and through the thinking of Descartes which was passed on through the rationalism of Spinoza to fall later into the hands of irrational atheistic existentialism.

According to Heidegger, authentic existence is the conquest of the true meaning of being, which is nothing. When this nothing is revealed to us in the form of anguish, we conquer true liberty which is "the liberty to die." Liberty consists, in a negative form, of accepting our destiny. Condemned to be free, condemned to living with others, Man is the owner according to Sartre until he enrolls in communism, of an absolute liberty rooted in pure subjectivity.

Both atheist existentialism and Marxism — which is the exact opposite of liberty — reject liberty. Existentialism shatters liberty with fragmentary isolated actions while Marxism ignores liberty by submitting Man to inexorable conditioning of his society and nature.

Through the Greco-Latin tradition Man can actually rediscover the roads to liberty.

Basic Freedoms

There is probably no other field of Greek influence which has been as decisive in the modern world as the area of liberty.

When Solon prohibited debtors' prisons, the have-nots gained a world of civil liberty. When he introduced *habeas corpus,* for the protection of the physical person, the world won justical liberty and political liberty was won when liberty was identified with democracy and both were defined as *obedience of the law within the framework of equality*. Liberty, among the Greeks, was dual-faceted: On the one hand, it was independence with respect for total personal control, while on the other hand it took in obedience for the law. From that time on, Man would try to seek the right balance between order and liberty.

History has shown that the Argentine people have a frustrated political vocation: They want to live in a world of liberty and democracy. Dazzled by the constitution-writing spirit of the French Revolution and that of the authors of the constitutional document signed in Philadelphia, we adhered precociously to constitutionalism, and from that time onward we have systematically violated the articles of our Constitution, modified it to suit the whims of politicians or simply ignoring its contents, instead of modifying them in accordance with provisions included in the text of the document for just such occasions. It would be to the country's benefit to research the origin of this lack of coordination between the people's vocation for liberty and the fulfillment (or lack of it) of the conditions laid down by the law which safeguards it. We would be able to find out then if this dissonance is caused by human interference over the course of a 60-year process of decadence, or if the problem can be found in a law which has not kept pace with the situation in our country today.

Along the lines of obedience of the law within a framework of equality has come, also through the Greek school, the thought that Man is at liberty to do anything the law does not prohibit and at liberty to not do anything the law does not oblige him to do.

"Liberty for all consists of each person's being free to live as he pleases," Aristotle was to say in *Politics*. While the laws of Sparta regulated everything right down to people's private lives, Athens defended individual liberty and the city from dominating its citizens. The people were free, within the ample boundaries of Athenian law, to lead the life they pleased. Thus Greece set one of the pillars of individualism in the place, which, centuries later, would form a part of the liberal man.

Attention focussed on the individual — as is confirmed by collectivists — does not dissolve social structures, but rather, in fact, tends to make them more cohesive. History shows that deterioration and decay in a society comes with the faltering of the personal ideal of each of its members. In a decaying society the concept of true individualism is replaced by egotism, isolationism and a placing of priority interest on material rather than spiritual values.

It is from a concept of individualism based on a theory of Man's having a living sense of freedom and human dignity that basic freedoms declared in a legitimate demand on the person in relation to his community are derived.

According to traditions followed by the United States, the four basic inalienable human rights are: 1) Freedom of expression and thought; 2) Freedom of religion; 3) Freedom to a life without need and 4) Freedom to a life without fear.

Both the often discussed right to free expression of ideas and the traditional right to free religious choice are expressly declared in the Argentine Constitution. In relation with the variable "political fear," they are indicators, the absence of which measure the distance between democracy and authoritarianism, and between liberty and repression. And if there is an "acid test" which proves the existence of liberty it is the *legal possibility of entering or leaving the country of which one is a citizen.*

The Right to a Life Without Fear

The right to a life without fear is a by-product of the other freedoms, since the creation of the others implies and takes for granted that life without fear already exists.

Two types of institutions which destroy liberty employ dictatorships: the hypnotic ones and those that rule through fear.

Mass arrest, summary executions, torture, concentration camps and permanent surveillance of the citizenry are some of the measures taken by tyrannies in campaigns to stamp our all opposition. This form of political repression is not based on precise laws, but on penal repression. As tyranny wants only its supporters in society, even lukewarm opposition is suspected. The result is a hazy feeling of guilt, an imprecise fear, an anxious pursuit of fleeting norms behind the cause of a single leader or party. There is a *thirst for vital security* which finds *tense calmness in propaganda*. And when the means of oppression begin to fail, the leaders of the reign of terror find a unique way of preserving their grip: war, foreign aggression.

"A person is a spiritual being, constituted as such by a form of subsistence and inner independence; he maintains this subsistence through his adhesion to a hierarchy of freely adopted values; assimilated and lived as a responsible commitment and constant development. All of his activity is thus unified in freedom and in addition he develops the uniqueness of his vocation through a series of creative acts." This is what Mounier had to say about the subject of the person while at the same time making it clear that as the *presence* of Man, the person is not susceptible to a rigorous definition because the person reveals himself as the experience of life progresses   Along the line of this characterization of "person," we find another basic freedom, a freedom which is different from those we mentioned before because it is an internal freedom, it is the freedom to think and decide, the freedom of intelligence and of will which is both a possibility for living and an axiological hierarchy.

"Neither Yankees nor Marxists, Peronists," is something more than the slogan we heard until we couldn't stand it any more in the period from 1973 to 1976. It is a definition of non-liberty, because liberty does not consist of choosing between given alternatives. It is, instead, the fundamental possibility of creating new alternatives. Liberty has no party leanings, nor does it have a name of its own. We must create our own alternatives and the Argentine alternative will consist of a declaration of what is Argentine without any popular pseudo-blessing.

When liberty is degraded through the manipulation of populist indoctrination, when it is tamed and drugged and turned into a complacent robot and dragged into the absurdity of identifying itself with slavery through the laws dictated by the party, it is the unifying nucleus of the person-conscience and responsibility — which deteriorates. In Mao's China, in Soviet Russia, in Castro's Cuba, in Hitler's Germany, in Mussolini's Italy and in Peron's Argentina, in every system where individual creative freedom and drive are opposed, the person — as in the Platonic story of the cave — is chained to the wall and takes liberty to be the shadows cast into him by those passing outside.

The manipulation of Man's will, which has turned the people into a mob, has not, by any means, replaced torture and other secret police action. It is just that the two techniques have been united to perfect, even more, sophisticated methods used by dictatorships to pursue and incapacitate mankind's will in the name of a particular ideology. Then it is no longer a matter of eliminating the liberty to act; it becomes then a campaign to destroy freedom of thought and desire.

George Orwell's *1984* foresaw for the 1980s something even less horrible than what Alexander Solzhenitsyn says is happening in the Soviet Union right now.

Thus the dictatorship of a few becomes the dictatorship of many. Unconscious that their will has been conditioned, "the many" become an instrument of a few who take power to conquer both the majority and the minority.

But it is the minority, whose will has not been broken, which is the true generator of liberty, which seeks to put the community to rights and get it back on the track to the goals history requires of it.

If this minority triumphs, the community will return to the business of building a nation and will be back on the road to liberty. If the minority is defeated, the community, as a nation, disappears or its possibility of living as such will be slashed.

If being a human being means being free, the theory the man we are electing follows is all-important because it is here that we will find his meaning of liberty. Man is not made of isolated subjectivity. His freedom cannot be absolute. If Man is a responsible being, this liberty cannot simply be consciousness of necessity. The human ego comes wrapped in the feasibility of body and world. This, Man's liberty is not utopian, but situated, which means that liberty is not isolated but is related to others; it does not move within a remote, abstract kingdom, but in a concrete society and in a definite place. It is out of some *situation* that Man begins to develop his duty to be free and just as duty done is no longer a duty, a "finished" human being is no longer a human being. To be a human being, he needs a constant project for his world, a constant anticipation of the future.

And we can, after considering these things, ask ourselves, "Liberty? What for?" There can be only one answer. We must be free in order to want and do everything necessary to keep the level of liberty in the community and in ourselves from dropping. We must be free in order to achieve *more liberty*.

Chapter XII

Sovereignty and Liberty

A Qualitative Category

According to a saying in the time of Louis IX of France, the king did not "have sovereignty over matters of time." This makes an interesting point concerning the difference between real power and the nominal power of feudal lords and others in a so-called powerful position.

Being that sovereignty is the essential quality of Power, it determines the relationship between Power and State and between Power and the rest of the elements in the political structure, within the limits of the law. There is a functional relationship between sovereignty and law and if the judicial system derives its strength from the existence of sovereignty, this constitutes the power of the State in terms of a politically and legally organized community.

Thus, "sovereign of the state" is an abstract title, while "sovereign of the community" is a concrete title, since it is the nation (community) which legally exercises power.

As one of the attributes of the Nation State, sovereignty is a synonym for self-determination, individuality and independence with respect to other nations, which means that if, on one hand, sovereignty is understood as external sovereignty, on the other hand its concept is one, not of supremacy, but of equality, by virtue of which all states are equally sovereign.

There are no degrees of sovereignty: A Nation State has sovereignty or it does not; there can be no in-between, since sovereignty is not quantative, but qualitative. This is precisely the meaning of the traditional notion of exterior sovereignty as political-judicial self-determination and consequently it is also the insubordination of any Nation State to another Nation State or power.

The independence of ancient kingdoms, like that of the City-States, was religious in origin and discussing or defining this independence seemed superfluous. Only much later, and after an intricate historical process, did the political question of sovereignty — and the word sovereignty itself — arise.

It was only during the transition from the Middle Ages to the Renaissance that nations and secular-based territorial powers began to assert themselves; and it was then that it became necessary to mark the territorial limits of one government's independence with respect to that of another's. It was then that the question of sovereignty first arose.

The concept of sovereignty actually first took shape in France with the opposition of Philip the Fair to the Papal State. Philip accused the Papal State of meddling in his kingdom's internal affairs, and thus the problem of achieving external sovereignty arose. Later the problem would be the internal sovereignty of lords of the diets.

The French Revolution, in the form of the Declaration of the Rights of Man (1789) and the Constitution (1791), by proclaiming the French nation to be sovereign, established the political principle that no group or individual could exercise authority except when that authority came directly from the nation.

Nations and Powers

Political power, which is a result of human interaction, is always a dominant power.

The political world of Medieval times comprised territorial lordships which were submitted to rule by national monarchies, while in the Modern political world, although oriented toward the formation of big supernational units, it is laid out in territorial units with a single center of dominant power.

From the point of view of power without nuances, a nation which exercises its sovereignty, could, theoretically, carry out any act, including the most open aggression. This hypothetical aggression against another, also sovereign, Nation State would not be judged in terms of a violation of international law, but on the basis of the consequences such an act would have on the aggressor and on the target of his aggression. We see in this the non-existence of effective international law in this area, and the temporary and fragile nature of every violated border pact. The problem is also pointed out by the disappearance in the 20th century of nation states like Latvia, Lithuania and Estonia.

There is no law to protect weak nations or effective judicial mechanisms which make them equal to the powerful. Only interaction between powers can create a no-man's land in which weak nations can exist. In nations where internal consensus can be freely expressed, and this is taken into account, wars of expansion have been limited by the people's wish not to participate in them. Expansionist policies are much less credible in a representative democratic system than they are in a dictatorship or other type of government which manipulates the people's will as it pleases. As long as there are powers in which public opinion has no influence on foreign policy, weak nations will have to form part of a chain of satellites belonging to these authoritiarian regines.

True Power

A trail of ever-more complex and hostile interdependencies has been blazed across the pages of history since the West entered the Industrial Era, from the amber route of ancient times to the migrations of the nomads of the steppes in the Middle Ages, to the spice route of Modern history and all the way to the colonialism of the XIX century. In both the field of competition and that of cooperation, the states of the world, in order to reach their interrelated goals, have become interdependent.

Even for the superpowers, the theory of absolute sovereignty and unlimited freedom of execution is restricted by world interdependence. International economic and political reasons are behind this, and will continue to be factors as long as more than one superpower exists.

On the other hand, dependence on foreign supplies and markets makes it necessary to live parallel to one another politically, as a means of putting limits on sovereign action. On the other hand, due to internal historical, cultural or political limitations, one's own sovereignty ends where that of another country which is in a position to keep its sovereignty begins.

Even though world economic interdependence rests firmly on a basis of agricultural and industrial production, progress of industrial build-up is an important measure for a nation to take in terms of its sovereignty. During World War II production played a decisive role in the Allied victory. Apart from that, the ways of war were perfected more from the time the Industrial Revolution began in

England in the XVIII century onward than in the 2,000 years before.

When a nation's sovereignty is measured in economic terms, a vital part of its power rests in raw materials or substitutes. Neither iron, nor coal, nor sugar, nor rubber, nor petroleum, nor wheat are evenly distributed anywhere in the world. But they are coveted by the powers, which try to insure that they will have maximum access, or total control, of these products.

Due to constant expansion of production, backed by private industry in the capitalist world, the domestic market cannot be expected to absorb the superproduction, and foreign trade is thus turned into another measure to insure sovereignty.

But it has a dynamic structure, it is a combination of inter-connected elements and stable relationships, so that each element affects the action of all the elements. As a whole, dynamic in nature, society is modified through the interaction of its elements over the course of history. The economic growth of a nation cannot take place without healthy ideology and political stability. Only through inter-action can republican institutions carry out their functions. And these institutions are not, as is supposed by Yrigoyen's heirs, an end in themselves, but a means of reaching real liberty. Something more than sentimental declamations, something more than patriotic rhetoric, and a lot more than repeated party promises is involved when we speak of sovereignty; sovereignty is a *real* power and as such, it must be outlined within the limits of reality.

Synonyms Among Savages

"As in the case of life, liberty is only deserved by the person who must win it every day," said Goethe in *Faust*. The truth of these words, evident in the issue of national independence, calls for a responsibility not all peoples want or can assume. It calls for daily work and drive which is a challenge that is easier to elude than to answer, a role that is easier to disguise than to assume.

Recalcitrant nationalism in our country has been nothing more than populist irresponsibility in disguise, with all its inward vision, its irrational hatred of foreigners, its rigidity of ideals and the static life structure it holds up as a model.

It is no coincidence that savage tribes consider foreigner and enemy to be synonyms, nor that every expansive era in history has coincided with the elimination of distances between peoples.

It would seem to be the general rule that he who only knows his own culture does not know the truth, because nationalism — that jealous hoarder and protector of what has already been acquired, instead of being a reorganizer and out to enrich its own experience — upn cutting geopolitical ties loses the meaning of the word, does not isolate itself under lock and key, but decides how to make, in the present and with experience from the past, the future for the nation, a future built on justice, with ample international relations, and liberty for all the nation's inhabitants. Real nationalism, like Faust, is ready to win life and sovereign liberty every day in a single, unique act.

Chapter XIII

Choosing Liberty

"Thou shalt earn thy bread by the sweat of thy brow," says the book of Genesis. Human liberty cannot develop alone in the high kingdom of metaphysics, nor is it absolute and unconditional. It is *dialectically related to need,* and this fact links it to economics.

The economy is a measure, and can even be a generator, of liberty. When the economy and system of distribution of wealth permit each member of society to exercise his basic right-liberty to eat the bread he earns through his own work, when they permit a reasonable freedom of choice of socio-economic roles, one of the fundamental demands of justice is satisfied. And we cannot deny the fact that a minimum level of social justice coincides with a minimum right to liberty.

All human societies contain some form of social stratification, which means that this is a universal trait of society and in consequence, that individuals' roles and status rise out of collective life itself.

But while social stratification exists in all societies, including those which insist they are free from hierarchy, not all societies permit their members to choose and carry out their socio-economic roles freely.

Only in those societies in which individual rights are placed above the rights of the State, only in those societies in which the individual is the only judge in the realm of his private decisions, only in those societies does each person choose, with the only restriction being his natural or acquired capability, the socio-economic role he will occupy, and is thus placed on a certain social level of responsibility.

In this way, when a nation's wealth makes it powerful, when it can subtract its chronic debts from the books, then a nation can achieve geopolitical self-determination.

But the economy is not merely a measure of liberty; it should also generate liberty. This is not true just by virtue of the fact that it creates the wealth the human being and the nation need, but also because it is the origin of multiple opportunities for human initiative, which create within the role of the economy, a free form of expression and a contribution to the well-being of the community.

Private initiative is an indispensable condition in the discovery of human liberty. This is shown clearly in the art, the science and the culture of the most brilliant periods in history. It is also obvious if we trace the development of capitalistic economy — which has raised the standard of living in large sectors of the world's population.

Capitalism

In analyzing the course taken by what we refer to today as the capitalist system, and especially when we analyze the various aspects of what is known as *liberal capitalism,* distinctive elements appear which constitute qualitative differences between it and other ideologies which seek to impose themselves on the world. It is distinguished, basically, by its attitude toward the outside world, by a tolerance which contrasts with the intransigence of the others.

As far as man's internal attitude goes, it represents humble but fertile submission in the face of the fragility and fickleness of our understanding. These are positive conditions and, because they are endowed with a solidity which makes them fit into a well-connected and coherent system, they have proven to be very influential in improving life and the quality of it.

Unquestionable proof of the fertility of liberal capitalism is provided by studies of demographic growth and progress in the quality of life, which undoubtedly began in England in the middle of the 18th century in unison with the advent of capitalist liberalism. The capitalist population of the world, which was to have its lifestyle transformed under the new system, stood at around nine million at the time — not much more than about one capitalist for every one hundred other people in the world then. Just over two centuries later, the population of the capitalist world numbers 700 million and accounts for a fifth of the world's population.[1]

Isolated demographic growth and limited improvement in the quality of life, though they may occur and last for a certain length of time, eventually lead to catastrophically different results from those sought. Extraordinary growth, for example, in a country with a tribal economy, ends up, for one reason or another, bringing collective destruction; excessive, unwarranted improvement in the quality of life for a small sector of society is also destined to bring collapse, as in the case of the imperial city-states. Because of this, liberal capitalism is not a projection of egoism interested simply in building up material goods, but rather, it is aimed at creating a progressive and orderly state of balance in which power is decentralized and personal idiosyncrasies are respected and which is rooted in liberty. Those who made John the Unlanded sign the great compromise were, without knowing it, laying the cornerstone of the wall which was to separate political power from economic wealth, and with this move, they set the wheels of liberal capitalism, which is based on private property, in motion.

This system, in which work potentiality is achieved through intelligent handling of capital, permits Man to reach a stage in which the machine, instead of putting him out of work, becomes an insensitive slave, capable of freeing Man's hands from menial labor and of permitting him to save energy he would normally spend on a tiring and boring task. The liberal capitalist system produces more free and creative leisure time than any naturalistic proto-economy; it has put the machine at the disposal of Man so that it will work for him and this represents the most effective move made in the constant quest for the domination of material things. In this sense, having surpassed promises of utopian paradise made by other politico-socio-economic systems, liberal capitalism should be considered the system which offers the most opportunites and possibilities. It is as if it had been made to order for the human being, who is differentiated by his love of freedom.[1]

---

[1] Armando Rivas, "La Crisis del Capitalismo," an article published in *Pensamiento Economico*, No. 404, First Quarter of 1976, Buenos Aires, Argentina. "Because of this, we can conclude that the increase in income and welfare which we have achieved had its origins in England in 1760, a country which has nine million inhabitants which represented a little better than 1% of the world's population.
"Some 225 years later, the population of the industrialized countries of the capitalist world totals 600 million inhabitants, which represents about a quarter of the world's population."

[1] Armando Rivas, (Article previously cited): "Liberal capitalism does not offer Man a utopia or a heaven on earth or a nirvana which permits him to escape the responsibilities which, as such, correspond to him."

Social Security

Western governmental activity over the second half of the 20th century has been impregnated with the concept of social security, since Man cannot survive without meeting minimum human requirements. The political concept of social security, however, ends up implying regret for the productive social system and puts a number of members of society outside that system.

In order to keep a social security system from putting limits on freedom, it must be molded to the relative situation of the society in which it is to be applied. It is impossible, for example, for a country which has just come out of the tribal stage of society to have as advanced a social security system as West Germany. And it is also impossible for Argentina, with an average per capita income of 1,800 dollars a year, to have a social security system equivalent to that of Sweden, with an average income of over 8,400 dollars per person.

Minimum social security benefits should insure a *decent* income, because *fair* is not always enough for a person who is willing to do what he can. And a *decent* standard of living should also be assured to all disabled people.

But there must be upper limits on this too. A social security system should not act as an anesthetic on the productive activities of the individuals in society. It should not cause the unemployment of anyone who is fit to work, nor should it authorize an unhealthy income that will keep people from trying to better themselves. There are several examples of imbalanced social security systems.

Due to the political power of its unions, Great Britian's social security system was maximized. Over the course of the past 30 years, Britain has fallen from the position of greatness it once held. Also through union influence, the social security system in New York has become a tempting invitation to idlers. Unemployment insurance, which pays the equivalent of working person's wages, stimulates the shirking of social responsibility which is the foundation of liberty. It is interesting to note that the United States, the typical example of libralism, has progressively increased its social security expenses as seen in the chart below.

Curiously enough, this trend toward disorderly proliferation of social security coincided with the return of the US to its isolationist policies. American influence over a certain sector of the world was unquestionable on the end of the 1950s. But the US hegemony began to crack in the late 1960s and was somewhat in question once again in

Percentage of total US Governemt expenses covered by payments
to individuals

YEAR	PERCENT
1955	11.7
1960	16.2
1965	17.3
1970	22.9
1975	34.0

Source: Daniel Bell's *The Cultural Conditions of Capitalism*, New York, 1976.

the mid-1970s. These factors correspond to the progressive satisfaction of a demagogic social security concept. A delicate balance exists between growth and power, on the one hand, and social security on the other. And this balance must not be thrown off in either direction.

While Argentina retires still relatively young people of 60 and even 55, countries like Sweden have a retirement age limit of 65 in order to give everyone a maximum useful life span.

The entire Argentine retirement system is mathematically impossible due to the fact that the proportion of retirees is too heavy a load for those who work. And if we transfer this thought from the financial to the economic, it means that people who work earn less, have a lower real wage than they would have if everyone who was able to work did so. From a standpoint of international competition our social security system places us in a dilemma: We must either reduce our real wages or we will be unable to compete with the rest of the world. No matter which thing we do, we will come out losing. The solution would be for more people to work so that all of us could earn more.

Summing up: In setting maximum and minimum levels of social security, we must not only insure the rights to these benefits of those who earn them, but also that the system encourages individuals to bear their proportionate load of social responsibility, or in other words, that everyone exercises his liberty.

Political Liberty and Economic Liberty

An article in *TIME* magazine of Dec. 22, 1975 included a

classification map of the world on various levels. From this study, conclusions can be drawn as to the relationship between political and economic liberty (See table, Appendix 4).

Nations can be grouped in the following categories:

A. Countries with concrete economic possibilities of offering freedom to its inhabitants (more than 3,000 dollars per inhabitant with the exception of petroleum producers).

These include countries which, over the last century and a half, and thanks to a liberal capitalist system, have reached post-industrial status. Economic development in these countries clearly correspond to cultural maturity and to the nations' political and industrial systems.

B. Intermediate countries in which economic but not necessarily cultural conditions exist which would permit it to achieve a state of liberty (1,200 to 3,000 dollars per capita).

C. Countries with less relative development than those above, and where the per capita income (750 to 1,200 dollars) is not high enough to initiate a social security system to protect the people from poverty and where civil and political freedom find no visible means of economic support. This category includes countries which despite having a high level of per capita income also have a very high rate of illiteracy (over 20%). These are basically the petroleum producers.

D. Countries with per capita incomes of between 150 and 750 dollars in which the people are economically in need, which has a definite effect on the existing level of liberty.

E. Countries which live in absolute poverty.

This grouping is by no means a classification of international justice, but rather, it is a picture of reality. Countries which have a Marxist economy are in categories B, C, D and E.

Growth, Distribution and Liberty

The just distribution of the fruits of economic growth should be the cornerstone of the government's socio-economic policy. Nothing, however, is gained by distributing what exists if the economy does not *grow*. And nothing is gained by growing, if the growth only means greater social injustice.

The government administration's responsibilities touch such important areas of economic freedom as:

1. Guarantees for the safeguarding of initiative and private property and protection of the community from practices or manipulation which limit freedom in the area of production or which restrict

the operation of the general market.

2. Defense of real wage growth as effectively received by the worker.

3. Elimination of exploitative practices by businessmen and unions.

4. Maintaining a decent social security system for the disabled and the aged.

5. Design, promotion and control of voluntary private social security systems in order to give the people a chance to raise the level of security of their own accord.

6. Promotion of equal opportunity education and professional training, with the only conditions being dedication and ability.

7. Progressive distribution of the fruits of growth.

Social justice cannot be achieved through political demagogy, which is not only not a solution to poverty, but also leads to greater irresponsibility. Social Justice is, after all, the result of the formation of the individual who is gradually liberated through constructive force, the fruits of which, he has right to. This justice, then, includes private ownership of the means of production, which are, in turn, the product of a system of captialism and private initiative.

National liberty is achieved through an economic growth which augments the Nation's defensive capabilities and signifies the increasing utilization of its territory. It is achieved by incorporating successive generations into the national productive process. It is also achieved by increasing the physical and technological capital of the nation for which it is necessary to step up commercial and cultural trade with the rest of the world. Only an economically strong country is listened to and respected. Only a constantly growing country offers its youth the active opportunities to which they are entitled.

Chapter XIV

The Hinge on which
History Swings

New Generation of the 80s

Just as the waters of a river flow on without stopping, time moves through the stages of history. Chopping this continuous time stream up into historical periods will be the task of the historian, whose singularly arduous occupation will force him to appraise the whole of society in each stage of history.

Neither a metaphysical nor a unique factor could be considered exclusive history-makers. The history of Mankind is not a mere natural process which makes no sense, and it is not about a series of disembodied spectators, but about real flesh and blood men.

Continuous history is a constant dialectic between the natural and the spiritual, but this spirit should not be understood — as it was by Hegel — as being the sole active factor in the process of history, but rather, as that reality which, based on the natural history and needing the natural, goes beyond continuous history because of its trajectory.

Each division of history, each life scene, is the result of the joint efforts of people whose coexistence in time is referred to by the deep-rooted term, *generation*.

But what people constitute a generation? Leaders in war, business, thought or politics? The anonymous people in general?

Let's make Ortega y Gasset's answer our own. "A generation is not a handful of illustrious men, nor is it simply a mass; it is like a whole new social body, with its select minority and its mob, which has been launched into an atmosphere of existence with a determined, vital trajectory. The generation, a dynamic compromise between mass and individual, is the most important concept in history, and could even be called the hinge on which its movements are executed.'' Based on Ortega's theory of generations, according to which each generation takes in a period of 15 years, Jaime Ferriaux has put Argentine history in order. He numbered from 1810 until 1970 (the year in which his book was published) eleven generations, the last one made up of people born between 1903 and 1917, whose 15 years of influence ran from 1955 to 1970.

We now add to this, the 12th generation of Argentines, made up of people born between 1918 and 1933 and whose influence on Argentine life began in 1970 and will end in 1985.

We have entered, then, the generation of the 1980s. If the leaders of this new generation are convinced that no one gets something for nothing and take the reins of real leadership in hand — and this includes the task of guiding the people towards goals for the good of the nation as a whole — successive generations will be able to reach what we have not, until now, been able to even approach: a nation which is sure of its identity and its meaning in the world.

Recent Political Experience

The will to assume responsibility, tenacious as it may be, is not enough. The generation of the 1980s will have to overcome the inherent perplexity of a still unclear situation, in order to later create a double hypothesis: the interpretation of certain events and the discovery of the tendency of these events to produce certain consequences. Out of this hypothesis, a true plan of action must be put together, that is, if we have that spirit to which Hegel gave so much importance and out of which we can milk power to formulate objectives and to make our process more dynamic. If the generation of the 80s does not do this, we will have to be content with a fatalistic concept of history — a concept which would be inadequate for a generation which plans to have any profound effect on the nation's destiny.

Experience is of key importance here. The traditional meaning of experience is *accumulated knowledge,* thus ascribing it on the one hand to reason and on the other hand, situating it in the past, in what has already happened; but we are going to use the term in a different sense, in accordance with its meaning in the field of modern philosophical pragmaticism. Expwrience in this vein is the relationship between Man and his socio-historical surroundings, which, based on reflection on the already irreversible past, is aimed at changing given factors and moving creatively into the future.

It almost seems superfluous to point out that the task we are assigning to the generation of the 80s must be preceded by a deep study of the factors which have led us to the present state of affairs before making final adjustments to the operative hypothesis we have chosen to call a plan of action.

In order to contribute to this basic stage of experience, we should look at a list of basic errors committed by political movements which contributed to national decadence.

1. Liberal Errors

Insisting on a unilateral plan for an agroimporter nation.

Having hampered — to some extent — social mobility by not absorbing the leaders of new classes into the Liberal movement.

Being economically dogmatic and politically infatuated.

Having failed to modernize and realize that the population had grown to 25 million.

Believing that the country had already "made it" and thus believing that it was enough to clean house and reimpose the ground rules of 60 years before without coming up with a new national objective.

Continuing to believe in the Constitution of 1853 as an eternally apt instrument.

2. Popular Errors

Reaching power through growing resentment and promises that were impossible to keep.

Believing, like the Liberals, although for different reasons, that the country had already "made it."

Supposing, because of the aforementioned, that the only thing left for the people — read populism — to do was govern.

Being incapable of governing.

Being short of basic geopolitical concepts and placing the country wrongly in the world.

Giving in to labor leaders, who, without respect for their followers, led a mass, the adhesion of which had previously been manipulated.

Forming alliances with enemy nations, the influence of which they thought could be absorbed and thus controlled.

Not having seen a need for generation renovation in its own ranks and thus creating an Old Men's Movement.

Committing and permitting disquieting acts which destroyed confidence in the state of law in the nation.

Believing — the Radicals — that the Constitution of 1853 and the Saenz Pena Law were *all* the country needed.

Defrauding the will of the people by irrationally trying to "cover all the bets."

3. Developmentalist Errors

Not being interested in means but only in ends as in the case of the Frigerio-Peron pact.

Founding growth on foreign capital alone without emphasizing aspects in which Argentina would have comparative advantage.

Proposing a national project of merely materialistic characteristics without explicit moral and social goals.

4. Military Government Errors

Pretending to be permanent — after 1951 — *post*-situation referees, removing those they did not like and turning over power later to the *uncontrollable consequences* of the voting laws.

Giving in to the temptation of populist sirens whom they promised electoral support.

Not having a national project.

Believing that the Constitution of 1853 was an eternally applicable instrument.

Supposing that order was enough.

Taking up their historical posts as rulers in a state of confusion because of not having done the necessary apprenticeship when young to be able to participate in the inherent problems of national economy and politics.

5. Non-aligned Errors

Carrying out only partial analyses, and as a result, joining up with one of three basic trends.

Keeping a purely technical level of commitments, for fear that global proposals would make them liable to anyone who took over power in the future.

But even if we rectify these errors, and others which, as an inevitable result, will follow them, Argentines of this generation must fight yet another battle, for which they will need subtle but very effective weapons: *the battle against the disrepute into which political life has fallen.*

Politics today are synonymous with the most vulgar and promiscuous type of disorder, after having become identified with the most vast ideological zones, the most weighted down with sentimentality, the coarsest of the political spectrum.

And public life is, like private life, the vital form of a person. We must reconstruct it into a series of institutions which do not tear down the whole person; we must give it back its old inner sense of learning for the good of all that goes into the making of Argentine welfare.

This should be the goal to which we devote our energies.

August 1976: The Alternatives

Even if this study makes certain attempts at being timeless, we cannot ignore the fact that it has been written in the third quarter of 1976. The acceleration of the process of Argentine decadence — the deep institutional, political and economic crisis in which it is culminating, obliges us to dedicate a few words to the present (August 1976).

We shall do this in order to analyze some facts, which, within a short time, could irreversibly affect the future of the Nation. Once again we shall see the concept of future. August 1976 is full of future.

On March 24, 1976, the armed forces deposed a populist demagogic government and replaced it with a military junta. Perhaps in no other case has there been such full consensus on the need for an abrupt change.

This military government came into power via an operation without violence, with complete control, and with all informative and operative variables covered, an operation which rivalled the precision of the most delicate surgery. Internally and internationally, it was considered totally justified and cleanly executed.

There is no question at all about whether or not the change should have taken place and no aspect of the change itself can be questioned. From this moment onward, the government is in the hands of the Nation's Armed Forces and the problem of a lack of vocation of military men to govern, which we have already analyzed, comes into play once again.

Thus, 50 days after the change, the nation is being administered, but not yet governed. The government has not formulated medium-term plans in the areas of politics, economy, labor and social welfare. The government is still ostensibly carrying out its cleaning up and purification process. What is still lacking is everything that has to do with broadening the nation as a whole and widening the base on which the government rests.

That which happens in the social and economic field is important to the future, but it does not set the conditions for the future, except through its political effects. But that which happens in political and institutional areas is a definite conditioning factor in the nation's medium-term future.

The principal, explicit aim of the Military Government is to wipe out subversion and along these lines, there have been successes and battles won, but the end of the war is not in sight. The violence which began to sweep Argentina in 1971 continues to haunt us. Every day claims victims within the ranks of combatants and non-combatants. In an undeclared war the heart of the enemy is out of range of our weapons, success is gradual and the end is unclear. The nation, which became a victim of the war through social, economic, political and ethical weakness, can only wipe out the enemy for good when it conquers, through maturity, growth, justice and moral re-activation, its own stagnation. If the Nation had not been in a state of decadence, subversion would not have found a fertile field in which to grow. Today we are confronted by two enormous challenges: that of conquering the foreign enemy and of transforming the Nation itself.

We should not fall into thinking that the heroic military successes of our Armed Forces are our only commitment even if, for the moment, the shooting war has priority.

Every time there is an institutional change and the Armed Forces take over, new hopes are opened up for the people.

The Nation breathes clean air, new air, fresh air and says: this time we are going to achieve government. From the non-government of Illia we went hopefully to the government of Ongania. From the anti-government of Isabel Peron, we have moved with hope to the government of the Military Junta. It is essential that our hopes not be dashed again.

We should, then, relive a little the climate of Buenos Aires in February and March of 1976. Total disorientation and ineptitude to the breaking point were shown by the political leaders in feeble attempts to find a solution to the drama the nation and its institutions were living through. There was also an absolute lack of greatness in those responsible, who never even thought to use the mechanisms offered by their own institutions as a means for solving the problem. There were also reciprocal accusations, and destructive criticism of those who tried to contribute to the finding of a solution. It is enough just to remember what the head of the Radical Party, Ricardo Balbín, said when he went on television on March 16, 1976 — just a few days before Isabel Peron was deposed — to address the people. His most important statement demonstrates the incapability of Argentina's populist politicians: Some may think that I have come to give solutions; I don't have them, but they exist.''

Populist politicians, as late as March of 1976, did not have any solutions to offer the Nation, as they have had no solutions for the past 60 years. Because of this they have no right to expect now that the Armed Forces, which had to take up the government role because of the failure of the Nation's political system, should, in a few months, resolve all the deep problems of all kinds that are assailing the country. The armed forces should know without a doubt that only they can solve the problem and that they must set the trends for a decisive national transformation. Politicians themselves and unionists turned spurious politicians have tried and have ended up realizing their own failure.

Despite all this, impatience, which comes from our lack of maturity, has already led to discussion, now, in August 1976, of a way to hand power back to civilian government.

There are probably two overall factions in the military, which, in themselves, are broken into many smaller areas of interest.

One line is called *soft* (read populist) which sees the current process as a cooling-off and arbitration period in which the Armed Forces removed Isabel Peron and they turn over power, as quickly as possible, to a Lanusse-type institutionalization program.

Adherence to this process would take the country into an institutionalized life, the basic rules of which are known and supported in party politics and trade unions as the Institutional Responsibility Act made public on June 24, 1976.

The other line is the *hard* line which makes the extermination of leftist terrorism its prime objective and says that until this terrorist defeat takes place, it is premature to commit the government to political or institutional plans.

The hard line has two variations with regard to the economy: a liberal orientation toward opening up trade, placement of foreign capital and technology and another based on autarchic ideology which considers the country basically self-sufficient and prefers to sacrifice stages of growth rather than contact foreign capital in basic development activities. In a way, this economic stance coincides with FORJA's utopian program (see Chapter IX).

Both of these lines and their branches are insufficient to solve the country's institutional problem. The first proposes a scheme which has shown itself time and again to be impractical and which coincides, strictly by chance, with guerrilla objectives. The second proposes no plan at all and will thus be trampled on any structured position.

The populist "institutionalization" could take place through elections in 1978, in which an alliance would take part, backed by the *soft* line, with a National Accord candidate, agreed upon by Unionists, Peronists and Radicals. If the candidate were a military man, what are supposed to be the four basic political forces of the country would be brought together. For all of us who lived through the 1971-1973 era of General Lanusse's Great National Accord (GAN) and through the tragic 49-day government of Héctor Cámpora with its Amnesty Law, this populist solution would be a suicidal leap that would pave the way for the birth of an Allende-like Marxist government.

It is not difficult to imagine that an electoral "solution" in 1978 would have a great deal in common with the "solution" proposed by Cámpora and his leftist activities. In the first place it would constitute without a doubt, a life-line for guerrilla ideology since, its activists would be better trained, its stance would remain strong in the face of populist divisions among those that would be included under the umbrella-Pact. In the second place, not reviewing the moral and political situation of the country and thus not finding a way to reverse the causes of our institutional decadence would leave the door open to new ideological action, through which the Republic would suffer a new attack of irrationality with its subsequent amnesty laws, labor contracts, retirement benefits for 50-year olds and all the rest of the traditional weapons in the demagogic arsenal. It would be a new triumph of distributionism over growth.

At the same time, the election process requires give-and-take. This process of concession would have to be carried out by the Armed Forces and would only serve to diminish their prestige, their internal unity and their overall cohesion and they will thus hand over an even weaker state than they did in 1973. Also, national and international subversive elements will not fail to use these circumstances to make a new takeover attempt with the added advantage that there is no Peron of '73 to make the Campora of '78 resign.

The process of institutionalization before a profound national transformation is a suicidal act and a gift to the enemy. The Armed Forces had better recognize this.

In this premature election call, practically all of the political and union figures responsible for the current situation would return: those responsible for the Cámpora elections, those who joined up with the Hour of the People, those who split up control of the country in a meeting at the "Restaurant Nino" on November 20, 1972. That time the result was Cámpora. There is nothing to guarantee that with the *same* ingredients, a *similar* system and *similar* ideologies we will not get the *same* results.

The building in the short space of a year of a national movement is a utopian thought. For this, much more time is needed and it also demands a well-rounded demonstration of governing ability by those who wish to organize a new movement.

Despite all this, as long as populism provides the only institutional plan in existence, it stands a good chance of ending up in power.

As a natural consequence of the decadence and destruction of the past three years, the economy has reached a dismal stage and has made this a bitter hour for society.

The natural opposition to all governments — subversive forces and those who have groups — take advantage of the lack of political planning for the future. We can add to this the economic recession, the causes of which originated in 1974 but the deep consequences of which we are suffering in the second half of 1976.

To oppose the populist line an explicit plan of how the country is to be governed in the future is needed. Institutional Responsibility Acts are not enough, nor will traditional ground rules be sufficient.

The question must be *what* is going to be done in Argentina, not *who* is going to do it.

The creative forces of the nation should be occupied with the making of a political plan that answers the fundamental question of *what* we are going to do. If not, the Republic will fall, as it did in 1973, into the hands of the enemy, who will use old national parties as vehicles for its proposals.

Chapter XV

Political Plan

Bases for the Proposal

Kant states in his "Anthropology" that liberty and the law that restricts it are the two axes around which the political world turns. But he adds that these axes should be accompanied by effort which is the element which makes liberty and law effective. Kant imagined various combinations of effort-law-liberty. For example, *law* and *liberty* without *effort* constitute *anarchy*. *Law* and *effort* without *liberty* make up *despotism*. *Effort* without *liberty* and without *law* is simply *barbarism*. Only when *effort* acts in conjunction with *liberty* and *law* do we have the bases for a *republic*.

Throughout this book we have been insisting on the necessity of Argentina's recuperating its lost identity and its sense of world significance. We have pointed out that this may be achieved through economic growth based on liberty which applies private initiative, with political stability, based on the power of consensus achieved through capability to govern and well-thought objectives based on the nation's current reality. Apart from this, it is achieved through respect for the law in the form of smoothly run republican institutions.

Out of a review of fundamental geopolitical and national political guideposts, comes a political proposal, of which we will only point out the bases without going into how it could be instrumented, since this goes beyond the limits of this study:

Argentina is part of the West. It is a Christian culture and has its ethnic origin and cultural roots firmly planted in Europe.

Argentina's geographical location, its natural resources, its technological and technical capabilities, its labor force, its climate and its cultural creations assign it an important role in Latin America and over the whole of the Southern Cone.

Argentine traditions are profoundly republican and broadly democratic. (Democracy is defined simply as government of the people and republic as government with the agreement of a judicial body).

Argentina, forming a part of the West because of its geopolitical location, is the object of growing aggression, which manifests itself in subversion and guerrilla warfare in terms of material war, ideological infiltration through manipulation of the people's will, in terms of the deepest psychology and through support of populist movements in the country's internal politics.

Argentina requires a long process of demographic, economic, cultural and political growth so that its generations can reach a higher level of civic maturity.

National sovereignty should be reaffirmed and increased through geopolitical realism, internal political stability, economic growth and progressively better distribution of wealth.

The Constitution of 1853 with the modifications made in 1958 has proven to be insufficient to insure the republican system of the nation.

From the year 1930 the Armed Forces have had to intervene decisively six times to eliminate governments which have come to power through elections carried out within the framework of the Constitution. From 1930 to 1976 the Constitution functioned only during the following periods:

PERIOD	YEARS IN EFFECT	YEARS OUTSIDE THE FRAMEWORK OF THE CONSTITUTION OF 1853
1930-1932	—	2
1932-1943	11	—
1943-1946	—	3
1946-1949	3	—
1949-1958	—	9
1958-1962	4	—
1962-1964	—	2
1964-1966	2	—
1966-1973	—	7
1973-1976	3	—
1930-1976	23	23

In 46 years of political life only 23 were carried out within the framework of the Constitution of 1853. From 1943, that is to say 33 years, the Constitution of 1853 has only been in effect 12 years.

The populist boom which has promised material wealth and no effort, as well as subversive foreign aggression, have made our Constitution an inadequate institutional framework for our country.

Native democracy of the 19th century corresponded to moral guidelines of conduct and respect which have no effect on mass minded people and less still for a traitor to his country and his local and foreign bosses.

The working of republican and representative institutions have been trampled on by populism, subversion and caudillos and has thus lost its meaning: that of being absolutely assured of freedom and of authentic participation by the citizenry.

The insensitivity of the Liberals and the personality cultist attitudes of Radicalism and Peronism have been obstacles to political mobility. The Liberals tried to turn themselves into a social elitist party, while the other two groups made no way for new generations, as can be seen in the advanced ages of their leaders in 1973. Perón, born in 1895, was 78, while Balbín, born in 1904, was 69.

Corporate groups invaded the political field, neglecting and confusing their specific role. Labor groups turned into a focus of unwarranted privileges and corruption, becoming rich and powerful by extorting money from both business and wage-earners alike.

Populism has falsified the Constitution by turning the people into a mob and the President into an idol to which the quality of being the sole owner of national will and thought is attributed; the opposition meanwhile has been declared the "enemy of the people."

Subversion infiltrated parliament, justice, political parties, the bureaucratic apparatus of the Executive Branch and the nation's unions. Subversive elements offered their activist support to populist parties and obtained a degree of power in return.

Both the party which governed from 1973 until March 24, 1976 and its prime opposition voted in favor of the Amnesty Law which led to a national situation of depredation, death and ruin. This vote alone rendered its leaders, its backers and its representatives unfit to carry on politically, and even less fit to lead the country.

The Armed Forces, which in 1976 saved the nation from falling into the hands of the subversive forces of a foreign enemy, should carry out a constant, active, political role.

The Role of the Armed Forces

It is a dog-eat-dog world and our optimistic Constitution of 1853 has shown its obsolescence in the fighting of an undeclared war, in the world of the Cold War and in the world of "detente" (with aggression).

Despite the fact that the past 46 years of Argentine history have witnessed the military's being obliged to assume a political role on a number of occasions, the Constitution of 1853 does not contain provisions governing the Armed Forces' performance of such activities, only assigning them the technical role of "armed hand of the Nation."

As a consequence, a serious conflict between the institution's real and formal roles arises, and reaches a climax every time the Armed Forces have to intervene in political life. While the phenomena of external aggression and internal subversion last, it is imperative that we provide, institutionally, for the role of the Armed Forces. History has proven it is inevitable that we should educate Armed Forces personnel in the field of politics, while making sure their military professionalism is kept intact.

It is also indispensable that a progressive, slow educational system on the working of the Nation's institutions be developed in which the Nation's political force can go through a real apprenticeship in governing Argentina.

If the Armed Forces, which today are the only custodians of national power, would not have liberated us from extremism, the nation would have been in a state of chaos, retaliation and death.

The current military government should stay in power long enough to achieve the following basic objectives:

The eradication of subversion.

Economic clean-up and creation of a basis for accelerated growth.

Purge on political and labor scenes to rid them of those responsible for the current situation.

Outline, without bending to pressure, of a gradually achieved political system and of controlled institutional functions.

The returning of power to civilian hands should, then, be gradual, according to trial and error, and employing sufficient prudence to keep us from being left at the mercy of a political situation. Only by discovering the cause and effect of the relationships of our situation will we be able to find the answer to what actions to take in this irreversible process.

Some Proposals

The following are some of the points on which a political system for Argentina's future should be based:

System of separation of powers should be maintained.

Parties, candidates and platforms should be made compatible with national objectives so as to avoid new Cámpora-type (or worse) situations.

Unions, business associations, social security and student and professional associations should have ample freedom to act in defense of their rights. Second and third category associations (those grouping several unions under a single heading), although having the power to protect union rights, should not, as in the case of the other types of groups mentioned, be permitted rights to obligatory association or compulsory dues. None of these associations should be allowed to take part in politics.

Promotion of Marxism in both party politics and union activity should be banned.

Amnesty law should be annulled. Legislators who voted for the law, those in the Executive Branch who approved the law as well as leaders of the parties which reviewed and backed the law, whould be excluded from Argentine political activity. Thus a new generation would be able to enter political life and remove those responsible for our national disaster from the scene for good.

A Republican Guarantees Council (CRG) should be created to review Presidential and legislative candidates in terms of their political seriousness and to prevent further Marxist-populist manipulation.

CRG should be made up initially of commanders of the Armed Forces and later by future elected presidents who have already completed their terms in office.

CRG should have the power to remove an elected official, through impeachment, and assume office for a determined period.

Presidents should have the right to be re-elected unless they are rejected by the CRG.

The first presidency should act without parliament, with the CRG acting as the Legislative Branch.

During the first three administrations after the first, the CRG should have veto rights on all legislation which, in its judgement, threatens national security or growth.

Once the country has an acceptable population level (33 million, for example), and a GNP of 3,500 dollars per inhabitant and when the CRG has determined that foreign aggression has ceased, the commanders-in-chief may leave the CRG, as long as three successive presidencies have been completed.

Provincial governors should be chosen by the President with the approval of the CRG. Provincial parliaments and municipal authorities should be elected.

Moral, political and geopolitical content in the nation's cultural formation should be supervised by the CRG, which will approve basic educational guidelines and those of the official news media.

Military education should include — on the Military College, Navy School and Aviation School level — political, legal and economic studies.

We have listed some of the provisions which would permit Argentina to bring together the *effort, liberty* and *law* that could someday lead us to the Kantian definition of Republic.

Careful management of time — the basic and politically, much discussed, variable — and action will permit the revival of those qualities of responsibility, security, greatness and spirit which characterize Argentines and which brought about the birth of the Argentine Republic. It is around these characteristics that we should build movements to orient the political participation of the people in public affairs.

Chapter XVI

Socio-economic Scheme

Capitalism Without Feudal Traits

As of the end of World War II, a virtual social revolution took place in the free world, brought on by the expansion of capitalism:

Feudal traits which had been evident in the process of capitalism in the XIX century and which could still be seen in parts of Europe began to disappear after the war — especially in the United States, the West's dynamic model of growth and equal distribution. The disappearance of feudal traits came in addition to a rise in the level of industrial production, greater concentration and a change in direction of big-business capital, the continuous growth of the number of individuals handling figures and personnel, the separation of ownership and administration, progress in working class politics and economy, and new methods of production in offices and factories.

The disappearance of these traits signified that no one tried to exercise superiority over his neighbor, by virtue of birth, the will of God, or membership in a power-holding group. All individuals were free and equal and if there was a system of hierarchy, it was because the leader had won his position on the free labor market. It was because they were free and equal that they were able to enter into a contractual relationship.

In a world in which the instantaneity of communications forced comparisons, prospects for social improvement (precisely because of the disappearance of feudal traits) formed part of the social and political climate. The working class — most evidently in the United States, but also, to a lesser degree in Europe — got a share of the economy's ever-increasing yield. The higher wages and better benefits the worker had begun to receive would have seemed a dream to even the most avid utopianist of 100 years before and at the same time, his social and economic capacity had increased in relation with his human and social role in production.

Faced with this panorama of constant improvement, the process in Argentina over the past 60 years has been the exact opposite. Instead of growing, we have been shrinking — which is obvious from our ever increasing inflation rate. Chapter I demonstrates, in figures, this sad reality which has become the predominant trait in Argentina.

Strangulation and Unilateral Formulas

Along lines of this decline, repeated balance of foreign payments crises in Argentine economic history signify, in practice, the dead ends of inadequate economic policies. These recurrent crises have been economically decisive in the lack of growth that has held Argentina down over the past 60 years.

Governments from various sectors which have taken office have failed to find a formula which simultaneously assures a solution to the problem of foreign debts and at the same time establishes enough internal political stability to give the measure enough time to prove its efficiency.

Being *unilateral* has been the sin of formulas put together by populists, liberals, developmentalists and others. They either pushed a *distributionist scheme* which was sure to use up national reserves in a short time, leaving the foreign sector high and dry, or they attempted to solve the foreign debts problem on the basis of an agroimporter country that *was not growing.*

They believed that the problem could only be solved through *massive foreign investment,* destined to go into *big national projects,* which slept the sleep of the just, or, like so-called "efficientism," made the nation focus its entire attention on the *solution to the problem in the foreign sector.*

Until a solution can be found for the recurrent problem of strangulation of the foreign sector, there will be neither political stability nor economic growth in this country. And this problem, together with that of economic growth, (generator of political maturity), will only be resolved with the combining of economic theories which, until now, have been unilateral studies.

We cannot deny that the country should maximize its agriculture and livestock sector in order to generate important foreign currency. But at the same time we must consider that the country in this last part of the XX century has a population of 25 million, and, because of this, real wage levels should be better than fair subsistance level for those who contribute to the general welfare of the nation with their work.   Of this 25 million inhabitants, 10 million constitute the standing active work force, and of these, only 1.5 million are occupied in jobs related to farm production.

We are worried also by the prospects of a country that does not have, nor will have in the near future, sufficient internal capital to develop, by itself, those large projects which require investments of hundred of millions of dollars.

And finally we are alarmed to think that without the conpletion of these projects the country will not be able to manage to make the qualitative leap it needs to make into an industrial nation and get it out of the dismal category of LDC (low developing countries) with which we identify ourselves and the Third World we aim to join.

The Economy as a Geopolitical and Social Instrument

The hour of truth, March 24, 1976, came to the nation when the Armed Forces felt obliged to interrupt the Argentine political process, and this should convince us of the shortcomings of uni-lateral economic ideologices, which by constantly contradicting themselves have kept the country from finding its direction.

By stripping each of the basic policies followed in the nation in the last 60 years of the ideological dimension which caused their inefficiency, we can extract the positive factors in which they agree. In order for the country to achieve the leap forward it needs, a compatible equation of these positive factors must bring together the interest of all those sectors which have banded together in one or another of these theories while the leaders of these movements design a country of the future with the most valuable traits of their philosophy.

It is necessary and possible to harmonize the following premises of the *Liberal Developmentalist efficientist distributionist and autarchist*.

The country should export agricultural goods and livestock, as a fundamental contribution to the balance of foreign payments.   In order to do this, maximum incentives for the agricultural production must be authorized, starting with incentive-price.   Tax instruments should discourage the holding of undeveloped land.

We must avoid evasion which might be promoted through an exchange and tax system linked to exports in general.

If we take into consideration the relative efficiency of agricultural production on similar land in the United States and Argentina we can figure that we could double farm production in general within the next few years and obtain an exportable surplus of about 7 billion dollars a year in traditional products during the 1980s. In order to do this the incentive price for the producer should be sufficient to permit intensive-capital exploitation of the humid pampa region and to open up zones which are at present marginal. Zones irrigated by the El Chocon complex should also be expanded. In the Chocon area alone a million hectares could be dedicated to production, but we must bear international prices in mind. The agricultural frontier should be broadened for grain as well as meat plus fruit and agro-industry products. The commercial effort called for in building up farm exports, especially as regards more sophisticated products, must include a stable promotion policy that private business can commit itself to permanently. More damage has been done to Argentine exports through fickle official policies than through competition from outside parties. As far as meat goes, a final offensive should be undertaken to conquer the great world market comprised by the US, overcoming bureaucratic, health and commercial barriers, and, besides that, negotiating with the EEC (European Economic Community) on a political level, for a more stable system of marketing and to progressively open new markets.

Agricultural exports are not enough to finance the growth and development of the country. They must be complemented with other primary products originating in our natural resources and with a high priority for the export of manufactured products where we may incorporate the comparative advantages of our primary production and our better labor, which compensates to a certain extent for our disadvantages in shipping and production scale. The state should apply, with great pragmaticism, reimbursements, refunds as well as tax and financial incentives in order to increase and maintain a permanent flow of industrial exports. Access to world markets demands growing quality and efficiency in our industry. In the 1980s our country should export more than 2 billion dollars a year in manufactured products. From then on the total should increase constantly and it will be industry's responsibility to provide this growth.

Incipient exportation of services and technology should receive ample official support — equivalent or superior to export of sophisticated manufactured products. Receptive tourism, which is really invisible exporting, also requires public and private action that is decisive and stable.

The substitution of imports policy should be emphasized along rational lines, concentrating on areas in which local production would not be forced to increase overall and sectorial costs in our own industry and without diminishing our capacity to compete internationally.   Areas like energy, oil, paper, petrochemicals, mining of copper, Solvay soda and steel generate opportunites to replace imports which in normal times come to more than 1.5 billion dollars.   This will permit a more flexible policy in the importation of more developed products that our industry requires in order to better its efficiency with the idea of competing abroad.   Basic industrialization will permit us to progressively achieve the industrial reorganization which the country needs in order to regain access to world markets.

This does not mean specific promotion of autarchy, but better competitive play between our natural and human resources.   We have already stated that autarchy is a step backwards.   Only powerful exportation which will permit us to import capital goods, technology and components, would better our efficiency and get us over our complexes, although the presence of certain finished foreign products on the local market would be beneficial in order to correct monopolistic deformations in our market's price scheme.   All this would happen through an integral adaptation of the customs tariff list, which is the one setting the final conditions for ups and downs in local prices and efficiency.   The current structure is about ten years old.   It should be modified to help industry make a leap.

We do not believe in price controls, nor in maximum prices, and we consider, as we have already said, that profitability and business growth are fundamental to the development of the nation.   The local market and adequate handling of customs tariffs are capable of generating a price-efficiency relationship which would get better progressively.   The supply of perishable products should be the responsibility of the public sector in so far as insuring an end to hoarding and cleaning up the market go.   Freedom is also fundamental in trade activities.   Acts which restrict free market should be exposed and their agents punished.

The challenge presented by theories of global growth limitations brought on by the eventual depletion of natural resources and by pollution create a special situation for Argentina.   In the first place, the situation permits Argentina to take advantage of foreign experience from now on in economic growth, incorporating from the very beginning agrarian, industrial and mining technologies which are less destructive to the ecology.   It will also permit us to impose already proven norms of hygiene and health in the area of urban and industrial waste disposal. Nevertheless this challenge invites us to fill in our waste space and to explore our natural resources to confront eventual crises from a more advantageous position.

Argentina's contribution to solving the ecological problem of an eventual lack of resources, the insufficiency of which is already affecting a good part of the world's population, should be a geopolitical space which is neither overpopulated nor a desert but which is evenly developed with a well-preserved environment and where plentiful human and natural resources are being developed.

Within the next 10 years the country must make progress on numerous, infrastructural and basic industrial projects.

In order to do this maximum available capital and technology must be mobilized. Nothing must stand in the way of this basis for the growth and integration of our territory. A brief list of important projects envisions a well-distributed economic growth throughout the country. This distribution can only be achieved by undertaking projects, not by restricting them.

Partial List of Basic Work Which Should Be Carried Out In Argentina within the Next Decade

National System of Electrical Interconnection
Alicura Hydroelectric Complex
Completion of Chocon-Cerros Colorados Hydroelectric Complex
Hydroelectric exploitation of Apipé-Yacyretá
Hydroelectric exploitation of Salto Grande
Hydroelectric exploitation of Parana Medio
Hydroelectric exploitation of Corpus
Hydroelectric exploitation of Río Santa Cruz I and II
Hydroelectric exploitation of El Chihuido
Hydroelectric exploitation of Cordón del Plata
Hydroelectric exploitation of Zanja del Tigre
Plan for Exploration and Exploitation of Offshore Petroleum Reserves
Plan for Secondary Petroleum Recovery
San Sebastian-Cerro Redondo Gas Pipeline
Centro-Oeste Gas Pipeline
Expansion of Cerro Redondo-Buenos Aires Gas Pipeline
Joint Projects with Southern Cone Countries
Cellulose Paste and Newsprint Plant to be Built
Expansion and Modernization of the Steel Industry (SIDINSA, SOMISA, ACINDAR, PROPULSORA, etc.)
Bahia Blanca Petrochemical Complex
Railroad Recovery Plan
Electrification of Suburban Railways

Expansion of Federal Capital Subway System

Telephone Modernization and Communications Plan (1 million lines)

Expansion and Renovation of the Merchant Fleet

Expansion of Grain Storage System

Building of Thermoelectric Plant to Take Advantage of Rio Turbio Coal

Building of Deep Water Port

Copper Mining (Pachon and others)

Iron Mining

The preceding list requires an investment of no less than 10 billion dollars, despite the fact that it is incomplete and does not include the modernization of the whole of Argentina's industrial complex, a need for social capital, (housing, health and sports) roadwork and other areas in which there have been practically no investments in the past five years. It is a well-known fact that the country does not have the cash or the foreign reserves to cover this kind of investments. Not even applying last-ditch regressive distributionist policies would we be able to achieve these objectives, apart from the fact that this would not be socially or politically realistic, nor would it meet the standards that we proposed for Argentines earlier in this book. We can only reach our goal of doubling our progress in ten years' time by following an open policy of foreign investment apart from the open trade policy already proposed.

The entire national tax system should be redone from scratch. It has quit functioning properly as a fund raising instrument and today operates as a perverse element which creates the opposite of the economic and ethical effect sought. Simplicity and tax collecting feasibility should be the guidelines for the new system, and it should also reward those who produce and save for the country. The tax capacity of an entity should be figured according, basically, to its spending power, its declaration of expenses and its fixed capital assets.

The objective should be to double the country's overall progress in ten years' time, so that the worker's real wages would also more or less double within this same period of time. That is to say, every worker should be able to measure his own progress in less than a generation. This is the basis for better social distribution. Spending power should grow at a slower rate than the others and with other factors taken into consideration, so that the worker, through the asymetrical distribution of growth and benefits, is able to feel the day to day effect of this growth on his life. Thus, an additional benefit of this objective would be the expansion of the local market.

The beneficiary of this overall growth will be the people. A pragmatic review of the withholdings list will quickly raise the real level of the wage-earners' pay, a social benefit he really obtains, and would quickly raise the real wage level, since current withholdings which go for the support of diverse bureaucratic departments would be eliminated. Today, for every 100 units of cost to business, the worker takes home less than 50. This does not mean that the basic element of social security should be eliminated, but that it should be adjusted in accordance to efficient cost-benefit criteria.

National capital savings would be an intrinsic objective of the plan, expecially as regards the flow of capital between the nation and its inhabitants. National savings should be protected from possible inflation and breaches of public trust. The feasibility and security of investing in Argentina should be made a firmer prospect than investing in US dollars or Swiss francs.

The nation's finance and exchange systems should be areas in which efficiency is highly rewarded, and where functional inefficiency, inherited or created privileges and changes in the state of the nation's economy cannot act as shelters for speculative profiteering.

In a nation which is growing, and to obtain national growth, there must be an ever improving standard of behavior of the nation's citizens. Apart from insuring the fruits of its activities, the Nation should also:

Do away with job stability, which hampers a psychological effect designed to make the worker care about efficiency. Stability should be replaced with effective social benefits.

Do away with all legal impediments to the Bankruptcy Law (No. 18.832) and any other legal instruments which hamper free competition and financial purification.

Within the area of economy, the State should have the responsibility of promoting, indicatively when possible, national economic growth in priority areas, by obtaining the:

—Creation and incorporation of capital
—Generation and incorporation of technology
—Utilization and preservation of natural resources
—Protection of the environment
—Formation of general and professional dignity among the people
—Opening of trade and cultural exchange with foreign nations
—Distribution of social justice and efficiency
—Creation of a balanced social security system

Above all, the State must achieve efficiency in its own administrative and business dealings. A nation cannot grow if it is not efficient.

A modern nation cannot be efficient if its public administration is inefficient. Because of this, the first thing it should do is remodel its public administration system from the bottom up, abandoning those activities which experience has demonstrated do not bring the social and economic effects sought. The state should, for example, give up its activities in companies it has nationalized over the past five years, in order to keep them from going bankrupt. The increase in the number of state, municipal and provincial companies and agencies since May of 1973 has been the result of purely political causes, and has obstructed the resources of productive sectors of the community. Perhaps, then, the remodelling of public administration is to be the most important factor in the nation's future growth.

Alberdi said more than 100 years ago that to govern is to populate. This is still valid today. An official 1973 projection indicates estimated rises in population until the year 2000.

Projection of Argentine Population Growth Until Year 2000
(in millions of inhabitants)

YEAR	TOTAL
1975	25.384
1980	27.064
1985	28.678
1990	30.189
1995	31.584
2000	32.861

This estimate presupposes a continuous reduction or drop in the demographic growth rate which has been noticable over the past few years. The projection shows an internal population growth rate of 1.04% per year, including the effects of migration. If we want to reach 40 million inhabitants by the end of the century, we must have an annual growth rate of 1.84%

In order to make up this difference through immigration, we would need an influx as of 1978 of 250,000 people a year (giving us a 3% rise in the internal immigrant population). The experience of the last several years has shown that Argentina loses university graduates and skilled laborers and tries to fill these gaps in the population through the immigration of unskilled or semi-skilled workers.

We must have a conscientious and wide-awake demographic program, especially as regards migration, since this area of planning will have an irreversible effect on our future.

A comprehensive program containing all of these policies would constitute the installation of a system which would insure socio-economic growth, adequate social security against unforeseen factors, maximum private initiative working in harmony with the progressive distribution of the product of national growth and emphatic personal responsibility for economic deportment.

Only a growing country with growing real wages can speak out about its national sovereignty and the freedom of its inhabitants, *but the economy is a social and geopolitical instrument, and is certainly not an end in itself.* The entire economic setup, with its objectives and processes, laws and institutions, is nothing more than a component of politics and a part of the spiritual realm of the individual and it must remain subordinant to these two areas.

What Is "The Greatest Number?"

Since all men are virtually equal, democracy is not a privilege. A right is not created by number. Otherwise Borges' ingenuous statement to the effect that "democracy is an exaggeration of statistics" would become an absolute truth. The sovereignty of law lies in its making the interests of the majority a predominant factor, while at the same time protecting the minority. This factor constitutes the greatest difference between democracy and its caricature, populism.

Since it is not a privilege, democracy belongs to no one and the principle of it comes before all ideologies. In a world in which ideas are used as weapons of war, the temptation is to inject democracy with any old orthodoxy, but it shies away from being fenced into an ideology, precisely because it goes beyond the limits of ideology. It is founded on a philosophy of freedom.

Since it is not, as many people mistakingly believe, a system of less effort for all, but a translation of moral values into political ones, democracy can never be the legalization of irresponsibility. More than in any other type of system, democracy calls for a select minority, which is militant in its spirit of abnegation. It also requires a continuous circulation through civic education of its values of freedom.

And since, as in the case of health and happiness, the only ones who worry about it are those who are losing it, hopefully we will make it the object of our collective will, to guide the orientation of our destiny as a free and sovereign nation.

Chapter XVII

The Second Founding
Of the Argentine Republic

To Govern is to Educate

More than 2,000 years have passed since Plato so comprehensively summed up the difficult task of governing. No other topic on the Nation's long and sad list is more demonstrative of the profound need for a total transformation. What do we have a right to expect out of our youth if, in terms of training and formation we have offered them: the portion of the budget set aside for education is smaller all the time; teachers' courses of study are eliminated; few new schools are built; the school dropout rate is permitted to rise; party songs and slogans replace national symbols and traditions; and subversive ideologies replace Christian ethics? What sort of men and women will we have reared to take charge of the nation if we take into account: idolatry of violence via the mass media; these same mass media being controlled by the State to serve the interests of the ruling party; adults in all sectors lending to a destructive process by satisfying their personal greed at the expense of a nation which is left unprotected and poverty-stricken? Of all the crimes committed by demagogic populist regimes, this is the worst and the most irreparable.

The consequences are already within view. The past 30 years of demagogy have produced the destruction of the Argentine educational system. Young students of 16 have been transformed by irresponsible or delinquent educators into killers, terrorists and nihilists.

The formation of Man is the fundamental responsibility of the Republic, and thus, of the government. The education policy must be the basis of the government's overall policy. If it permits the Nation's educational system and mass media to be conquered by subversive elements, the country will, upon losing its ethos and sense of identity, become nothing more than a Communist satellite. It is in the area of education where there is an absolute necessity for an immediate and profound change. This should be our top priority in what really amounts to a new founding of the Republic.

While teachers must introduce new content to the methodology, it is up to the government to define *political, moral and ethical content* in Argentine education. If there are people who should not be permitted because of their culpability and impunity for the damage they caused to the Nation, there are also educators the results of whose irresponsible actions are reflected in our troubled youth.

Educational content on all levels should be based on moral and political principles which are compatible with the philosophy of the Nation. The following basic guidelines should be revived to keep us from running the risk of alienating the Argentine of the future: The Nation has the obligation of rearing its children within the framework *of Christian ethics*. Only in this way will the Argentine people inherit common rules for conduct which insure coherent and responsible views for the future. This should be done on top of guaranteeing the right to free choice of religion and even the liberty to have or not have faith in God.

It is imperative that the people, from infancy, understand that a *future* exists and that they should learn to feel and think about this future — a future which, depending on their behavior today, holds growth and improvement for them.

Idolatry of the present should be eliminated since it causes permanent tension in the lines of our youth. Once they have made a deep study of the past they must necessarily relate to the future. Only through knowledge, through this *consciousness of the future* will we be able to make our youth understand the concept of responsibility which they must have for their actions of the present. The existence of God, the insurance of a future, generate a concept of responsibility, religious responsibility, responsibility before God and for eternal life, and responsibility to the future in present day life.

Consciousness of moral values in the actions for which they must respond is the best weapon with which to confront life's decisions which our youth must gradually assume.   Without this moral conscience, and the deep faith from which it is derived, decisions become elusive and produce the alienation of our youth. The prime concept of the May Revolution (1810) and the country's subsequent independence (1816), that is to say, *liberty*, should make a comeback in Argentine classrooms. Liberty, within the limits of the law, should be an *ideal* of Argentine education. In this country, which has opened its doors to all immigrants, Alberdi's concept of *tolerance and pragmatism* should be reiterated.

Once the Argentine has insured his ethical upbringing, this concept should also be put into practice. The best kind of *background* is one of *work*. The only *freedom* which exists is that *which is exercised,* and the only *law* is that which is *practiced.* And the priority of ethics over action is worth repeating. But without action ethics have no means of expression.

Pragmaticism and tolerance are the two criteria which define the West. It is imperative that our youth should know and absorb the concept of *human solidarity*. Solidarity should be understood with a sense of Christian love and with a feeling of social feasibility. Giving help to one's fellow man is still valid 2,000 years after Christ.

But the whole of society is also our fellow man in need and requires the drive of each individual in order to build a nation. The behavior of the Argentine should be based on Christian solidarity and social function.

Responsibility, liberty and solidarity make the existence of *private initiative* possible in a world of *private property*. Without solidarity the world is changed into a world of exploitation. Solidarity, defines as meaning that no inhabitant of the country who is willing to make an effort in his field should suffer from need, will insure a system of social security, at a tolerable cost to the nation and of measurable effect on its beneficiaries.   If Argentine upbringing includes this concept we will have *social security* and will be able to set up limits to put a stop to the mad wanderings of the demagoges.

Initiative and private property, the basic concepts of Western capitalism, the first as the driving force behind growth and the second an expression of the rights of each individual to the fruits of his actions, must be part of Argentine upbringing.

Even our youth should have a *geopolitical view of Argentina's situation,* They should know that Argentina, because of its history, geography and politics is part of the West. They should be familiar with the world and its battles and how they develop. They should cast off fear of aggression while at the same time being conscious of its existence.

Argentina is ethically and culturally *Christian* and geopolitically *Western*. The same concepts of liberty and solidarity exist on world levels as on individual levels.

In a country which is basically made up of the children of immigrants and which channels itself toward a new flow of immigration it is absurd to instill hatred for that which is foreign in our youth. A *practical, ecumenical, cultural* and *commercial opening* should be made in the conscience of our youth so that they see the world as it is, an ever smaller planet which is the center of operations for the entire human race which is born on it and the chess table on which countries rally for their future and their survival. *The foreigner is not an enemy* but, is rather, *a possible friend,* and a sure *interlocutor* with whom to exchange culture, wealth and technology.

The youth of Argentina should also know the difference between the various regimes which exist in the world. *They should be familiar with the reign of terror,* kidnappings, killing of hostages; they should know about the modern versions of Auschwitz, Warsaw and the Gulag Archipelago in order for them not to be taken in by ideology.

The old concept of living in a *country which has "made it,"* should be replaced with the concept of *Argentine greatness* and the people should be convinced that greatness is within their reach and that they should make *the greatness of their country their objective.* The country is for everyone who lives in it, the nation is superior to its inhabitants and only national sovereignty can guarantee individual liberty. The nation is above any class. In Argentina there exists no class struggle and the nation, because of this, cannot be subjugated to the interests of any class.

In a world which calls for improvement and growth, for *success,* that is to say, improvement, the growth of each individual must be considered a positive guideline and not a sin. Success in sports, artistic success, and material success, as it applies to individuals, constitutes the basic building blocks of the collective success of a society. The adults of the future should see the success of their fellow men from their earliest years as dignified examples to be emulated and not envied and destroyed.

These guidelines, applied to the education policy and to the content of mass media information would signify a complete transformation of the contaminated cultural medium into which our youth has been dumped. Rereading the political, economic and social prospects and adding them to the problem of bringing up our citizens assures us of the tremendous size of the task to be undertaken, which does not consist of merely changing direction, but, of founding a new Republic.

In Part I we analyzed the political, social and economic state of the nation in its last stages of decadence. In Part II we turned a critical eye on the deterioration and displacement of the nation geopolitically. In Part III we analyzed basic problems in the workings of the nation's culture. In Part IV we concluded that there is a total absence of a valid national project.

The problems cannot be resolved through the application of plans whose failings are familiar to us. It is not merely the form of government which is being discussed, it is the entire personality of a nation in crisis. Fundamental problems require fundamental solutions.

The Need for a New Basic Form

Instances of interference in the constitutional life of the nation which have occurred since 1930 have been carried on with the supposed object of defending the Constitution of 1853. There is an intrinsic contradiction here, which has paved the way for the repeated frustration and failure of these half-hearted revolutions or mere coups.

There is an overall contradiction here because the Armed Forces, which came to power by interrupting an institutional process, try to rule by the Constitution, while the civilians who come to power through an institutional process slant the meaning of the Constitution and transform the country's institutions into a dictatorship of the majority: This situation is perhaps the best example we have of just how contradictory Argentine politics are.

By convincing ourselves that the Constitution of 1853 requires basic amendments and that the Republic should be refounded, we will win the war in which we are entangled and also win the peace that should follow it. The country needs a new Constitution to cover the new circumstances it must confront. Never has the nation's very existence been in such danger as it has over the last few years.

In a new organization act, a true founding of this Republic, necessary amendments to renovate the Constitution should be introduced.

This is what is meant by Revolution. This Revolution has the formulation of a new Constitution as its objective, and were this not so it would only be a violation of the Constitution with its subsequent damage to judicial order. The forming of a new Constitution generates new ground rules and justifies the Revolution (H. Kelsen, Teoria pura del Derecho).

The Constitution of 1853 has changed into an Argentine myth. The positive conditions it considers abstractly are undeniable, and undeniable too are the benefits it has given the country in almost 80 years of use. But it is also undeniable that circumstances have changed. Until March of 1976, we witnessed an orgy of corruption which used the Constitution as a shelter. We saw the legal publicizing of doctrines which were totally against the Constitution and against our republican norms and we witnessed, too, murder as a method of expressing ideas.

The Constitution of 1853 is not adequate for a country which is involved in a non-conventional war, nor for a country subjected to international aggression, nor for a country which has been declared the prime objective of subversive elements in Latin America.

The basic principles of the nation should find adequate protection in the Constitution.

These principles should be given a defense mechanism to insure their stability and permanence through a new basic law.

In this way, 1977 is similar to 1853. Thirty years of battle and anarchy ended in 1853. On February 3, 1852, an illustrious and open country won out over a closed barbarous country.

On March 24, 1976 a civilized and ethical country triumphed over the anarchy and disorder which, since 1945, has tried to take the nation by assault and which manifested occasional and concealed alliances with international subversive elements.

In 1853 the victors had no doubt over the necessity of giving the country a new Constitution since the early one was no longer applicable.

In 1979 the victors of March 1976 should have the same conviction. In 1853, as on all earlier occasions the Constitution was written and approved by representatives of the effective forces in the country. There was no election of a constitutional congress by means of a voting process.

Along this line Ricardo Levene says, in his *Historia de la Nación Argentina:* ''... it was decided that the election should not be carried out by number of inhabitants, and that each province should elect two deputies. Although the system of election by the people was adopted, Urquiza sent *confidential messengers to the provinces... and the result was excellent.* Santa Fe (the provincial government), elected Leiva and Seguí; Entre Ríos elected Gutiérrez and Pérez; Cordoba elected Derqui and Campillo; Santiago del Estero elected Gorostiaga; Mendoza elected Zapata and Delgado; Corrientes elected Torrent and Díaz Colodrero; San Juan elected Godoy and Del Carril; San Luis elected Huergo and Llerena; Salta elected Zuviría and Blanco; Jujuy elected Padilla and Quintana; La Rioja elected Regis Martínez; Tucumán elected Zavalía.''

The basic laws of the nation have always been laid down by a revolutionary creator, from the laws of Solon to the American

Revolution. The 5th French republic was founded by de Gaulle. New basic norms for this Republic were not set through an exhaustive electoral process, in which everyone would have commented on topics in which they had no experience. Instead, these basic norms were set down by means of a creative revolution by those who had the responsibility of founding the Republic.

A Revolution defines the *"what"* of the country's *essence*, of its future. It is a revolutionary act, the formulation of new basic precepts to define the prime characteristics of a Republic. In Argentina there is no current definition, since during the last thirty years the definition given in the Constitution of 1853 has been trampled on and the demagogy of sixty years has suffocated essential cultural values and guidelines.

The new basic form will acquire legitimacy as did that of 1853, through its application over a period of years. Revolutionary acts are legitimate if they triumph and last. Only time and application will lend legitimacy to the new Constitution. It is thus that the Constitution of 1853 has lost legitimacy — through lack of application.

We find in the strange dialectic of a modern war that is subversive, an extremism which declared in 1972 and 1973 that it would defend constitutional precepts to the death. It served their ends to say this since it gave necessary freedom of action to ideological subversion. Once in power they would be sure not to be so naive as their predecessors if someone whould decided to try to recover the Republic.

If within the ruling "party," the military "party," there truly exists a hard line, it should be a completely revolutionary line. It should not merely be a tactical hard line. A line is not harder or softer than eventual punishments it applies to those responsible for the country's problems. It is harder, firmer, more decisive if it carries the Revolution to its logical consequences and if it does not content itself with eliminating an inept government in order to see later if, through already disproven procedures, a capable government can be found.

There is a danger that some will see the necessity for the intervention of the Armed Forces in March, 1976 as having been carried out only as a means of replacing inefficient people who had taken over power, and that because of this the change itself is enough. The illness goes deeper than that, affecting every part of our political, social, economic and cultural body. It requires well-founded remedies.

Because of this the authors of the March, 1976 revolution must feel obliged to make it a true Revolution and not a mere act of unconstitutional arbitration on constitutional matters it says it is defending. There would be important advantages to publishing a new basic norm over the mere amendment carried out through a revolutionary act or any other type of legal instrument. A new Constitution signifies a reaffirmation of all aspects of the old Constitution which are still useful. And it also signifies that the modifications to be introduced are to bear in mind the overall constitutional context. That is to say, a new Constitution is a positive act, a truly revolutionary act.

A mere amendment is an instrumental act and is passive in all that is not amended by it. Only a new Constitution has a level of conscience which touches on all constitutional themes, and because of this it is a conscious and wide-awake act.

In producing a new Constitution, all the defense mechanisms which our liberal Constitution does not contain should be incorporated.

The freedom our forefathers bequeathed us should be defended by its own institutions.

The second founding of the Republic should be effected by those who hold the power and sovereignty of the nation in their hands through a system of preparation and approval which they select. The new founding should foresee circumstantial alliances since leadership requires that alliances be built around clear ideals which will not be submitted to negotiation. Negotiations are valid in the process of electing those who will govern but not in defining what the Republic is to be. Populism subordinated these ideals to the number of its allies. Leadership achieves alliances, affiliations, and a consensus on ideas.

Translated by Dan Newland

APPENDIX I
FOREIGN TRADE DEVELOPMENT

CHART I
**Foreign Trade Per Inhabitant in U.S. Dollars (1964 value)
In the 30 Top Nations in the Field**

	1973	1964	1948	1928	1913
1 Belgium	2.498	1) 1.235	424	7) 372	355
2 Holland	2.028	2) 1.072	295	3) 413	—
3 Switzerland	1.867	3) 1.061	426	5) 390	274
4 Sweden	1.596	5) 990	365	257	134
5 Denmark	1.592	4) 1.006	327	4) 409	228
6 Norway	1.570	6) 858	370	9) 280	170
7 Canada	1.250	7) 824	481	2) 444	241
8 West Germany	1.139	12) 550	—	167	126
9 Finland	999	9) 607	253	174	92
10 Austria	938	16) 459	98	196	—
11 Ireland	925	11) 570	249	—	—
12 New Zealand	913	8) 782	542	1) 559	338
13 France	792	17) 397	133	175	126
14 Israel	771	14) 478	385	—	—
15 Great Britain	706	13) 524	302	6) 373	214
16 Australia	702	10) 577	397	8) 365	263
17 Italy	519	20) 264	57	82	56
18 Venezuela	416	15) 463	396	121	27
19 Japan	395	24) 151	12	52	20
20 United States	376	21) 246	141	133	73
21 Jamaica	306	18) 288	96	—	—
22 Malaysia	286	19) 285	185	—	—
23 Costa Rica	242	27) 128	121	—	76
24 South Africa	203	22) 226	187	187	127
25 Nicaragua	166	23) 159	47	—	39
26 Chile	144	25) 144	102	—	130
27 Uruguay	133	26) 138	164	—	161
28 Argentina	**129**	**30) 110**	**198**	**10) 274**	**209**
29 El Salvador	92	28) 120	47	—	20
30 Guatemala	89	29) 113	58	—	19

Source: Federico Pinedo's "La Argentina, su posicion y rango en el mundo";
U.N.O. Statistics Annual.

CHART II
Trade in Millions of Dollars (1964 value)

	1928-29	1948	1964	1973
United States	15,813	20,747	46,833	79,022
Great Britain	15,056	15,104	27,779	39,478
West Germany	10,772	2,546	30,839	70,596
France	7,133	5,455	19,065	41,282
Canada	4,350	6,338	15,648	27,655
India	3,564	3,079	4,360	3,990
Italy	3,315	2,616	13,187	28,462
Japan	3,268	942	14,622	42,814
Holland	3,215	2,895	12,862	27,252
Belgium	3,073	3,736	11,491	25,253
Argentina	**3,018**	**3,191**	**2,487**	**3,130**
Australia	2,303	3,060	6,351	9,213
Spain	1,635	855	3,213	8,364
Switzerland	1,561	1,962	6,257	12,005
Brazil	1,528	2,307	2,696	7,607
Denmark	1,485	1,283	4,733	7,905
South Africa	1,463	2,233	3,840	4,811
Austria	1,304	688	3,309	7,059
New Zealand	821	943	2,035	2,706
Norway	795	1,186	3,275	6,217
Mexico	787	1,045	2,548	3,754
Finland	592	988	2,796	4,651
Venezuela	360	1,858	2,895	4,702
Singapore	—	1,543	2,039	4,939
Hong Kong	—	922	2,508	6,078

Source: Federico Pinedo's "La Argentina, su posicion y rango en el mundo"; *u.n.o. Statistics Annual*

CHART III
Growth in Percent of Total Trade

	1928/29-48	1948-1973	1928/29-1973
United States	31.2	280.9	399.7
Great Britain	0.3	161.4	162.2
West Germany	−76.4	1,772.8	555.4
France	−23.5	656.8	478.7
Canada	45.7	336.3	535.7
India	−13.6	29.6	12.0
Italy	−21.1	908.8	758.6
Japan	−71.2	3,445.0	1,210.1
Holland	−10.0	841.3	747.7
Belgium	21.6	575.9	821.8
Argentina	**5.7**	**−1.9**	**3.7**
Australia	32.9	201.1	300.0
Spain	−47.7	878.2	411.6
Sweden	58.5	422.9	728.8
Switzerland	25.7	511.9	669.1
Brazil	51.0	229.7	397.8
Denmark	−13.6	523.1	438.4
South Africa	52.6	115.5	228.8
Austria	−47.2	926.0	441.3
New Zealand	14.9	187.0	229.6
Norway	49.2	424.2	682.0
Mexico	32.8	259.2	377.0
Finland	66.9	370.7	685.6
Venezuela	416.1	153.1	1,206.1
Singapore	—	220.1	—
Hong Kong	—	559.2	—

Source: Federico Pinedo's "La Argentina, su posicion y rango en el mundo" (page 434); *U.N.O. Statistics Annual.*

CHART IV
Commercial Trade Per Country in Millions of U.S. Dollars

	1898	1907	1913	INCREASE PERCENTAGE 1898-1907	1898-1913
United Kingdom	3,128	4,760	5,407	34.9	45.7
Germany	2,250	3,713	4,966	61.1	19.8
United States	1,797	3,318	4,689	142.4	210.4
France	1,540	2,210	2,914	33.4	85.8
Holand	1,325	1,957	2,819	49.6	121.2
Belgium	729	1,162	1,696	67.8	142.6
Austria-Hungary	659	944	1,323	42.1	120.0
Russia	697	868	1,257	12.2	82.1
Italy	498	889	1,172	97.8	157.9
Argentina	**232**	**561**	**872**	**167.9**	**294.7**
Japan	220	460	680	77.0	161.8

Source: Federico Pinedo's "La Argentina, su posicion y rango en el mundo" (page 428); *U.N.O. Statistics Annual.*

APPENDIX II
QUALIFIED IMMIGRATION

Number of Argentine immigrants (by classification) admitted to the United States during the period from July 1, 1950 to June 30, 1966.

Fiscal year (7/1 - 6/30)	Total	Professionals & technicians	High-level administrators	Skilled workers
1950-1951	190	78	41	71
1951-1952	231	114	48	69
1952-1953	333	153	68	112
1953-1954	424	212	84	128
1954-1955	510	218	85	207
1955-1956	684	354	124	206
1956-1957	1,805	362	429	814
1957-1958	1,348	717	138	493
1958-1959	848	478	98	273
1959-1960	991	508	137	346
1960-1961	1,151	552	125	474
1961-1962	1,003	531	98	374
1962-1963	1,672	781	197	694
1963-1964	2,614	1,159	336	1,119
1964-1965	2,133	973	257	903
1965-1966	1,404	699	166	529
Total	17,341	8.089	2,431	6,621

Source: U.S. Department of Justice, Immigration and Naturalization Service.

APPENDIX III

Reciprocal Exports Among Latin American Nations Included in the Andean Pact

Entire Andean Group	Total Exports	Exports to Nations Within The Group	Each Nation's Export as % of Group Total
Bolivia	—	—	—
Bolivia	165	2	1
Chile	1,163	17	1
Colombia	777	56	7
Ecuador	303	25	8
Peru	1,048	21	2
Entire Andean Group	3,456	119	4

Source: A. Krieger Vasena y J. Pazos', "Latin America: A Broader World Role," London, 1973.

APPENDIX IV
A Partial List of Armed Conflicts
Throughout World History

B.C.
2800	Conquest of Sumer by the Akkadians
2000	Invasion of Babylonia by the Hittites
1800	Conquest of Babylonia by the Khasites
674-675	Egypt surrendered to the Assyrian Empire
612	Assyria falls
586	Nebuchadnezzar destroys Jerusalem
525	Egypt conquered by the Persians
492-479	Greek and Persian Wars
490	Battle of Marathon
480	Battle of Thermopylae and battle of Salamis
431-404	Peloponesian war between Athens and Sparta
338-335	Greece falls to Macedonia
334-323	Alexander the Great's conquests
325-304	The Etruscan Wars
323	India rebels against Macedonian domination
281-272	Battle between Tarranto and Pyrrhus
264-241	First Punic War
218-201	Second Punic War
149-146	Third Punic War
146	The fall of Carthage and Corinth
55	Caesar invades Britain and completes the invasion of Gaul
48	Julius Caesar defeats Pompey and Pharsalus
43-41	Caesar's wars of succession
25BC-9AD	Conquest of Bavaria, Austria and Bulgaria

AD
9	Teutoburg disaster
20-35	Roman border wars
387	The Gauls sack Rome
395	Visigoth rebellion
406	Barbarians invade Gaul
410	Alaric leads Visigoths to victory over Rome
429	Vandals invade Africa
439	Vandals take Carthage
449	Anglosaxons conquer Great Britain
451	Huns invade Gaul
493	Italy defeated by the Ostrogoths
568	Northern Italy conquered by the Lombards
633-750	Formation and expansion of the Arab empire
732	The Franks defeat the Muhammadans at Poitiers

804	Annexation of Saxony by the Frank kingdom
1066	William the Conqueror of Normandy completes his conquest of England
1099	Crusaders take Jerusalem
1147-1149	Second Crusade
1187	Jerusalem fallw into the hands of Saladin, Sultan of Egypt
1110-1227	Genghis Khan's conquests
1190-1192	Third Crusade
1202-1204	Fourth Crusade
1204	Crusaders take Constantinople
1214	Battle of Bouvins. Consolidation of the French Monarchy
1337-1453	Hundred Years War
1346	Battle of Crecy
1356	Battle of Poitiers
1415	Battle of Agincourt
1429	Joan of Arc saves Orleans
1453	Constantinople falls to the Ottoman Turks
1455-1485	War of the Roses
1498-1750	Conquest of America
1571	Battle of Lepanto (Navpaktos)
1588	Defeat of the Spanish Armada
1618-1648	Thirty Years War
1690	Battle of the Boyne in Ireland
1701-1714	Spanish War of Succession
1750	General Wolfe takes Quebec
1756-1763	Seven Years War
1772	First partition of Poland
1775-1782	American Revolution
1793	Second partition of Poland
1796	Russia, Prussia and Austria united in Third partition of Poland
1796-1797	Napoleon's First Italian campaign
1800-1801	Napoleon's Second Italian campaign
1805	Battle of Trafalgar
1803-1813	Peninsular War
1812-1814	War of 1812
1813	Venezuelan War of Independence
1818	Waterloo campaign
1820	Naples rebellion
1821	Revolt in Piedmont
1845	U.S. annexes Texas
1846-1848	Mexican-American War
1848	Italian war against Austrian and Papal domination
1854-1856	Crimean War
1854-1858	''Bleeding Kansas'' strife
1859-1861	Italian liberation war
1861-1865	U.S. Civil War
1864	Austro-German-Danish war

1866	Seven Weeks War
1870	Franco-Prussian War
1879	Zulu War
1896	Italians defeated in Ethiopia
1898	Spanish-American War
1899-1902	Boer War
1900	Boxer Rebellion in China
1912	Balkan war flares up
1914-1918	World War I
1917	U.S. declares war on Germany
1935	Italy begins Ethiopian invasion
1938	Annexation of Austria by Germany
1938	Germany occupies a portion of Czechoslovakia
1939	War between Germany and Poland
1939-1945	World War II
1939	Russo-Finnish War
1950-1953	Korean Conflict
1964-1973	War in Indochina
1967	Six Days War in Middle East
1970	Biafra conflict
1971	War in Bangladesh
1973	October War in the Middle East
1976	Lebanese conflict

Chronology until 1945 based on Joseph Reiter's "Panorama de Historia Universal," Buenos Aires 1972.

APPENDIX V
SUMMARY OF ARGENTINE POLITICAL PARTY
PLATFORMS IN MARCH 1973

1. Type of government and planned legislation

National policies — Justice — National defense — Municipalities — Federalism — Cooperativism.

FREJULI

Minority to be guaranteed its rights in legislative checks and balances. Power structure to be reinterpreted in accordance with world trends and overall development, so as to guarantee judges' immobility in their posts, since their independence is threatened by *their ties with the social group to which they belong.* Repressive "state of siege" laws to be repealed. Legislation to be appeasing and to contain ample amnesty laws for all people on trial or in prison for having broken the law through their political actions. Executive branch to be endowed with as many technical teams as it needs to carry out its role as the nation's liberator. New life to be pumped into the provincial economies in order to establish a truly federalist state. Nation's interior to be moved toward regionalization by means of establishing centers of economic·and social development.

INTEGRATION AND DEVELOPMENT MOVEMENT (MID)

Electoral legislation to be introduced to guarantee the ruling party a majority in the National Congress. Respect and representation for minorities. Repressive "state of siege" laws to be repealed. Total amnesty law to be introduced. Freedom to be granted to both social and political prisoners. Constitutional reform and any moves to limit freedom of expression or the will of the people to be rejected. Human rights violators to be severely penalized, no matter what the circumstances under which the violations are committed and no matter whether the violator is an instigator or one who takes active part in the violations.

PROGRESSIVE DEMOCRATIC PARTY (PDP)

Democracy to be restructured without suspending its guarantees, and through the development of public opinion to foment broad socio-economic reform. All violent revolutionary action which brings contentment at the expense of liberty to be opposed. Access to the election of governors and representatives to be free, with the sole condition being loyalty to essential principles. No person's democratic rights to be withheld because of his religious or political beliefs. Self-assembly rights to be assured in Congress. Law against conflict of interest in public service to be introduced. 'State of Siege'' to be modified to include option right accorded by the Constitution to prisoners. Severe penalties to be introduced for use of illegal pressure or torture. All groups employing repression and persecution to be suppressed. Principle to be defended by which police investigation is auxiliary and subject to judicial control and also by which the extra-legal creation of police and armed civilian groups is prevented. Provincial governments to be given the right to establish their own tax system. Each province to be given a larger proportion of the national taxes derived from that province. National government to help municipal administrations by equipment destined to bettering public services. Active Federalistic economy to be promoted, without which, Federalist politics cannot exist. Cooperativism to be backed and state interference to be limited, in order to prevent impairing freedom of association and freedom to work. Consumer and productive cooperation to be free from taxation. Banking and Savings cooperatives to be created, protected and developed. Law giving judicial power to the executive branch to be repealed. Oral trial to be instituted. Institute of Criminology and criminal rehabilitation to be implemented. Judicial boards of standards made up of lawyers pertaining to each court's jurisdiction to be formed. Military justice to be independent of the high command and to be regulated by military tribunals with established jurisdictions and which should enjoy the same guarantees and independence as all other tribunals in the nation.

INTRANSIGENT PARTY (PI)
Seeks the political, economic and social autonomy of the municipal governments.

POPULAR CHRISTIAN PARTY (PPC)
Seeks the transfer of the Federal Capital to a site in the interior of the Republic.

DEMOCRATIC SOCIALIST PARTY (PSD)
Mayor of Buenos Aires to be elected by popular vote. Municipal elections not to be held at the same time as other voting. Cooperative movement to be represented in socio-economic council and in all other economic decision-making centers. Consumer councils to be set up within public service organizations which are to be represented in the cooperative movement. Electrical facilities to be organized on a national level and guided by federative principles and development of electric cooperatives to be encouraged. Administrative and share-holding cooperatives to be created for the exploitation of public services. Tax exemptions to be limited to non-profit cooperatives. Divorce to be made legal. The rights of partners in an extramarital union to be recognized. Laws covering person to be restructured. Repressive legislation or institutional reforms brought in by the military government to be annulled or revised. Citizens to be protected from administrative injustice, and control organization to be designated by Parliament. New political parties statute, eliminating state interference, to be introduced. Legality of all public opinion to be recognized. Separation of

church and state and freedom of religion to be recognized. Proportional electoral representation to be upheld.   Armed Forces to be reduced. Military service to be reduced. Military budget to be kept under 50 per cent of the amount allotted to education. Military Ministers in the cabinet to possess a technical post, but not to represent an autonomous force within the government. Possession of sophisticated weaponry or *prestigious* arms to be renounced. Continental arms race to be renounced. Barracks living to be slowly eliminated. Function of the military to be progressively transformed into a technical operation. Wages to be paid to draftees.

RADICAL PARTY (UCR)

Legislation imposed by military governments to be revised. Constitutional convention in which amendments to the constitution would be discussed to be recommended. Repressive legislation to be imposed to counter administrative immorality. Repressive laws, ideological discrimination, military mobilization of civilians, exiling of foreigners, special courts, the death penalty and torture to be abolished. Current system of obligatory military service to be revised. Military medical examination to become a part of a permanent national campaign of preventive medicine. Military program to teach illiterate soldiers to read and write to become part of the nation's education policy. All discrimination against women to be eliminated, putting the nation's women on an equal footing with men in all cases except those in which she already has additional benefits. Article 264 of the Civil Code to be modified giving equal rights as parents to both progenitors. Office of Women's Affairs to be organized in the Labor Ministry to increase the number of women in the labor sector. Investigative organization to be created to study female capability and to help promote the employment of women in decision-making sectors at a governmental and inter-governmental level. Women to be integrated into social, economic and political development process. Protection of minors to be promoted through the technicalization of the sector, and by backing foster home policies, the creation of new orphanage services, giving backing to families, creating a special juvenile affairs court and by sanctioning a juvenile code. Municipality to be defended as a natural and necessary institution, which should enjoy broad autonomy. Full autonomy of the municipality of Buenos Aires, with popular election of mayor to be ratified.

II Foreign Policy

FREJULI

Country to be oriented in accordance with Third Position principles. Commercial and diplomatic relations to be carried on with every country in the world. Sovereignty of Antarctica, the Malvinas (Falkland) Islands and the River Plate Basin to be defended. Latin American unity against North

American imperialism and Brazilian sub-imperialism to be sought. Andean Pact to be adhered to. Pacts with the OAS and the ALALC to be repudiated or modified.

INTEGRATION AND DEVELOPMENT MOVEMENT (MID)

International polices to spring from the projection of national ideals and interests abroad. Effective national unity to be promoted as a preliminary stage in the development of regional and continental unity. National interests to be defended in the utilization of common geographical resources and in environmental protection. Principles of non-interference and self-determination of the people to be maintained. Relations to be maintained with all countries as a means of breaking down ideological barriers. Relations to be re-established with Cuba.

PROGRESSIVE DEMOCRATIC PARTY (PDP)

Solidarity with all people fighting for their freedom from foreign domination or internal dictatorship to be promoted. Organization of American States to be denounced for not having tended to the economic interests of Latin American people, and for having refused to back the returning of the Malvinas (Falkland) Islands and Belize to their rightful owners. Peaceful coexistence and assurance of self-determination to be maintained with all countries. Active anti-imperialism and independence from foreign influence to be re-established. Closer ties to be established with other Latin American republics. Secret international accords to be rejected. Regional pacts which could bring about present or future wars to be repudiated. A strengthening of the United Nations and the repealing of the veto right among the most powerful nations to be sought. Nuclear arms ban to be sought. International control of thermo-nuclear experiments to be sought.

INTRANSIGENT PARTY (PI)

Independent international policy along guidelines set by Yrigoyen and in solidarity with the nation's Latin American brothers and with countries which have submitted to colonial exploitation to be implemented.

POPULAR CHRISTIAN PARTY (PPC)

Awareness of ties between Argentina and the Third World, especially as it relates to Latin America, to be promoted. Cooperation with international organizations to be developed. Relations to be established with all countries and *without ideological barriers*. Agreements which limit the nation in its decision-making capacity to be reviewed. Cooperation and ties with Latin American nations to be strengthened as a means of reaching economic, cultural and political unity. Sovereignty and self-determination to be defended; interference to be rejected. OAS to be denounced as an instrument of imperialism. False policies of ALALC which slow the process of Latin American independence to be denounced. River Plate Basin and Andean Pact to be supported. Aid to be given to countries fighting to free themselves from colonialist, neo-colonialist and imperialist oppression. All accords to be reviewed and those which are contrary to the nation's principles to be denounced. Foreign service to be restructured so as to serve the nation more efficiently.

DEMOCRATIC SOCIALIST PARTY (PSD)

Popular participation in a Latin American common market through representation in a Latin American parliament to be sought. Acceptance and development of the idea of continental solidarity in the fields of social justice, democracy and free institutions to be promoted.

RADICAL PARTY (UCR)

Policy of non-interference and self-determination of the people to be adhered to. Judicial equality of nations and the protection of human and civil rights to be upheld. War pacts, totalitarianism, imperialist penetration and colonial exploitation to be repudiated. Universal disarmament as a means of ending war without prohibiting countries to maintain a means of self-defense to be backed. Party to fight for the prohibition of nuclear arms tests. Support to be given to the UN and suppression of the veto right to be sought. Relations to be maintained WITH ALL COUNTRIES. A national mass media office to be set up abroad. Stockholm declaration on human environment, aimed at preventing pollution and ecological destruction, to be backed. Latin American unity to be supported. Action to be taken within the OAS to insure the observance of human rights. Latin American regional action to be pushed throughout the CECLA, ALALC, the River Plate Basin agreement and the Andean Pact. Backing to be given to direct or judicial solutions to all border disputes. Accords to be formulated covering waterways which flow into the Basin, in order to assure the use of the Parana as a means of intercommunication and to prevent its contamination. Radical party initiatives to be pushed: The Alta Gracia Charter, the River Plate Basin agreement, World Nutrition Fund and free navigation for neighboring countries on international rivers. Backing to be given for deals based on a system of non-reciprocal generalized preferences with industrialized nations. At the same time the elimination of tariffs and restrictions which oppose expanding sales of basic products would be sought. A strengthening of Latin American joint action and the maintenance of a united front with developing countries which form part of UNCTAD and GATT to be sought. Greater institutionalized Latin American interdependence to be sought in place of non-institutionalized dependence. Political independence within international organizations to be maintained. Maritime policy to sustain the principle of Free Navigation, sovereignty of coastal states and the defense and exploitation of the continental shelf and epicontinental sea.

Recovery of the Malvinas (Falkland) Islands and the establishment of national sovereignty in the Antarctic territory to be pursued.

III Culture and Education

FREJULI

Universal primary education, the elimination of illiteracy and semi-illiteracy to be sought. Party to try to cut the dropout rate (50% in primary schools) in the nation's schools. Intensive plan for the building of new schools, in which the national government would cooperate with the local community, to be implemented. Universities to be self-governing. Universites to be opened with no type of limitation. Priority according tomerit to be given to institutions as regards national education and cultural budget. Education to be free of religious overtones so as to safeguard the rights of parents to bring their children up in their faith. Science and technology to be supported through institutes, laboratories and universities.

INTEGRATION AND DEVELOPMENT MOVEMENT (MID)

National system of education to be supported. Public education to be fortified. Private education to be stimulated. Teachers' law to be respected. Government backing to be given to scientific and technological research and to the spread of national culture so as to strengthen our traditions and at the same time to permit and facilitate the flow of modern international thought. Growth of the intermediate level technology to be provided for. University system to be restructured.

PROGRESSIVE DEMOCRATIC PARTY (PDP)

Common, non-religious, free, primary and secondary education to be reinstituted and university level to be reformed. Education budget to be increased so as to reach 4% of the Gross National Product within a six-year period; greater proportion of national tax money to go into provincial funds. Illiteracy to be attacked on all levels, with special courses being set up for adults. Enough schools to be built to cover all national needs. School boards to be elected. Secondary education to be reworked to fit the demands of the nation. Universidad Tecnologica (Technological University) to be restructured and given more importance. Law authorizing private entities to issue university certificates to be repealed. New university law based on reform to be introduced. Public and school libraries to be established. Mass media to be used as a means of offering basic knowledge and civic education to the general public. Artistic activities to be developed and protected through the creation of schools of fine arts. Party to cooperate with UNESCO in seeking to eliminate the obstruction of scientific, artistic and literary works.

INTRANSIGENT PARTY (PI)

Nation's responsibility to assure free and obligatory primary education, to make available technical high school and higher education without limitations and to support the nation's culture, to be recognized. Scientific research to be stimulated.

POPULAR CHRISTIAN PARTY (PPC)

National budget for education to be increased by 25%. Education to be based on the principle that Man is a critical and creative subject and to satisfy his need to develop. Educational system to be made to order for the community. Educational programs and pedagogic methods to be revised. State subsidies to be awarded only to private non-profit educational establishments.

DEMOCRATIC SOCIALIST PARTY (PSD)

Budget for education to equal 25% of total expenses as a minimum and 5% of the Gross National Product. Minimum school attendance to be set at 6,000 class hours. Schools, classroom space, books and other incidental items to be free of charge to the children of the nation. Plans for youth technical education program to be implemented. Organic law for education to be introduced. Permanent School Fund to be re-established and increased. Educators to participate in the autarchic education administration, Authentic University Reform to be put in practice. Sex education to be introduced in school. Cooperativism to be taught as a subject in primary and secondary cycles. School building program to be implemented. School cooperatives to be promoted and recognized. State to be prohibited from backing private schools and other educational establishments with the exception of those which are free of charge. All professional titles to be awarded by state universities. Teachers' training and professorial education to be an exclusive function of the state. Primary and secondary education to be organized federally. Illiteracy, semi-illiteracy and dropping out to be eliminated. Education to be obligatory on primary level. Common, obligatory, free and non-religious education described in law 1.420 to be defended. The formation of extra-curricular and continuous education to be guaranteed. Patrimonial culture to be upheld and its repression prevented. Tri-annual conference on science, education and culture to be held.

RADICAL PARTY (UCR)

Indians to be integrated into the nation's culture. National artistic and cultural values to be promoted. Program of culture and education for the people via the mass media to be implemented. National conscience of patriotic values to be revitalized. Argentine books to be stimulated. Public libraries to be supported. A National Cultural Expansion Plan to be developed. Cultural exchange to be promoted throughout the territory.

Artistic institutes throughout the country to be increased. Non-religious, free and obligatory education to be re-established in accordance with law 1.420. Private education to be controlled and diplomas to be awarded ONLY by official institutions. Private education to gradually omit financial aid it receives from the state. Organic education law to be introduced according to law 1.420 and the University Reform. National Education Council to recover its full powers. Education to receive 25% of the general budget. Normal school to be rehabilitated and brought up to date. Party to work toward making education obligatory through first years of high school. Teachers' statute to regain its full strength. Benefits for retired teachers to be freed. Education to be insured for the minor, the adult and the mentally deficient; institutes for the mentally deficient to be returned to the jurisdiction of the Culture and Education Ministry. Scholarship program to be created in order to permit young workers to study. Teacher training institutes to be created. More kindergartens and nursery schools to be created in accordance with the needs of the neighborhood. Number of rural schools and agricultural training schools to be increased. Technical training to be intensified. School construction and maintenance program to be created. University Reform to be re-established, providing autonomy for the university and freedom of educational program, tripartisan administration and educational exemption.

IV Economy

Transport — Public services — Energy — Agriculture and livestock.

FREJULI

Productive factors to be fully employed. System to be progressively socialized. Financial system to be nationalized and brought under state control. Tax reform to be implemented as a means of producing more just distribution of wealth, the simplification of the system, and the elimination of tax evasion, Reorganization of Public Administration to be imposed in order to achieve better service oriented toward investment and social and economic decentralization. Export control organization to be created. Party to take advantage of multipolarity and contradictions within imperialist systems when it appears to benefit the nation. Preferential treatment to be given in trade with Socialist countries. Public and private debts to be controlled. Foreign capital to be freed so that it may make an effective contribution to our balance of payments. Remittances of all types to be limited and controlled. New technology to be incorporated. Investments to be gradually nationalized. Foreign companies to finance their own operations. Complete agrarian reform to be implemented covering property and use of land. Cooperativism to be fomented. Local production to be developed. Industrial policy to be imposed which covers nationalization of monopolistic companies and of companies involved in strategic activities, and which also covers decentralization. Socio-economic structure to be reformed according to a popular and Christian national doctrine. Energetic policy based on article 40 of the Constitution of 1949 to be followed; this article establishes that all natural energy sources with the exception of those in the vegetable category, are the inalienable and untransferable property of the nation. Hydroelectric energy to be exploited. Mining to be reactivated. New systems of transport and communications to be introduced, not with economic objectives, but based on the needs of the population.

INTEGRATION AND DEVELOPMENT MOVEMENT (MID)

Real wages to be brought up to date. Tax pressure to be reduced. Ample tax moratorium to be introduced. Companies strangled by recession to receive credit. Customs protection to be increased. Closed factories to be reopened and new ones to be built. De-nationalized companies to be offered re-nationalization. Reproductive and heavy industries to be developed. Recovery of self-sufficiency to get backing in the mining sector. Small miners to receive backing. Roads to be modernized, transformed and expanded; energy, transport and communications sectors to receive backing. No fewer than 200 airports to be built. Aeronautic industry to be promoted. Air transport firms to receive backing. Merchant fleet to be expanded. Domestic maritime and river transport to be promoted. Plans for port improvements to be executed. Country's interior to get backing through defense of prices on primary products, the industrialization of production regions and the placement of new industries in the interior. Patagonia region to receive energy from Chocón-Cerros Colorados complex. Credit and taxes aimed at channelling national savings and at taking advantage of foreign capital, to be implemented. Repatriation of lost capital to be sought; foreign capital to be rejected if it signifies selling controlling interest in national companies. Federalism and decentralization to be in force. New roads plan to be implemented to replace the current one which mirrors the anachronistic railway system. Provincial governments to participate in the management of their respective ports. Official banking policy to impede transfer of deposits in the interior to the capital and greater Buenos Aires area, a practice which reduces local credit possibilities. Administrative and control organizations aimed at promotion of regional production to be decentralized. Provincial participation in taxes to be raised by up to 50%. Federal Investment Council to be returned to the provinces. Policy of compensatory tariffs and of public services promotion to be introduced. Interest rates to be conducive to investment by those who require financing. New tax systems to be formed which would take promotion and integration of the country's interior into account. National Farming Council to promote colonization of state land. Means to be sought to put idle and unexploited land to good use. Investment in expansion of livestock, especially cattle, pigs and sheep, to be stimulated. Red meat production to be promoted. Export trade to be oriented toward these products through a higher level of industrialization. Exports of livestock on the hoof to be eliminated. Fowl production to be stimulated. Policies to be aimed at stimulating the development of farm production in general. Fishing industry to be promoted. Forestry and lumber industry to be promoted. Export bank to be created. Cooperative activity to be backed. Administrative rationing, modernization, maximum efficiency and financial feasibility to be promoted in state firms.

PROGRESSIVE DEMOCRATIC PARTY (PDP)

Tax plan to be based on direct taxes. Tax system to be reformed so as to limit big profits and decrease the load born by low-wage earning taxpayers. Tax collecting to be perfected. Minimum taxable salary level to be raised and family allotments also to be raised. Confidentiality of sworn statements for tax exemptions to be discontinued. Profits from farming to be considered fourth-category profits — farming is more personal than commercial. Sales tax rates to be reduced because of the effect they have on prices the consumer must pay. Of revenue from sales tax, provincial governments should receive no less than two-thirds of the money collected in their territory and this revenue, in turn, should be put into public services. Internal taxes affecting prime necessity items to be reduced unlike those which are placed on luxury items; thus double taxation is avoided. Wholesale and retail prices to be controlled on all articles of prime necessity. Economic and social planning to be introduced to promote national development, to better the people's income and to better distribute the nation's wealth. This plan would be carried out by a socio-economic council made up of workers, businessmen and university students. The budget policy will center on problems of poverty, illness and ignorance. The nation's expenses are to be justly divided so that economically privileged sectors of the population bear more of the burden. Secret clauses in budgets to be eliminated. Credits obtained by the country to be employed in the development of petroleum production, the steel industry, energy resources and transport, while investment in non-productive areas and/or military equipment would be avoided. Immigration and residence of foreigners in this country to be fomented. All factors which tend to limit the consumer and raise prices to be repressed. The autonomy and position as a state entity of the Central Bank to be preserved with its board being made up of state, provincial, consumer, and business representatives. Central Bank to recover direct loans made by the government and to avoid taking a role as provider of state funds. New orientation of banking system to be placed in action, which will include socio-economic planning. Industrial Bank to be declared a development bank. Declaration to be made to the effect that these banks should not contract loans which could be damaging to national sovereignty. Foreign investment should be developed, subject to specific and concrete legislation. Adhesion or submission to foreign credit agencies such as the International Monetary Fund should be avoided and the country should also avoid having these organizations influence our monetary policy.   Expenditures to be balanced with state resources.   Special law to transform agriculture to be introduced.   More equal distribution of land to be promoted.   Legal and tax reform to be introduced in the farming sector.   Roads and education to be made more available in rural areas, and harvests to be protected against monopolized commercialization.   Free cooperatives to be set up and loans to be made available to these cooperatives.   The setting up of monopolistic light and power companies to be impeded and the assets of those which exist would be expropriated.   Legislation to be introduced to give the province in which hydrocarbons, solid mineral energy sources and hydroelectric energy sources exist ownership rights on the resources.   In the case of petroleum, exploitation, construction of pipelines, refineries and other installations, to be the sole right of the nation.   Provinces would receive proportional royalties from the state company YPF on all petroleum extracted by the nation.   Sale of rights of national and provincial resources and concessions to private companies to be prohibited.   Private firms could only carry out limited, temporary job contract work in any mining operation.   Distribution, production and refining operations to be the exclusive right of YPF, the state oil firm.   Exploitation of uranium — under the same conditions as those set for oil — to be assured.   Electric cooperatives to be promoted.   Country's electrical potential to be developed.   New networks of highway links, the nation's ports and railroads to be developed.   Railway administration to be reformed.   New ports and new access channels to those already in existence to be built.   Provinces to be given jurisdiction over their ports.   Port administration to be put into the hands of an independent board made up of municipal and provincial members, as well as representatives of the shippers who use the ports.   Opening of navigable channels to be accelerated.   Mitre Channel from Rosario to Buenos Aires to be stretched to La Plata and made navigable for high-sea-going vessels.   Work to be carried out on the Rio Bermejo and on channels to the north and middle of the nation.   Channel network to be built.   Big city transport to be cut back. Industries to be set up in the country's interior, in order to prevent centralization.   State to be kept out of all but strategic areas of industry.

FEDERALIST PARTY

Foreign participation in the national economy to be promoted — through capital, labor, technology or credit, taking care to insure that its contribution would be a genuine one.   Export of traditional and non-traditional goods to be encouraged and not to be limited by ideological borders; exchange rates, taxes and tariffs to be adjusted to facilitate exports.   Exploitations of services and industrial activities to be subsidized.   Stable rules to be established for economic activity. Just distribution of income and equal economic relations to be assured. Human resources, seen as the main basis for development, to be mobilized and training to be promoted. Small and medium-sized businesses to be protected and their growth stimulated. Unemployment and inflation to be fought.

INTRANSIGENT PARTY (PI)

Banking to be brought under state control; finance and insurance institutions to be run according to a system of cooperative credit. State to have dominion over strategic sectors of foreign trade, which would be operated on a legitimate cooperative basis. Central Bank to have complete control of foreign currency. All mining, industrialization, marketing and transport of energy and mineral resources to come under state control. Areas of economic activity to be handled by State, private and foreign private companies to be defined so as to promote stability. All basic industries to be reserved for the state. State to back recovery of national firms which have been the object of foreign plunder. State to divide planning into areas of interest. Economic activities based on domestic capital to be defended and promoted. All public service, communications and transport companies to come under state control. Laws and the holding of the land to be transformed through an AGRARIAN REFORM act. State to control production standards. Tax system to be reformed to eliminate indirect taxes and replace them with taxes on profits and patrimony. Buying power to be protected. Administration to be decentralized and regionalized according to Federalist principles.

POPULAR CHRISTIAN PARTY (PPC)

Ties with the International Monetary Fund to be broken. Banking activities to be regulated according to a Plan for Development. National income to be redistributed among wage-earners in order to promote more equal distribution of wealth. Prices and monopolistic activities to be controlled. Wage increases to be based on productivity. Workers to eventually become shareholders in companies for which they work. Dual foreign exchange markets — one official and the other free — to be created. Official: Divise from exports; divise for essential imports. Non-essential imports to be prohibited. Free market: for financial remittances. Foreign Trade Corporation to be created for the promotion of non-traditional exports, to facilitate traditional export operations, expand markets and handle trade operations. Foreign trade law to be introduced to regulate and orient activities in this sector. Foreign debt to be renegotiated. Factory councils to be set up with the participation of administration and workers. Cooperation between workers and management to be promoted. Firms owned by workers and worker cooperatives to be set up both in public and private sectors. Selective location system to be set up for foreign companies. YPF to have top priority. National firms, both state and private, to tend to absorb marketing. Self-sufficiency in petroleum to be insured. Petroleum exports to be incorporated into economic system as a source of foreign currency. New hydroelectric complexes to be initiated and work to be continued on those already begun. National firms working in the field of energy to be fortified. Agrarian reform to be introduced in which land would be given to those who work on it. Tenants to become owners of the land they work. Taxes to be paid on the profit potential of land in accordance with its quality. Transfer of available land to small landholders so that they can bring their farms up to optimum size. Increased agrarian productivity to be stimulated through a system of agricultural credit. Greater investments and better technology to be stimulated in farming. Direct assistance to be accorded to the farmer through INTA and similar groups. Greater mechanization to be promoted in agriculture. Anonymous ownership of land to be eliminated. Farm cooperatives to be promoted. Farm unions to be created. Investments to be made for the building of more grain elevators. Access routes to ports and centers of consumption to be created. Packing house facilities to be improved and expanded. Rural electrification to be promoted and telephone network installed. Institute of Colonization to be created.

DEMOCRATIC SOCIALIST PARTY (PSD)

Inflation to be considered as robbery. Promotion of monopolistic maneuvers and industrial privilege to be considered crimes. Technological development of basic and intermediate industries to be promoted, superfluous or redundant industries to be avoided, unnecessary patents and trademarks to be rejected. Obstacles to production and exportation to be suppressed. "Equality Book" to be published each year and to include (a) amount of personal patrimony; (b) amount of income; (c) amount paid in taxes. Commission to be formed to control production costs and rates of payment within state firms, and including technicians and consumers. As a means of solving the current emergency and when the Treasury deficit cannot be financed through normal means, forced credit from large capital and high income sources to be imposed. Foreign capital to be incorporated as a substitute for import and to promote export. Natural resource wealth to be defended. Swamps and erosion to be fought. Intensive reforestation planned, water policy to be formed, rational use of water resources (in the fields of consumption, energy and irrigation) to be promoted. Hydroelectric development to have a goal of 100 KW of consumption per capita per year. Greater use of hydroelectric energy to be promoted. Basic industrial costs to be controlled. Consumption Ministry to be created. Multinational companies to be controlled. Tax payments by personnel with incomes of up to 5,000 pesos (according to current values) per month to be limited to fourth category level. Non-productive truck farms to be done away with. Land of big landholders to be subdivided through taxes and/or expropriation. The economic misuse and/or non-use of land to be prohibited. Rural electrification to be the responsibility of farm cooperatives. Rural cooperative groups to be formed in farming areas. Indian population to be incorporated into rural and urban life through a program to make land ownership accessible to them, through professional training, and through attention to the health and education of their children.

RADICAL PARTY (UCR)

Rural electrification to be promoted. By-products to be utilized. National farm machinery industry to be developed. Production cooperatives and farm marketing to be supported and developed. Reforestation to be increased. Quotas to be established in the lumber industry. General improvement of Argentine products to be promoted and importation to be coordinated with backing being given to the principle of self-sufficiency. Consumption of fish to be promoted. Modern industrialization methods to be promoted. Fishing for unexploited species to be promoted. Equipping of the fishing industry in unexploited zones to be supported. Maritime construction industry to be developed as regards fishing vessels. Access to individual or family ownership of farmland to be facilitated. Conservation and improvement of soil to be promoted. Marketing process to be implemented which would insure reasonable and stable long and short-term benefits. Balance to be effected between dirt firming and livestock products, with incentives being given to producers of items in greater demand on national and international markets. Grain, meat and by-products foreign markets to be developed and consolidated. Export prices and the marketing system to be defended to assure the country of the divise it needs for its development. Principle to be established that land is a productive asset, not a capital good and thus should not be an instrument for financial speculation, nor should property rights be permitted to be exercised unconditionally. Agrarian Reform to be founded on social, economic and political factors. Unexploited holdings of vast lands to be prohibited. These large lands to be transformed into workable units and to be awarded to those who work the land. Public domain to be utilized in colonization schemes. Lands not included in the humid pampa zone to be incorporated into the productive process. Construction program to be created which will promote settlement in rural areas. Colonization system to be reformed so that former owners do not unduly benefit from profits brought by the new productive process. Tax policy to favor the farmer. Counter-productive small farms to be eliminated through regrouping. Resettlement and consolidation of farmland into productive units. Rural sector to be benefited by credit policies. Rural social security to be complete and obligatory. Petroleum to be in the hands of YPF and its agents and representatives but this does not mean that the state firm cannot contract work and services it considers necessary; provincial governments to receive a portion of profits from oil produced. Aggressive policy of exportation and diversification of markets to be followed. Sales to be intensified in countries which sell us more than we sell them in order to build up their purchases of Argentine products. Local self-sufficiency policy to be enforced. Mass marketing plan with credits for the transformation of small businesses to be introduced. Commercial centers to be instituted in new urban areas. Businesses to be rationally organized so as to assure their efficiency, their participation in the market, their individuality, and the honesty and efficiency of their officials. Workers to participate in the administration of state firms. Budget to be increasingly aimed at education, housing, and public health. Provinces to take an increasing part in the distribution of resources. Provincial co-participation to be automatic. Tax system to be restructured so that it serves as an instrument for redistribution of income. Tax burden to be taken off labor sector, and tax rates which affect consumer prices to be reduced. Taxes on family assets to be eliminated. Monetary and budgetary policies to be coordinated. Credit system to be nationalized. National Institute of Underwriters to be fortified. Cooperative credit system to be backed and regulated. Limits to be established for foreign companies which make use of national credit. All use of national savings funds is prohibited to foreign companies. Systems of control of the movement of capital to be implemented. Transfer of foreign currency to be limited to areas in which a return on this money is assured. Immediate cashing in of foreign currency produced by exports to be required. Foreign debt regulations to be imposed. Gradual adjustment of foreign quotations for the Argentine peso to be made in accordance with variations on our domestic costs. Superfluous or non-essential imports to be prohibited. Non-traditional exports to be promoted. State to control foreign trade. ''Foreignization'' of our economy to be eliminated through an independent policy toward foreign capital, national organizations and the interests of national minority groups which are contrary to the good of the community. Maximum use to be made of existing productive potential of natural resources. Social movement to be promoted, mainly through the participation of workers in company profits. State to intervene in the fundamental aspects of the economy or when the need to correct distortions arises. Private initiative to be backed. Cooperative system to be implemented. National Development Plan to be formulated with regard to investments, based on long-term policies for specific sectors. Income policy to promote rational distribution of economic resources. Decent wages to be guaranteed. Economic and Social Council to be organized to carry out the democratic planning of the economy. New legislation covering placement of foreign capital to be introduced. State to participate in basic sectors of the economy and in those which lack sufficient investment possibilities, through the formation of state-owned or mixed corporations. State to regulate transport services and to reduce tariffs as much as possible. A National Transportation Law to link all means of transportation in one system. Electric energy to be exploited only by the state. Industries which produce semi-finished products to be given priority. Capital goods industries and those which develop regional industry to be supported. Production to be modernized. Technological research to be intensified. Heavy industrial concentration to be corrected through direct and heavy taxation. The importation of finished goods to be prohibited when national industry produces these goods within the same quality standards. Merchandise confiscation by customs officials to be destroyed or re-exported. Mineral resources to be researched. Credit to be extended to the mining industry. Mining market to be regulated. Idle ownership of mines to be repressed. Mining legislation to be brought up to date.

V. Labor

FREJULI

Labor Contract law to be sanctioned which takes in labor in all aspects: responsibilities of workers, suspensions, lay-offs, death, stability, risks, dismissal, child labor, working women and workers of advanced years. Priority to be given to credit which is to the worker's advantage. Monetary and inflation adjustments and long-term payment to be included in labor credit plans. Basic statutes to be introduced to update collective wage scales. Law 14.250 to be perfected. Vital and mobile minimum wage to be introduced. Professional fees to be set by collective contracts. Law 14.455 guaranteeing labor representation to be upheld. Decrees or portions of decrees (14.455, 969/66 and 2.477/70) which tend to undermine the strength of union groups, or which prohibit the natural right to strike to be repealed. Union delegates to sit on company boards. Gradual labor representation in the management of companies and popular self-management of public services. Workers to be permitted to choose between strikes and arbitration, but the latter would not affect the right to strike. Substitution of workers during a strike to be prohibited.

INTEGRATION AND DEVELOPMENT PARTY (MID)

Collective work contracts to be implemented. Professional Association Law to be reinstituted. Decree 969/66 and all other regulatory dispositions which altered the spirit of law 14.455, to be repealed. Government to be absolutely forbidden to interfere in union matters.

PROGRESSIVE DEMOCRATIC PARTY (PDP)

Workers and administrative employees to participate in company profits. Profits of large companies to be limited. State employment agencies to be created. Baby-sitters to be provided for children while their mothers work. Constitutional disposition to back public servants' stability on a national, municipal and provincial level. Preventive medicine to be implemented for workers. Labor and Social Security Ministry to be formed and to be sanctioned in a future Constitution. Obligation of provincial governments to uphold existing social legislation to be inserted in the national Constitution.

Backing to be given to strong unions to be brought together in a single Argentine union movement, which would be formed as a consequence of wage earners' wishes and would not be an institution imposed by the state. The state cannot set the rules for professional associations nor can it pretend to be a judge of the quality of a union, nor can it propose to stimulate the division of the union movement. The workers themselves to be the only judges of union organization, and the state would recognize and negotiate with the largest union organizations. The state cannot declare strikes legal or illegal, but simply just or unjust.

DEMOCRATIC SOCIALIST PARTY (PSD)

Minimum, vital and mobile wage to be guaranteed. Salaries and work conditions to be contracted collectively. Right to strike in both public and private sectors to be upheld. Workers to receive indemnities for dismissal, work accidents, and pregnancy at current rates. Age limit for enrollment on payroll of state companies to be eliminated. Seniority to be recognized, including years worked in both prior and current post, when establishing annual vacation period. Legislation to be introduced to protect the rights of (fine arts) artists. Actors' rights to be recognized. New contract for teachers and professors to be negotiated and teachers' statute to set pay scales and seniority.

RADICAL PARTY (UCR)

Legislation to be sanctioned to instrument the rights upheld by article 14 of the Constitution, and a work and social security code to be implemented. Legislation to be introduced to give workers participation in profits and management of private and state companies. Right to strike to be upheld in according with existing legislation and as an expression of the will of the majority, voiced by secret vote in places of work. Collective contracts, commissions and updating of conciliation and arbitration to be implemented. Vital and mobile minimum wage established for a former UCR government in the form of law 16.459 to be upheld. Internal democracy in union life with representation of the minority and jurisdictional power of the administration to interfere in same to be reaffirmed. Stability of union leaders to be increased and insured. Unity within the union movement to be promoted and aimed at the formation of a center for workers in accordance with the will of the union members. Union authorities not to be elected for more than two terms. Voting to be obligatory for all union affiliates. Discounts or extraordinary dues and special quotas subject to legislation, to be voted on by secret ballot in places of work. Party politics prohibited within the union movement. Labor justice to be made more energetic throughout the country. Legal jurisdiction over union activities — management of funds, electoral process, violation of prohibition on party politics, compulsive discounts and all other infractions committed or in question of having been committed on union rights — to be established. Legislation to be introduced by government on labor organizations in business. Business councils to be set up with members elected by all personnel in the firm. Legislation to be introduced covering social benefits which assure that authorities administering these benefits are completely independent of the decisions, funds and administration of unions. Top priority status to be guaranteed within a federal organization to secondary category associations (unions) by channelling money collected in union dues to its treasury. All laws introduced by de facto governments to be revised, including all those sanctioned since 1966, and those which are aimed at labor repression or limitation will be annulled.

VI Social Welfare

FREJULI
Social security to be administered by an entity comprising workers, employers and the state. Social security, workers' self-management, with state control and via union structure, to be imposed. Retirement benefits for the disabled. Voluntary retirement for women. Work risks and work-related illness to be considered and included in the framework of the social security system. Family benefits to be restructured to assure proper control of these benefits and to penalize non abidance. Useful and adequate employment to be guaranteed in every field before resorting to subsidies for unemployment. Health insurance to be implemented.

INTEGRATION AND DEVELOPMENT MOVEMENT (MID)
Plans for construction of new housing to be implemented, centering particularly on the housing deficiency among fixed income sectors. Complete system of social security which takes in health problems, old age benefits, availability of recreation and sports to the entire population, to be implemented.

PROGRESSIVE DEMOCRATIC PARTY (PDP)
Legislation to be introduced defending minority. Municipalities to take part in effecting immediate social services. Specialized benefits to be administered by provinces or inter-municipal organizations. Schools of medical science to sign agreements with health centers throughout the country in order to facilitate decentralized medical education. Organizations linked to socio-medical research to be incorporated into medical schools. Housing construction to be carried out by the private sector with financial and technical aid from the state and municipalities. Taxes on construction material to be suppressed. Public works to be limited to only the most necessary, as a means of lowering the prices of materials and permitting a sensible increase in the construction of housing for the population. National Social Security Code to be sanctioned covering death, disability, illness, retirement and unemployment for all workers, public and

private. Social security to be established by means other than taxes on labor. Unemployment funds to be established. Autarchic security system divided into funds to be established. Retirement funds to be used only for the purpose for which they were created and not to cover tax deficits. Governing boards of retirement funds should include representatives of those affiliated with the fund. System of preventive medicine for workers to be implemented. Health policy to be oriented toward complete socio-medical benefits. Research centers aimed at bettering health standards to be created. Health centers to be opened.

Bio-statistics to be compiled. Health education to be implemented. Health insurance to be implemented. Well-equipped surgical centers to be created. Specialists in social medicine to be encouraged. Periodical medical examinations to be obligatory in places of work. Protection to be given to unwed mothers, natural mothers and orphan children. Out-patient dispensaries to be created. Government control to be imposed on the making and sale of medication. Health organizations to be autarchic. The creation of professional organizations to be encouraged. Medicines and medical equipment to be free of taxes and customs tariffs.

INTRANSIGENT PARTY (PI)

Real wage increases to be guaranteed. Complete social security coverage and access to housing to be imposed.

POPULAR CHRISTIAN PARTY (PPC)

Federal Housing and Planning Institute to be created. Unification of retirement funds to be re-structured, and benefits and withholdings to be adjusted. Deep and urgent study to be carried out with the idea of replacing the current system which tends to use money destined to social security benefits to cover budgetary deficits. System to be independent and to be administered by representatives of the retired, business and union sectors. Evasion to be eliminated, and benefits to be paid in checks cashable in any bank at any hour.

DEMOCRATIC SOCIALIST PARTY (PSD)

Unemployment insurance to be instituted. Indemnities to be alloted to the families of draftees hurt or killed in accidents. Retirement to be given to housewives. Social service to aid the aged to be created. National Savings Bank to be created. National Health Service to be created and to be financed by proportional taxes on profits excluding taxes on personal work. Decent wages to be paid for both professional and non-professional work in the medical field. Medication to be controlled as regards composition and price. Making of medicines which are the same but are sold under different names to be prohibited. Research to be carried out to discover what part advertising costs play in the retail price of medicine. Non-profit institutions to be created to carry out plans for family housing. Progressive tax to be levied on the sale price of vacant land. Taxes to be placed on gambling, on large landholdings, on excessive profits and to be used to finance housing plans. Urban land expropriated as part of the popular housing plan not to be returned to private hands. Uncontrolled growth of urban centers and the arbitrary plotting of lots for financial gain to be limited. Study to be made to determine what percentage of social income received by unions is to be used in housing programs.

RADICAL PARTY (UCR)

Housing deficit to be absorbed through public and private resources, with priority being given to needy regions and low social levels. Payments on home loans to be kept at a level which will not endanger the family budget of the loan contract signer. A National Housing Plan to be created and supported through taxes on wages, fees and profits payable by the employer through an additional tax levied on state evaluation of real estate, through foreign credit awarded on long-term low-interest basis and through special bonds issued by the state. National Mortgage Bank to be instituted as a tool for government action in the housing area. Private banking must apply 30% of all funds assigned to housing to economical living quarters. General coordinated urbanization plan to be enacted in order to achieve rational growth of the country's centers of population. National Physical Education and Sports Policy to be implemented. Aid to be given to Indian communities. School cafeterias to be supported. Recreation centers to be stimulated. Direct assistance to be given to the needy. Tourism to be developed as fringe benefit for workers. Slums to be eradicated through a national plan. Health to be considered a basic right and to be given absolute national priority. Importance of public health to be re-established on a ministerial level, by returning former decision-making power to health authorities. Proper funding to be assured to cover health expenses. Insurance against illness to be established and later health insurance aimed at equal medical assistance to be brought into effect through a prior study of all conditions. Health code to be established. National plan aimed at the protection, recuperation, physical rehabilitation and mental rehabilitation of the population to be introduced, which would also bring the improvement of the nation's hospitals and the broadening of medical attention. Battle against infectious diseases to be revitalized. A mother-child maternity program to be introduced. National nutrition policy to be introduced which would permit nutritional improvement among vulnerable sectors of the population. Health action to be taken in rural areas. Program to rehabilitate the handicapped through a special labor system to be revitalized. Mental health plan to be created. National plan to be introduced as a means of fighting drug addiction. National health education plan to be implemented. Environmental protection plan to be established. Medicine to be considered a social benefit and to be covered by a Medications Development Law. National pharmaceutical industry to be supported and drug producing cooperatives to be placed under government auspices. System of benefits to be reorganized so as to eliminate evasion of payment. System of retirement benefits to be reorganized. System of health benefits to be introduced. New system of family allowances to be introduced. Retirement pay to guarantee a decent minimum living. Allotments to be adjusted periodically. Pensions to be brought more in line with retirement benefits. Administration of pension funds to be autarchic and to be in the hands of the state, affiliates and management on an equal basis. Red tape to be reduced in order to shorten the time beneficiaries must wait to start receiving their benefits. National and/or provincial professional pension funds to receive money from professional enrollment fees. Better distribution of funds so as to cover all types of benefits. Priority to be given to age, with respect to retirement, from unhealthy jobs. Social security code to unify regulations covering retirement benefits. Right to sue to be given to applicants who, after one year from application, have not received benefits. Sociological research to be maintained in order to establish social reality in rural, urban or industrial areas. Family institution to be protected by decreasing economic and health risks. Nursery schools to be set up to aid working mothers. National Youth Council to be formed for vocational stimulation and orientation. Legislation to protect those who are out of work and are unable to find a new position to be introduced. Laws governing indemnities for dismissal and work accidents to be brought up to date. Labor medicine and industry safety law to be adjusted according to guidelines set up by the International Labor Organization.

APPENDIX VI
Classification of Countries According to Political And Economic Freedom (Chapter 13)

Based on material contained in the article entitled *Poor vs. Rich: A new global conflict* which appeared in *Time* magazine on December 22, 1975, the author of this book has compiled his own classification list.

The prime criterion for classification has been the gross income per inhabitant as listed in *Time*, with some omissions in cases where *Time* uses averages of countries belonging to the same region.

The figures correspond to the final quarter of 1975 and do not necessarily reflect current values.

In a very few cases countries have been included in a category to which they would not belong if only their gross income was taken into account but which reflect generally sufficient resources, population and culture to warrant this placement.

It should be noted that *Time* places Argentina at a gross income level of 1,250 U.S. dollars per inhabitant. In the text of this book a gross yearly income of 1,800 U.S. dollars per inhabitant was used, which corresponds to the conversion in dollars of Argentine money based on buying power. This does not change Argentina's position in the following charts: A. Countries with concrete economic policies to offer their inhabitants (more than 3,000 U.S. dollars per inhabitant, with the exception of oil producing countries).

Country	Income Per Capita in U.S. dollars	Rate of Illiteracy %
United States	6,200	2
Sweden	6,149	1
Switzerland	6,048	1
Denmark	5,560	1
West Germany	5,378	1
Canada	5,370	1
France	4,908	2
Belgium	4,834	1
Luxembourg	4,804	1
Iceland	4,596	1
Norway	4,535	1
Australia	4,000	2
Holland	3,950	1
Finland	3,657	1
Austria	3,581	1
New Zealand	3,930	2
Japan	3,810	2
Britain	3,607	1

B. Intermediate countries in which economic conditions conducive to a state of liberty exists, although political and cultural conditions are not necessarily conducive to freedom (1,200 to 3,000 U.S. dollars per inhabitant).

Country	Income Per Capita in U.S. dollars	Rate of Illiteracy %
Italy	2,899	7
Bahamas	2,240	15
Israel	2,730	16
East Germany	2,716	1
Czechoslovakia	2,550	1
Ireland	2,544	1
Poland	1,940	1
Greece	1,780	20
Spain	1,730	14
Hungary	1,695	1
USSR	1,530	1
Bulgaria	1,402	1
Portugal	1,310	35
Argentina	1,250	9
Trinidad Tobago	1,200	11

C. Countries with a relatively low level of development in comparison with the others mentioned here and with an income per inhabitant (750 to 1,200 U.S. dollars) which is insufficient to embark on programs to cover the people's needs and where political and civil liberties are not sustained and where there is no clear economic structure. Countries are included in this list which despite having high per capita incomes, demonstrate a high rate of illiteracy (more than 20%). These last are basically oil producing countries.

Country	Income Per Capita in U.S. dollars	Rate of Illiteracy %
Kuwait	8,450	45
United Arab Emirates	6,740	80
Quatar	5,940	85
Libya	2,980	73
Venezuela	1,360	23
Saudi Arabia	1,300	85
Rumania	n/a	n/a
Gabon	1,150	88
Surinam	900	21
Panama	880	16
Albania	n/a	n/a
Lebanon	870	14

Jamaica	870	18
Mexico	870	22
Uruguay	860	10
Costa Rica	780	11
Chile	780	13
Iran	760	77
Brazil	750	33

D. Countries with incomes of between 150 and 750 U.S. dollars per inhabitant and where the population feels economic need which has a definite influence on the level of liberty which exists.

Country	Income Per Capita in U.S. dollars	Rate of Illiteracy %
Belize	700	11
Taiwan	660	16
Iraq	640	76
Peru	620	39
Turkey	580	49
Malaysia	550	57
Dominican Republic	510	36
Ivory Coast	510	80
Nicaragua	500	42
Algeria	500	80
Zambia	500	80
Angola	490	85
Tunisia	460	70
Guatemala	450	62
Cuba	450	22
Zaire	420	80
Colombia	410	27
Rhodesia	410	70
Paraguay	400	26
Guyana	380	20
South Korea	380	29
Ecuador	370	33
Papua	360	68
El Salvador	340	40
Mozambique	330	93
North Korea	320	n/a
Jordan	315	69
Honduras	290	55
Ghana	290	75
Morocco	290	86
Egypt	260	74
The Philippines	250	28

Nigeria	250	75
Senegal	250	90
Liberia	250	91
Thailand	230	32
Cameroons	230	85
Bolivia	200	60
Mauritania	200	95
Sri Lanka	200	24
Central' Africa	180	90
Togo	180	90
Republic of Malgache	170	61
Kenya	170	75
China	170	75
Uganda	160	80
Sierra Leone	160	90
Gambia	160	90

E. Countries which live in a state of absolute poverty (less than 150 U.S. dollars per inhabitant per year).

Country	Income Per Capita in U.S. dollars	Rate of Illiteracy %
Haiti	140	90
Guinea	140	90
Sudan	140	85
Vietnam	135	33
Tanzania	130	80
Pakistan	130	84
Indonesia	120	57
India	120	66
Niger	120	95
Malawi	110	78
Laos	100	75
Bangladesh	100	78
Yemen	95	90
Chad	90	90
Nepal	90	91
Burma	80	40
Cambodia	80	59
Cambodia	80	59
Upper Volta	80	90
Afghanistan	80	92
Somalia	80	95
Ethiopia	80	95
Mali	70	95
Rwanda	70	90
Burundi	70	90

Bibliography

Aberg Cobo, M., *Cuatro Revoluciones Argentinas 1890-1930-1943-1945*, Buenos Aires, 1960.

Aizcorbe, R., *El Mito Peronista*, Buenos Aires, 1976.

Atebcui, J.E., *Que es geopolitica*, Bs. As., 1957.

Balestra, Juan, *El Noventa*, Buenos Aires, 1959.

Bell, O., *The cultural contradictions of capitalism*, New York, 1976.

Celerier, P., *Geopolitica y Geoestrategia*, Bs. As., 1975.

Coleccion Economic Survey

Chajotin, S., *Le viol des foules par la propangande politique*, Paris, 1954.

De Felice, Ph., *Foules en delire, extases collectives*, Paris, 1956.

Del Maza, G., *El Radicalismo. Notas sobre su historia y doctrina*, Buenos Aires, 1955.

Diamand, M., *Doctrinas Economicas, Desarrollo e Independencia*, Buenos Aires, 1973.

Diaz de Alejandro, C. F., *Ensayo sabre Historia Economica Argentina*, Buenos Aires, 1975.

Di Tella, G. y Zymelman, M., *Las etapas del desarrolio economico argentina*, Buenos Aires, 1967

Ehrlich, P. R., und Ehrlich, A. H., *Bevolkerungswachstum und Umweltkrise*, Frankfurt, 1972.

Ferns, H. S., *Gran Bretana y Argentina en el Siglo XIX*, Buenos Aires, 1966.

Ferrer, A., *La economica argentina*, Mexico, 1963.

Floria, C. A. y Garcia Belsunce, C., *Historia de los Argentinos*, Buenos Aires, 1971.

Frischknecht, F., *Govierno*, Buenos Aires, 1976.

Frondizi, A., *El Movimiento Nacional. Fundamentos de su Estrategia*, Buenos Aires, 1975.

Frondizi, A., *Petroleo ye Politica*, Buenos Aires, 1954.

Galvez, M., *Vida de Hipolito Yrigoyen*, Buenos Aires, 1948.

Gambini, H., *El 17 de Octubre*, Buenos Aires, 1970.

Garcia Venturini, J. L., *Ante el fin de las Historia*, Buenos Aires, 1964.

Golberry do Conto e Silva, *Geopolitica do Brasil*, Rio de Janeiro, 1967.

Grondona, M., *La Argentina en el Tiempo y en el Mundo*, Buenos Aires, 1967.

Guglialmelli, J.E.; Golberry do Conto e Silva, *El "destino manifesto" brasileno y el Atlantico Sur. En Revista "Estrategia,"* no. 39, Buenos Aires, 1967.

Ibarguren, C, *La historia que he vivido;* Buenos Aires, 1969.

Irazusta, R. y J., *La Argentina y el Imperialismo Britanico*, Buenos Aires, 1934.

Kahn, H. and Wiener, A., *The Year 2000*, New York, 1967.

Kaiser, R. G., *Russia. The people and the power*, New York, 1976.

Kelsen, H., *Teoria pura del derecho*, Buenos Aires, 1973.

Kissinger, H., *The necessity for Choice*, New York, 1961.

Krieger Vasena, A., y Pazos, J., *Latin America: A Broader World Role*, London, 1973.

Levine, L. W., *U.S. - China Relations*, New York, 1872.

Lezama, H. E., *Balcarce 50*, Buenos Aires, 1972.

Luna, F. y otros, *Que Argentina queremos los argentinos*, Buenos Aires.

Madison, A., *El crecimiento economico de Occidente*, Mexico, 1966.

Massuh, V., *La Libertad y la Violencia*, Buenos Aires, 1968.

Massuh, V., *Nihilismo y experiencia extrema*, Buenos Aires, 1975.

Meadows, D. H.; Meadows, D. L.; Randers, J. and Behrens, W. W., *The Limits to Growth*, New York, 1972.

Mihajlo, and Pestel, E., *Mankind at the Turning Point*, New York, 1974.

Mounnier, E., *La Revolution contre les Mythes*, Paris, 1934.

Navarro Gerassi, M., *Los Nacionalistas*, Buenos Aires, 1968.

Perriaux, J., *Las generaciones argentinas*, Buenos Aires, 1970.

Pinedo, F., *La CEPAL y la realidad economica en America Latina*, Buenos Aires, 1963.

Pinedo, F., *La Argentina: su posicion y rango en el mundo,* Buenos Aires, 1971.

Potash, R., *El Ejercito y la Politica en la Argentina (1928-1945). De Yrigoyen a Peron,* Buenos Aires, 1971.

Riyas, Armando, *La Crisis del Capitalismo. En Revista Pensamiento Economico,* No. 404, Buenos Aires.

Scenna, M. A., *FORJA, una aventura argentina,* Buenos Aires, 1972.

Smith, H., *The Russians,* New York, 1976.

Solzhenitsyn, A., *Warnung an den Westen.* En el periodico *"Die Zeit",* Frankfurt, 9 de Abril de 1973.

Solzhenitsyn, A., *Archipielago de Goulag,* Barcelona, 1974.

Thompson, R., *Peace is not at Hand,* London, 1974.

Villegas, O., *Tiempo Politico argentino,* Bs. As., 1973.

Index